AMERICAN HERO

AMERICAN HERO

The True Story of Tommy Hitchcock—Sports Star, War Hero, and Champion of the War-Winning P-51 Mustang

NELSON W. ALDRICH JR.

Prologue and Epilogue by Richard L. Jackson

Guilford, Connecticut

An imprint of Rowman & Littlefield

Distributed by NATIONAL BOOK NETWORK

British Library Cataloguing in Publication Information Available

Library of Congress Cataloging-in-Publication Data
Names: Aldrich, Nelson W., author.
Title: American hero : the true story of Tommy Hitchcock : sports star, war
  hero, and champion of the war-winning P-51 Mustang / Nelson W. Aldrich, Jr.
Other titles: Tommy Hitchcock, an American hero
Description: Guildford, Connecticut : Lyons Press, 2016. | Originally
  published under title: Tommy Hitchcock, an American hero. Gaithersburg,
  Md. : Fleet Street Corp., 1984. | Includes index.
Identifiers: LCCN 2016012800 (print) | LCCN 2016024261 (ebook) | ISBN
  9781493022878 (hardcopy) | ISBN 9781493022885
Subjects: LCSH: Hitchcock, Thomas, Jr., 1900-1944. | Polo players—United
  States—Biography. | Bankers—United States—Biography. | World War,
  1914-1918—Air pilots, Military. | World War, 1939-1945—Air pilots,
  Military. | United States. Army. Air Service. Aero Squadron, 103rd. |
  Mustang (Fighter plane)—Merlin engines—Design and construction—History.
Classification: LCC CT275.H62573 A54 2016 (print) | LCC CT275.H62573 (ebook)
  | DDC 940.54/81092 [B] —dc23
LC record available at https://lccn.loc.gov/2016012800

To Margaret Mellon Hitchcock, her children, and descendants

Contents

FOREWORD

I AM HIGHLY GRATIFIED THAT THIS BOOK ON TOMMY HITCHCOCK'S LIFE is being published and that I have the opportunity to contribute to it.

Tommy was a great athlete; one of the greatest athletes of my generation—by far the best polo player of our time. I don't know of anyone who could compare to him in every aspect of the game. He could not only hit the ball from every side of the pony, forward or back, but he had a great ability to block players. Tommy was also a great team player. He brought out the best in all of us, whether we were good, bad, or indifferent. He never shouted at others as some polo players did, but he encouraged his teammates in every way by his own excellence. Both as a player and team player, he had no rivals anywhere.

Tommy and I were in London at the same time during the Second World War, when we saw a lot of each other. I was very fond of Tommy and admired him enormously. His friendship contributed greatly to whatever pleasure was to be found in those troubled times. It was a terrible tragedy that he was killed in an airplane accident. Amidst all the sadness of that era, his death was, for me, the greatest sadness of all.

—W. Averell Harriman
Washington, DC.

ACKNOWLEDGMENTS

THIS BIOGRAPHY COULD NOT HAVE BEEN WRITTEN WITHOUT THE invaluable material gathered by James Claggett. Long before I began my work, Mr. Claggett interviewed most of the people whose reminiscences are the backbone of this story: Joseph Gaeta, H. S. Henriques, Joseph Thomas, William Jackson, David K. E. Bruce, Merion Cooper, William Laurence, Arthur Krock, George Gordon Moore, Helen Hitchcock Clark, Edward Weeks, Douglas Burden, Esq., and Upton Sullivan.

I myself interviewed Julian Peabody, Elwood Quesada, W. Averell Harriman, Ethel Leary, Avy Clark, Seymour Knox Sr., Eric Pedley, and James P. Mills.

I would also like to especially thank Mrs. Hitchcock, without whom this book could not have been written, and her two daughters, Louise Hitchcock Stephaich for her assembly of the photographs, and Peggy Hitchcock for her comprehensive editing of the manuscript.

I am grateful as well for the help of Tommy and Suzanne Hitchcock, Billy and Jane Hitchcock, and Alexander M. Laughlin. I also want to thank Luba P. Harrington for helping with last-minute revisions, Clara C. Bolger for her invaluable assistance, Carey Clark, and Anita W. Biddle.

Prologue

THE DAY NEWS CAME OF TOMMY HITCHCOCK'S DEATH, MY MOTHER
sat outside alone on a terrace wall and smoked her first cigarette, a habit
she continued for the next forty years. My father never spoke to me
about it, but he kept Hitchcock's photo front and center on his desk all
his life, wherever he moved. He worshiped Hitchcock, and some of his
feelings show through in the appendix to this second edition. I can still
remember on weekend outings from New York going with my mother
for tea at the Hitchcock house in Westbury with Peggy Hitchcock,
Tommy's widow. While I did not understand the mournful atmosphere
of the house, I have never forgotten her kindness and interest in me as
a mere small child.

Hitchcock had died on April 18, 1944, test flying the Mustang
P-51B, the revolutionary fighter that he, more than any other man alive,
brought into being. As Nelson Aldrich writes, just six weeks later the
Mustang ensured Allied air superiority over Normandy. And during the
Battle of the Bulge, it decimated the remaining five hundred fighters of
the German Luftwaffe.

Born in late 1939, I have no memory of Tommy Hitchcock and could
never have imagined writing a prologue to this second edition of Nelson
Aldrich's biography. After thirty-four years of foreign service and eleven
years as president of Anatolia College in Thessaloniki, Greece, I found
myself in Hangzhou, China, as a Ma Yinchu Fellow in 2011. There,
improbably, Vic Currier, a New Mexican historian and Vietnam veteran,
single-mindedly researching my own father, began to email me sections
of his two-volume biography of William H. Jackson to proofread. The
close friendship of Jackson and Hitchcock and their critical partnership
during World War II, summarized in the epilogue to this edition, jumped

out from the pages, and for the first time I was really drawn into the inter-war years and World War II. "So we beat on, boats against the current, born back ceaselessly into the past," wrote Scott Fitzgerald, whom we will have occasion to come back to soon enough in these pages.

Hitchcock's image, among those who knew him, has remained constant—a curious mix of optimism, daring, caring, and quiet humor. What has changed in the nearly seventy-five years since his death is the world around us. Hitchcock is no longer a household word and remains a largely unknown figure to today's readers. It would be hard to exaggerate, however, the attention he received as indisputably the preeminent world polo player of the twentieth century. During his heyday prior to World War II, before the advent of most professional sports, polo was a top spectator sport, drawing up to 45,000 fans for major matches. By comparison, the 2015 USPA championship match, polo's premier event, drew only 11,000, the largest crowd in many years.

As a World War I hero and ten-goal player, Hitchcock was widely known and admired in the close-knit society of that time. Personal contacts on both sides of the Atlantic with figures such as the Roosevelts, Winston Churchill, Averell Harriman, Jock Whitney, David Bruce, and many more facilitated his rare ability to cut through government red tape during World War II. For many, Tommy came also to personify the spirit of the inter-war years. Wherever he went, he was mobbed. Whatever he wore, polo shirts or polo coats, which he was among the first to sport, became the instant fashion and remain so to this day. A 1932 *New Yorker* cartoon showed Hitchcock thrown from a polo pony, probably a higher profile than being on the cover of *Time*, where his mother actually appeared in 1930, since every reader knew instantly just who and what Tommy Hitchcock was.

And then there is the F. Scott Fitzgerald phenomenon. Fitzgerald was besotted with Hitchcock and saw in him everything that he was not and so intensely envied. Tommy obviously stood out for Fitzgerald among the crowd, "wherever people played polo and were rich together" in his famous phrase. Scott and Zelda, extravagant and impecunious, were frequent guests, invited or not, at Tommy Hitchcock's summer compound in Sands Point and also turned up from time to time at his parents' farm,

Broad Hollow, in Westbury, New York, where Hitchcock kept his string of polo ponies. From 1922 to 1924 Fitzgerald lived in Great Neck in what, according to Fitzgerald's biographer, Matthew Bruccoli, Zelda described to her friend Xandra Kalman as a "nifty little Babbit home," looking across Manhasset Bay at Sands Point, an enclave of wealth where Tommy summered and that became the fictional East Egg of *The Great Gatsby*.

Everything is relative, however, and what Zelda dismissively called her "Babbit home," built in 1918 and still nearly new when they moved in, was decidedly not modest. As Mary Jo Murphy points out in her September 30, 2010, *New York Times* article, Scott and Zelda lived at 6 Gateway Drive in Great Neck and drove a second-hand Rolls Royce, but at the same time Fitzgerald complained to his editor, Maxwell Perkins, that if he could not lay hands on $650, he would have to sell the furnishings and furniture. The contradiction highlights Scott and Zelda's extravagant devil-may-care life in the Jazz Age. As of early 2016, their opulent faux mansion at 6 Gateway Drive was still going strong and sold for a whopping $4.2 million. Brucolli, for his part, cites Fitzgerald's monthly budget for "house liquor" while in Great Neck of $80, equal to $1,000 today. Together, Scott's drinking and Zelda's emotional problems often spelled trouble.

Scott and Zelda, nevertheless, parleyed their charm and Scott's literary reputation into the upper reaches of Long Island's swinging 1920's Jazz Age society, but they were by no means ideal guests. In her *Inventing Great Neck: Jewish Identity and the American Dream*, Judith Goldstein recounts an out-of-control, perhaps dubious, episode at one of Herbert Bayard Swope's parties in Great Neck where an inebriated Zelda stripped off her clothing and pursued Mrs. Swope's terrified sixteen-year-old nephew upstairs, pounding on his locked door. Swope allegedly threw the Fitzgeralds out, and they were banned forever from the household, Goldstein writes. The sordid details of Zelda's behavior at the Swope mansion are quoted by Goldstein from Frederick Lewis Allen's *Only Yesterday: An Informal History of the 1920s* (NY: Harper and Brothers, 1931, p. 128). As editor of *Harper's Magazine*, Allen may in fact have been among the crowd at Swope's infamous party, although curiously the episode was deleted from later editions of his book.

For many summers, Tommy had shared a bachelor's bungalow complex at Sands Point with Jock Whitney, Averell Harriman, and George Moore. Even in this easygoing atmosphere, the Fitzgeralds' drop-bys were likely, nevertheless, to have been a nuisance. Innately polite, Tommy must have been at his wits' end as the Fitzgeralds lounged about his place, although at the same time fascinated by their banter. A private man, despite public adulation of Tommy the polo hero, he often probably just couldn't get rid of them.

After the Fitzgeralds had departed Long Island, Tommy married in 1928, bought out the Sands Point complex from his partners, and had noted Palm Beach architect Maurice Fatio tear down the main building and design an Art Deco white brick house, one of the first with central air-conditioning, preserving, however, one of the bungalows for the children.

In later years, in New York and Long Island, when Tommy was married, the indigent Fitzgeralds kept in touch, presenting the Hitchcocks with troubled self-portraits dashed off by Zelda. Peggy Hitchcock particularly empathized with Zelda's problems and may have visited her in the Baltimore asylum and also paid her dental bills.

Identifying real life models for characters in *The Great Gatsby* has become a sort of long-running parlor game for literary sleuths. Fitzgerald was a creative and brilliant writer, however, capable of drawing on a vast Rolodex of friends and acquaintances for inspiration. He was, after all, a Princeton man, although he withdrew in 1917 to enlist. To label this or that person as the basis for a single character or, worse, to slice and dice people into exact components of a character frankly seems to me an insult to his genius.

An exception, however, was Tommy Hitchcock, with whose physique, gentle character, war record, polo exploits, and social status Fitzgerald was obsessed. Fitzgerald acknowledges in his "Notebooks" that Tommy was in part the inspiration for the characters of both Tom Buchanan in *The Great Gatsby* and Tommy Barban in *Tender is the Night* (both Toms or Tommies). Starting with physique, he writes of Buchanan that "you could see a great pack of muscle when his shoulder moved under his thin coat. It was a body capable of enormous leverage—

a cruel body," and Tommy Barban too is described in stark physical terms. Some readers have taken these references to imply that Hitchcock was himself arrogant and aggressive like Buchanan, but Fitzgerald was at pains to dispel this notion. Aldrich writes, for example, that as late as 1938, Fitzgerald took umbrage with a playwright, Mrs. Edwin Jarrett, whose adaptation of *Tender is the Night* had misconstrued the Hitchcock-like character. Tommy Barban was, he wrote to Mrs. Jewett, "in a way" Tommy Hitchcock but not like Barban a creature of the "boudoir." The reality of Hitchcock, Fitzgerald insisted, was "that you can feel the strong fresh-air current in him."

At about the same time, not long before his death, Fitzgerald wrote to his daughter Scottie at Vassar College comparing her studies there to Tommy's "humility" as a "newspaper hero" from World War I and "the greatest polo player in the world" going back to school at Harvard. Hitchcock would forever be, he wrote Scottie, in his "pantheon of heroes." More recently, a lost copy of *The Great Gatsby*, warmly inscribed to Tommy from Scott, turned up on the Internet in 2012 for the eye-popping asking price of $750,000.

As for the remaining cast of *The Great Gatsby*, including the title character himself, there is a cottage industry promoting a spectrum of candidates seeking immortality in the pages of Fitzgerald. Certainly Scott and Zelda in Great Neck must have gazed across Manhasset Sound at the twinkling lights of upscale Sands Point, imagining the green light at the end of Daisy's dock and "the orgiastic future that year by year recedes before us." Exactly whose twittering lights they were looking at is, however, by no means clear. As Mary Jo Murphy again points out in her September 30, 2010, article "Eyeing the Unreal Estate of Gatsby Esq.," the summer Great Gatsby Boat Tour around Manhasset Bay always labeled the impressive Swope Mansion at Sands Point as "Gatsby's House," at least until it was bulldozed in 2011. Never mind that Herbert Bayard Swope only bought the place in 1929, years after the Fitzgeralds moved to Europe, and had supposedly been declared persona non grata at the Swope house in Great Neck or that the mansion was in East Egg (Sands Point) rather than West Egg (Great Neck) where Gatsby held forth.

Equally, Horst Herman Kruse in his 2014 *F. Scott Fitzgerald at Work: The Making of "The Great Gatsby"* develops a compelling and detailed case for Max von Gerlach, a disreputable used car dealer and minor bootlegger, as Gatsby. Gerlach may well have sold Fitzgerald a car or delivered booze to his back door, but, as Kruse acknowledges, Gerlach could go only so far in filling Gatsby's shoes, and Fitzgerald himself and others were part of the character. I suspect that major liquor dynasties before, during, and after prohibition, like that of Julius and Max Fleischmann, were also part of the picture. Gerlach, of course, saw benefit in boasting of being the real Gatsby, and Fitzgerald himself was not above hinting to social contacts that they too were or might be inspirations for one or another book.

Fitzgerald and Hitchcock must have encountered each other at parties the Fleischmann brothers threw, where they were both entertained, and at the mansion of Mary Rumsey, Averell Harriman's sister, who shared with Fitzgerald a passion for the faddish new "science" of eugenics and whose estates abutted those of the Hitchcocks in both Westbury and Sands Point. According to Kruse, Fitzgerald ascribed part of the inspiration for Gatsby to the "glamour of the Rumseys and Hitchcocks." Scott and Zelda also undoubtedly attended occasional Sunday polo games at the Sands Point Polo Club, where Tommy starred. While their paths may have often crossed, however, their trajectories were clearly different. Hitchcock was, after all, an insider dominating a major spectator sport, well bred and connected, while Fitzgerald remained an outsider, like Gatsby, looking in enviously from across the Bay. Both, however, became avatars for the Jazz Age, Tommy as a war hero and champion poloist and Scott for defining the age in *This Side of Paradise* and *The Great Gatsby*.

Tommy always had a rebellious, highly competitive streak, favoring the underdog. As a child, he deliberately overturned a donkey cart as a pretext to avoid attending a wedding, commandeered the Whitney Phaeton roadster for an unauthorized joy ride, and, at age fourteen, insisted on entering an expert, adult skeet-shooting competition in Aiken, South Carolina, defeating all comers. He was also a very competent boxer and tennis player. In World War I, he rejoiced in the pure joy and adrenaline of one-on-one aerial combat against the Germans, shooting down a string of Nazi aircraft before being ambushed and shot down himself. In later years, he reveled in verbal and legal jousting with the legendary founder of Pan American Airlines, Juan Trippe, whom Tommy knew well and considered a worthy opponent. With his competitive juices flowing, he bested Trippe before the Civil Aviation Board (CAB), frustrating the latter's plans for exclusive flight routes across the Atlantic. Trippe had boasted that Pan American carried the American flag, but Hitchcock won equal rights for his fledgling American Export Airlines, sold after his death in 1944.

At Harvard after World War I, under a two-year program for veterans, Hitchcock struggled with chemistry and relied on a fellow student, William Laurence, later a noted *New York Times* journalist, for tutoring to get him through. They formed a close friendship, and Laurence, a Lithuanian Jew, the orphaned son of a rabbi, and an impoverished immigrant, opened Hitchcock's eyes to a previously unsuspected world. On Hitchcock's advice, he adopted the name Laurence in place of Leib Wolf Siew to improve his career prospects.

Nelson Aldrich writes that the Meadow Brook Club, like most clubs at that time, discriminated against Jews, as well as not offering polo on Sundays. When the Sands Point Polo and Golf Club was founded on a property purchased in 1921 by Julius Fleischmann, Hitchcock became a founding member of its first board. Under the leadership of Averell Harriman, the board included luminaries like Vincent Astor, Max Fleischmann, Ralph Bloomer, Harry Guggenheim, Bernard Baruch, John Schiff, Herbert Bayard Swope, JH Whitney, Marshall Field, Robert Lehman, William Randolph Hearst, and Charles Schwartz. Hitchcock certainly wanted to play polo both days of the weekend, and the club was close to his summer home in Sands Point, but he was clearly also a pioneer in this early venture to break the barriers of discrimination. The club enlarged his circle of friends, and his fellow board member and nearby neighbor, Robert Lehman, soon made him a partner at Lehman Brothers, where he took the initiative to buy American Export Lines.

Ever the devoted family man, Hitchcock wrote to his wife, Peggy, on April 17, 1944, the day before he was killed, with concern about his four-year-old son Tommy's tonsillitis and threatened measles, as well as looking forward to his nephew Avy Clark's wedding which he planned to attend in London on April 19. He expressed particular pride that Clark's Mustang P-51B squadron "was now the highest scoring U.S. group in England," making "deep penetrations into Germany and chasing German planes all around the tree tops."

Hitchcock's sudden death on April 18, 1944, devastated his loving wife, Peggy, who had relied so much on his business and day-to-day management skills and left behind twin sons Tommy and Billy, aged 4, and daughters Louise, 14, and Peggy, 9, as well as his stepson, Alex Laughlin, 19, with whom he was always close. In his absence, Hitchcock family life of course continued, albeit in a lower register. Peggy, born into the civic-minded and philanthropic Mellon family of Pittsburgh and Gulf Oil, never remarried and became a loyal backer of both the United Hospital Fund and the Albert Schweitzer Hospital in Haiti, as well as a compassionate supporter of any family member in need, paying for operations and whatever exigencies arose. After the war, she sold the Sands Point house, which no longer exists, and bought the family's old homestead at Broad Hollow Farm in Westbury.

Louise, Tommy's eldest daughter, lived in Egypt briefly until Suez, and, for many years, in Paris, and has championed the Albert Schweitzer Hospital in Haiti, founded and run by her Uncle Larry Mellon. Her sister Peggy has made her life in Arizona, becoming a Buddhist and founding a non-profit, American Friends of Tibet, for the promotion of Tibetan culture. Hitchcock's twin sons, Tommy and Billy, childhood playmates of mine growing up in New York, wisely did not follow their father's path in polo, no longer an amateur sport and now dominated by Argentine pros. Instead, Billy has pursued a successful career in the energy sector and Tommy as a lawyer and public defender. The many grandchildren and great-grandchildren, whom Hitchcock never had a chance to meet, have distinguished themselves in diverse fields and would also have made Hitchcock very proud.

Poring over long-ago photos of Hitchcock and his family for this new edition reveals both inspiration in the family's obvious closeness and joy in living and immense sadness in the way that things worked out. In hindsight, the Hitchcock years (1900–1944), despite two world wars and the depression, were also in some ways golden years. Certainly nostalgia for the inter-war period has continued to grow, and there have now been six film versions of *The Great Gatsby*.

Tommy Hitchcock was a uniquely iconic figure in his own lifetime, representing for many the exuberance and can-do optimism of the first half of the twentieth century, an era long gone. Whether in aerial combat, on the polo field, or in business and engineering, he was a force of nature. Yet he was also a very private person, understated and modest about his achievements. It was probably this contrast between the public image and the real man that most fascinated F. Scott Fitzgerald. Both dimensions shine through in this new edition of *American Hero* and should help to restore Tommy to the "pantheon of heroes" for a new generation of Americans.

—Richard Jackson
Wellington, FL
May 2016

INTRODUCTION

He was a sturdy straw-haired man of thirty with a rather hard mouth and a supercilious manner. Two shining arrogant eyes had established dominance over his face and gave him the appearance of always leaning aggressively forward. Not even the effeminate swank of his riding clothes could hide the enormous power of that body—he seemed to fill those glistening boots until he strained the top lacing, and you could see a great pack of muscle when his shoulder moved under his thin coat. It was a body capable of enormous leverage—a cruel body.

So F. Scott Fitzgerald describes Tom Buchanan in *The Great Gatsby*. And so, perhaps, he saw the man on whom that character was based—Tommy Hitchcock, member by birth of America's High Society, internationally famous athlete, fighter pilot, investment banker with Lehman Brothers, and pioneer in the area of commercial airfreight transport. Other men saw him differently. The diplomat David Bruce, the statesman Averell Harriman, the lawyer and Central Intelligence Agency official William Jackson, Will Rogers, John Hay Whitney, the movie director William Wellman, the businessman A. Charles Schwartz, these men and many others, it is no exaggeration to say, worshiped Tommy Hitchcock. He was for them the beau ideal of that segment of the upper class that flourished on the Eastern Seaboard and that until the twenties—Hitchcock's twenties, too—occupied the most prominent place in America's social imagination.

At first glance he must have seemed an almost perfect representative of this class. His ancestral roots spread from Boston to New Orleans, from New York to Washington, and in each of these cities his family had been notable since before the Civil War. He was rich by inheritance, though his family's wealth was trivial compared to that of many members of their set. His family connections in Europe, especially France and England, were long established and actively cultivated. His education included graduation from two of the then most resoundingly upper-class institutions in America, St. Paul's School and Harvard, and attendance at Oxford. He lived most of his adult life in and around New York, the stage that held the spotlight of publicity for the rest of the class. He married, as one said in those days, extremely well. His business career after a few false starts took him into investment banking, which in the esteem of his class was the highest occupation next to law. Finally, though he was not in the least "social," his background, travels, and fame gave him an extraordinarily wide circle of acquaintance.

But in one respect the role he played within his class was historically unique: he was one of the greatest athletes in American sports. In the twenties and thirties, he was ranked with Babe Ruth, Bill Tilden, Bobby Jones, and the other stars of the Golden Age of Sport. He was the first and last "gentleman athlete," or "amateur," to achieve national, indeed international, celebrity. Before him there were amateurs in all sports. There had to be, for most sports before his time were college sports and therefore "amateur" in principle, if not always in fact. But none of these athletes achieved the worldwide prominence that he did, thanks to his skill and to the phenomenal new outreach of the media.

His game was polo, the most dangerous and difficult, and one of the oldest, most beautiful sports ever played. Hitchcock, poloists believe, played it better than anyone else, before or since. William Jackson, an otherwise caustic lawyer who nevertheless wrote a reminiscence of Hitchcock called "Memoirs of a Hero-Worshipper," recalled one afternoon when he had the misfortune to play against the man. Tommy rode him off the ball so hard that Jackson's horse fell to its knees. Only the arm of God could have saved him. "As I was falling off, Tommy reached across with his left hand, still holding the four reins, and pulled me back in the saddle. And then in the next split second he hit a near-side backhander faraway in the opposite direction." Inevitably the image of the polo player on horseback summoned another: the perfect, gentle knight. Jackson was not alone in making this leap, but he put it down on paper, celebrating the horseman's "generosity of spirit, his courage, his security without the slightest need for self-assertion or conceit, and his natural leadership without regard to rank."

David Bruce said of Hitchcock, with whom he shared an apartment in London during World War II, that he was the only "perfect" man whom he'd ever met—a rather sacrilegious remark, but a sample of the idolatry that he attracted. In the view of Douglas Burden, a childhood friend and college roommate who later became a naturalist and conservationist, Hitchcock could transform a pigeon shoot into a shootout on the Yukon. He saw his friend as one of those rare and enviable men who seem to be the near-perfect instruments of their will, captains of their fate. "His life," Burden wrote, "was controlled by a directness of purpose. There was never anything remotely ambivalent about him. He always seemed to know just what he wanted to do, and when he made up his mind, he did it."

Above all, Tommy Hitchcock's life was exciting. At seventeen, in World War I, he was a pilot with the Lafayette Flying Corps. Before he turned eighteen he had participated in many battles and had killed at least one man, maybe more, among the enemy. A year later he was shot down and captured by the Germans, then made a dramatic escape to Switzerland. Finally, in World War II, he played a crucial role in the development of the P-51, a plane without which the Allied victory in Europe would certainly have been postponed and possibly even prevented.

Aviation played a haunting refrain throughout much of Hitchcock's life. He employed his knowledge of aircraft in his business, buying a controlling interest in American Export Lines, a shipping line; then, foreseeing an era in which commercial aviation would flourish, he established the American Export Airlines in 1937. Eventually, he would die in an airplane crash in 1944.

It is said that Fitzgerald, with his reputation for idolizing the rich, saw Tommy Hitchcock as everything he himself wished to be. That Fitzgerald was as proud as an autograph collector to have known Hitchcock can be seen from his correspondence. In 1929 he wrote to his editor, Maxwell Perkins, from Paris, recommending that Scribner's translate a book that was just then all the rage in France, *Evasions d'Aviateurs*, because it contained the story of Tommy Hitchcock's escape. Years later, after reading the script of a play that someone had made out of *Tender Is the Night*, Fitzgerald warned the author that she had gotten the character of Tommy Barban wrong. Barban was based on Tommy Hitchcock, he said, who wasn't at all the sort of boudoir figure he seemed in her play. Hitchcock's "realities" were those of another sort, of "strong fresh-air current."

Again toward the end of his life, Fitzgerald remembered Tommy Hitchcock as a model of behavior for his daughter Scottie. He wrote her at Vassar College to say how much he admired her for going to college even though she didn't need to: "like Tommy Hitchcock who came back from England . . . already a newspaper hero in his escapes [sic] from Germany and the greatest polo player in the world—and went up to Harvard in the same year . . . because he had the humility to ask himself, 'do I know anything?' That combination is what forever will put him in my pantheon of heroes."

It is difficult to say when, exactly, Hitchcock and Fitzgerald met, or how well they knew each other. They did meet, perhaps first in London during the Westchester Cup tournament of 1921, certainly after October 1922, when Scott and Zelda took a house near the Ring Lardners' at 60 Gateway Drive in Great Neck, Long Island. It doesn't much matter how intimate they were. There was an extraordinary clarity about Hitchcock the man, and a storybook richness in his legend, that made intimacy unnecessary for knowledge—at least for a novelist.

The Fitzgeralds came to Great Neck from St. Paul, Minnesota, in the fall of 1922 and left it for France in the spring of 1924. In between, except for a four-month period in which he locked himself away to write short stories, and another few weeks in which he assisted at the birth and death of his play *The Vegetable*, Fitzgerald and Zelda did little except go to parties. When they weren't going to parties—in Manhattan, on Long Island, in speakeasies and private houses, on lawns and beaches, small parties and enormous parties—when, that is to say, they weren't at someone else's party, they were giving parties of their own.

By November Fitzgerald's play had flopped and he was flat broke; he shut himself up in a small room over the garage and wrote and wrote. In four months he wrote eleven short stories and earned more than $17,000—good money in those days—but at the end of his ordeal, in the clear financially, he felt that what he'd written was "trash" and that doing it had broken his heart. He and Zelda decided to rent a house in the south of France; they wanted to get away from the tradesmen who were persecuting them, and he wanted to finish his novel on which he'd been working intermittently for the past three years. He did finish it, somehow or other, at St. Raphael, and it was his masterpiece, *The Great Gatsby*.

In those years Hitchcock himself was going to a good many parties. He and two friends lived in a brownstone on East 52nd Street with a man who might have sat for the portrait of Jay Gatsby. His name was George Gordon Moore, and the parties that he gave were filled with music, lovely girls, handsome men, good food and wine, frequent laughter, and tears. One could never tell whom one might meet at a George Moore party. There were movie stars and reporters, hairdressers and art dealers, Irish nationalists and playboys, bankers and debutantes, stockmarket plungers and bootleggers, prizefighters and chorus girls, tennis bums and opera singers, and more than a sprinkling of the well-born sons of the Eastern upper class. One knew who would not be there: not one representative of the provincial, conservative, industrious, conscience-driven majority of Americans, not one person supporting Prohibition. The parties were iridescent with promise: the promise of love, of wealth, of power, of fame, and success. People came with delicious intimations that tonight, there on 52nd Street, they could meet someone who would change their lives. For some, it hardly mattered how. The suddenness of it all was the thing—the randomness, the sense of new beginnings endlessly renewed, canceled, renewed again, as the race of life ought to be.

At these parties—the same sort of parties that Fitzgerald went to, of course—Tommy Hitchcock stood out. In the first representation that the novelist made of him, as Tom Buchanan, the resemblance to the man is distorted. It had to be, in a novel. Moralistically, though, one might say that the image is distorted by envy. Fitzgerald once claimed (to Edmund Wilson) that he'd grown up "among nothing else but the rich." This was not true. Financially, the Fitzgeralds were rarely better than "well-off." One result of this was that even after Princeton and a studious observation of the boys from St. Midas—as he called schools like St. Paul's—Fitzgerald came to envy the rich: that is, to hate and to admire them. He himself confessed in "The Crack-Up" that he could not look at a rich man without wondering where his money came from, what crime. Toward the rich, he said he felt the "smoldering hatred of a peasant." This, despite the fact that no good American writer, with the possible exception of Mark Twain, has wished so fervently for the rich and wellborn, as Fitzgerald put it in a short story called "The Rich Boy," to be "different from you and me." He believed that wealth should somehow transform a man, open possibilities to the spirit that are denied to grubby little strivers of the middle class. He believed that wealth, inherited wealth in particular, ought somehow to impart a luminous quality to its possessors, an aura of power and ease, all the more mysterious and compelling because it was unearned. To Fitzgerald, money was romantic. He saw a rose-colored hue in gold, and a golden hue in the possessors of gold. The rich, his rich, would always be handsome and willful (or, if girls, irresistible and willful), but they would invariably let him down by proving, in the end, to be also wasteful and destructive and irresponsible—in other words, not at all "different from you and me," certainly not very different from F. Scott Fitzgerald.

Physically Tom Buchanan and Tommy Hitchcock have much in common, and the resemblance is reinforced by the fact that when the reader is first introduced to Buchanan he has just come in from riding. Yet what is important about the description is not the details of physique and face but the expression that Fitzgerald imposes on them. The body is "cruel," the shining eyes are "arrogant," the manner is "supercilious." No one who knew Tommy Hitchcock, above all not Fitzgerald himself, ever suggested that he was arrogant or supercilious or cruel. On the contrary, everyone who knew him was astonished at his modesty, his kindness, and his good humor. Perhaps one could say that the fictional character is the revenge that Fitzgerald takes on the real character, not because the real character was evil (or even, as Fitzgerald's final version has it, "careless"), but because the real character fell short of an ideal, a romantic ideal of aristocracy.

Tommy Barban in *Tender Is the Night* is Tommy Hitchcock in a much deeper sense. The hero and heroine of the novel are Dick Diver, an intelligent, charming, and sensitive psychiatrist, and Nicole, a young heiress whom he met and cared for in a sanitarium and later married. Together they create what Yeats called a perfection of the life, a feat that proves unbearable to Diver, who slowly falls apart, physically and morally. Tommy Barban enters this story at the beginning and figures strongly at the end. He is half English and half French (as in a sense Hitchcock was), taciturn but friendly, interested in what goes on around him, above all in Nicole, but unmoved. As such he stands out against the party scenes that open the novel: in the midst of a scuffling hedonism, he seems a creature of classical stability. Unlike Buchanan, the college athlete gone soft on drink and on the returns from a well-diversified portfolio, Barban has a clear-cut function in the world and an uncomplicated knowledge of his own interests: He is a soldier, a European, and a man of property. He is also in love with Nicole, and at the end of the novel he takes her from Diver as easily as ancient warriors took captive the daughters of their vanquished foes.

Everyone else in *Tender Is the Night* is in passage toward some pitiable self-destruction. This is a social set fading in its pursuit of the "orgiastic future" that Fitzgerald saw as the culmination of the American dream of success. As a counterpoise to this movement, Fitzgerald might have chosen a figure of New England probity and cultivation, an honorable lawyer like Squire Montague in *The Gilded Age* or Lambert Struther in *The Ambassadors*. But Fitzgerald could never concede that a middle-class way of life might, after all, be the best. Instead, inspired (as he admits) by Tommy Hitchcock, he brings on stage an antique hero, the oldest form of aristocrat, the warrior, a man who risks his life, not his health, a man whose "simplicity of . . . ideas" combines with a "complexity of . . . train-ing" to create what is the only thoroughly purposeful male character in the novel. Barban is simple while the rest are complicated; he is straight-forward while they are devious; he is concentrated while they are diffuse;

he has a code of behavior while they have a hunger for feeling; he deals in realities while they dwell in dreams.

The twenties, among what passed then for the upper class, bred a conviction that the good life was approachable not through work and love but through a continuous immersion of the self in something that they called experience. Experiences could be good or bad: it depended on who "had" them, and what he made of them. This was doubly convenient. No one had the confidence to make judgments anyway, but everyone felt that he could analyze. Experience, being continuous, has no objective, no goal, no term. It can't be judged good or bad, because whatever it is, it can always be said to teach something. Experience can be analyzed; it can be searched for its meaning (invariably psychologized). The second convenience was that it gave everyone something to talk about, as endless as the flow of experience itself.

The contrary of a life lived for experience is a life constructed of events. The difference is like that between a cocktail party and a game, or a game and a battle. These are extremes, but the point where Hitchcock stood was far closer to events, to games and to war, than to the twenties immersion in experience.

That is the kind of hero that Tommy Hitchcock was—a man of action, an embodiment of the social myth of prowess.

CHAPTER ONE

Aiken, Westbury, and St. Paul's School, 1900–1917

THOMAS HITCHCOCK JR. WAS BORN ON FEBRUARY 11, 1900, IN AIKEN, South Carolina. Had the event fallen in the summer, he would have listed his birthplace as Westbury, Long Island. It mattered little: The fresh-air currents blew strong in both places. Until he was twenty-two, he never lived in a city.

Not that Aiken and Westbury were rural. Aiken was then, as it is now, a resort, and like Newport it had been discovered by well-to-do people of Charleston in the eighteenth century. It was sufficient, in a resort of those days, that it have a large and comfortable hotel, with good food and drink, and ample verandas on which to walk about, or sit and rock, while talking of how fortunate everyone was to have escaped from the stupefying heat of the city. Aiken had such a hotel, called the Highland Park, and until the Civil War broke out (180 miles away in Charleston), the place numbered among its clientele some of the most prominent families of the city—the Ravenels, Williamses, Fords, Percivals, Townsends, Finleys, Coffins, Condes, and Legrees.

The war, of course, took its toll on the lives and fortunes of many of these families, and after it was over, Aiken, and the Highland Park Hotel, suffered a brief decline. Its resurrection was almost entirely the doing of a Miss Celestine Eustis, who came to Aiken in 1873 with her recently orphaned niece, Louise Corcoran Eustis, called Loulie.

They were a curious couple. Miss Eustis was then thirty-seven, a stocky woman with a Roman nose, piercing dark eyes, and a manner that alternated bewilderingly between fluttery femininity and forthright decisiveness. The child was six, a little slip of a thing, at once frail and bursting with restless energy. What was curious about them, at least from the local people's viewpoint, was that they spoke French.

The Eustises came originally from New England, the first of that line, William, having arrived in Massachusetts Bay sometime before 1627 (the recorded date of birth, in Chelsea, Massachusetts, of his first child). The family prospered so that by the Revolution, two Eustis brothers, William and Jacob, were deeply involved in the politics and business of the colony. Jacob, a merchant, lived in Brookline, a town just outside Boston, where his son, George Peabody Eustis, was born in 1796. George went to Harvard College and was graduated in 1815, at the age of nineteen. Thereafter he went abroad as private secretary to his uncle, William Eustis, a former governor of Massachusetts, who was then U.S. minister to The Hague. On his return he studied law in Boston and was admitted to the bar.

At that point in his career, one would have supposed that young George Eustis, with his family connections, his diplomatic experience, and his legal training, enjoyed more glittering prospects of success than most men of his generation in Boston. But sometime before 1822 he and his father had a falling-out (over what is not known), and in that year George left Boston and moved to New Orleans. It was a strange choice. In culture, religion, manners, and law, New Orleans was as far from Boston as he could have gone without leaving the United States. New Orleans was cosmopolitan where Boston was provincial, Catholic where Boston was Protestant, sophisticated where Boston was simple and sober, its law based on the Code Napoleon where Boston's was based on English common law.

Nevertheless, George Eustis's success in Louisiana was astounding. By the time of his death in 1855, he had been repeatedly elected to the state legislature, and he had served successively as secretary of state, attorney general, associate justice, and then chief justice of the Louisiana

Supreme Court, where his work was of such national renown that Harvard, in 1849, awarded him a doctor of laws degree.

Socially, too, he achieved a prominent position in his adopted city. In 1825 he married Clarisse Allain, the daughter of Valerian and Celeste Allain, a well-known Creole family in southern Louisiana with strong ties to France. Even after her marriage, Clarisse Eustis went often to Paris, and her last child, Celestine, the woman who rediscovered Aiken in 1873, was born in France in 1836. Clarisse's second child, Marie, though born in New Orleans in 1831, spent most of her life in France, as did her daughter, also called Marie, later Mme. Auguste DuBos. Clarisse lived until 1876, dying at Pau, a resort in the French Pyrenees.

The first child of George and Clarisse Eustis was a boy, who was born in 1828 in New Orleans and named for his father. After graduation from Harvard, he practiced law in New Orleans and then ran for Congress in 1856 and again in 1858, winning both times. George Eustis Jr. was by all accounts an extraordinarily attractive man. Intelligent, witty, bon vivant, handsome, fluent in French, he was a rarity in American society, a truly civilized aristocrat, gaining from his New England heritage an appreciation of the life of the mind and from his French ancestry a love of grace and beauty.

If there was any household in Washington, D.C. on the eve of the Civil War where the young congressman from New Orleans might have felt perfectly at home, it was that of W. W. Corcoran. Corcoran (1798–1888) was also a Southerner of broad interests and great civility. He was a merchant banker and had extensive business relations all along the East Coast, in England, and on the Continent. He had acquired a large fortune, which he spent liberally on good works in his city of Washington and in putting together the first major collection of art in America, which became the Corcoran Gallery. He also founded the Louise Home* for destitute women in Washington and was a major benefactor of the University of Virginia.

In 1858, in a brilliant ceremony that briefly dispelled gathering tensions in the capital, George Eustis and Corcoran's only child, Louise,

---

*So named for his wife and daughter.

were married. With the outbreak of the Civil War, Corcoran, despite his Southern origins, remained loyal to the Union. Eustis chose the Confederacy. Yet both men deplored the war, and their relationship seems to have remained cordial. When Eustis's House colleague, John Slidell, was appointed by the Confederacy as minister to France, George Eustis agreed to go with him as secretary to the legation in Paris. This mission brought about a serious diplomatic crisis known as the Trent Affair, and a minor crisis in the Corcoran-Eustis family.

On the way to Europe on board a British vessel, the *Trent*, Eustis, Slidell, and James M. Mason, minister to England, were captured by the USS *San Jacinto* and interned in, of all places, Boston—a city whose ruling class contained large numbers of Eustises and some very highly placed business associates of Eustis's father-in-law. Consequently, his stay in Charlestown prison was not onerous; he supped well and was provided with the best wines, the bills being paid by Corcoran. In a few weeks he and the two commissioners were released, thanks to diplomatic pressure from the British. He arrived in Paris with Slidell early in 1862 and was joined there by his wife and sister Celestine.

The couple had three children in close succession, William Corcoran, George Peabody, and Louise Corcoran. Even before the war was over, however, their mother fell ill with consumption. By 1865 she was virtually an invalid. The family took a villa in Cannes in the hope that the climate might prolong her life. It did not, and she died in 1867 within three weeks of Loulie's birth. George Eustis had come down with tuberculosis himself by that time and had only five years to live. He bore the disease with fortitude, fearing more for his children than for himself. With Celestine and governesses protectively hovering about, they were encouraged to spend as much time as possible in the open air—then believed to be the only therapy for lung disease.

When George Eustis died in 1872, Celestine became the guardian of his three children. To little Loulie she was Tantine (a contraction of Tante Celestine), and Tantine she would remain into the next generation as well. Quite possibly Tantine would have chosen to keep the family in France—she herself was more French than American—but she accepted the claims of W. W. Corcoran on his grandchildren and returned with them to Washington in 1873. For a time she and the children lived with the elderly widower in the city; then, largely because of the young girl's frail health, she moved to Aiken. They bought a big, rambling house, winged and elled and eventually (thanks to Miss Eustis) almost covered in wisteria.

Apart from the climate, the potential that Miss Eustis saw in Aiken was chiefly horticultural. The soil was sandy but rich in clay, well watered with ponds and streams and the tributaries of the Savannah River, which lay thirty miles to the southeast. Almost her first act after buying Mon Repos, as she christened her new home, was to transplant a small orchid sprout that she'd brought with her. It was the progenitor of six huge pots. She was also responsible for the japonicas, flowering honeysuckle, bamboo, and olive trees that are found throughout Aiken. She recognized, as well, that the greatest glory of the area was its stands of magnificent pine, acre on acre of towering trees, their trunks bare of branches for fifty feet or more, then feathering outward in sun-streaked canopies of dark green a hundred feet above the soft forest floor. She bought as many of these woods as she could, to protect them, as well as two other landmarks, Lover's Lane and Burton's Pond. Ironically, in view of what lay ahead in Aiken's future, equestrian sports were not among the possibilities that Celestine Eustis envisioned. She was not a horsewoman, and when, by the 1890s, her niece had made Aiken into one of the principal equestrian centers of the country, she used to remark, "I was raised a lady, and here I am practically living in a stable."

In Aiken, Loulie Eustis was educated by tutors and governesses, as were most young ladies of her class and generation. She learned to read and write in both French and English, and she was instructed in music and painting and drawing. To "broaden her outlook," as one put it in those days, her aunt frequently took her to Paris and every summer to one or another of the coastal resorts of the Northeast—Boston's North Shore, Newport, Saratoga, Bar Harbor.

It was a childhood and youth barely conceivable today, at once disciplined and free. Loulie grew up primarily among adults, and whatever the liabilities in not having friends her own age, she more than made up for them in developing a lively imagination and a strong knowledge of who she was and what she wanted. Moreover, when the time came for her to meet people of her own age, her brothers, William and George, having gone to school in the North, and having been amply endowed with the Eustis capacity for joie de vivre, knew lots of eligible young men. One of these young men was Thomas Hitchcock Jr.

Hitchcock was the eldest of three sons of Thomas Hitchcock, who, under the pseudonym of Matthew Marshall, was one of the best-known newspapermen of his day. He wrote for Charles Henry Dana's *New York Sun*, the liveliest, the best-edited, and often the most controversial newspaper in the country. He wrote on many subjects, but the one for which he became famous was financial affairs. When he died, one of his obituaries read: "It was sometimes difficult for those who knew him to decide whether he was abler as a writer or as a financier, or whether his profound appreciation of music . . . equaled his knowledge of art . . . [He] was the first among American journalists to demonstrate that it was possible to treat financial questions with literary finesse."

The Matthew Marshall column appeared every Monday. People from all over the country subscribed to that one issue, and all Wall Street waited for it. The reason, as one historian of the paper put it, was that "unlike any other financial article it plunged deep into the fundamentals. Neither a tipster, nor an I-told-you-so, Matthew Marshall laid bare the basic causes of market movements. He was a financial scholar, philosopher and seer."

He must also have taken his own advice, for he had become a multimillionaire long before he died. Generous to his family and friends, he was also famous along Newspaper Row for his frugal habits. To his colleagues on the *Sun*, for example, he used to boast that he paid less for his suits than anyone else in the office.

"See this suit?" he once said to Dana, expansively displaying a sporty tweed. "It cost me six dollars."

"Hmm," Dana is supposed to have replied, "probably a lot less than you paid for your butler's."

Hitchcock's face fell. "You're right," he confessed, "I paid 140 dollars for his."

Contemporaries described him as a stern, almost angry-looking man, with fierce powers of concentration. He was a familiar figure downtown.

Every lunch hour he could be seen threading his way through the crowds on his way back to the office, carefully balancing his sandwich and pie on a glass of milk. His penchant for always paying the lowest price was eloquently expressed on days of panic in the market, which he often foresaw before anyone else. The other *Sun* editors would be roused from their labors by ecstatic chortlings of "Bargain Day! Bargain Day!" as Hitchcock bustled through the room on his way to see his broker. They soon learned to follow him.

His son and namesake was born in 1860 and grew up in a large house on 29th Street. Matthew Marshall was renowned for the indulgence with which he raised his sons. They were educated (badly, according to his son Thomas) by tutors, but no expense was spared to give them the attainments and adornments that the elder Hitchcock considered fitting for young gentlemen. They went to dancing classes in the winter and to the Rockaways and Newport in the summer, which (along with their father's wealth) assured them places in New York society, close to, if not actually among, the Four Hundred.

About 1876, when he was sixteen, young Thomas with some difficulty persuaded his father to send him to England, to prepare for Oxford. A place was found for him at the home of a Gloucestershire vicar who supplemented his meager income by tutoring boys in the classics. It was there, according to family legend, that Hitchcock got his first glimpse of what would forever remain his vision of the country life.

The vicar was a hunting man, and he introduced the young American to the perils and delights of the sport. By the time Thomas Jr. went up to Oxford he was an accomplished horseman and became a member of the Breister, a gathering of local gentry and undergraduates who hunted, in season, at least three times a week. Oxford itself made a strong impression on him: He enjoyed his studies and made many friends (among them Douglas Haig, the future commander in chief of British forces in World War I).

Returning to the States in the mid-1880s, Hitchcock for a few years played the young bachelor about town. He also played polo, a sport that had been introduced to America in 1876 by James Gordon Bennett Jr., the madcap proprietor of the *New York Herald*, and Hitchcock became one of the two or three best players in the country. In 1886 he was on the U.S. team chosen to play against a British quartet in what became polo's most celebrated series of contests, the International matches, for the Westchester Cup. The Americans lost that match, but Hitchcock had the satisfaction in subsequent years of seeing his son participate in every International but one from 1921 to 1939, all winning efforts.

The first International had been played in Newport, but even by 1886 the resort had become less than satisfactory for amateurs of horses, hunting, and polo: It was simply too populous. And neither geographically nor spiritually was it the sort of place to re-create English country life. Newport was Fifth Avenue bent around a small peninsula in New England. Young Hitchcock consequently began looking around for a more suitable landscape in which to realize his vision. He found it in some rolling farmland in and around Westbury, Long Island, which had been cultivated by a community of Quakers since the seventeenth century. It was ideal land for what he had in mind: well watered, with pasture and wood and sturdy fences, all laid out as beautifully as the park of an English nobleman. He and Edwin Morgan, son of the Civil War governor of New York, began buying up these properties at bargain rates, keeping some for themselves and selling others as the area became increasingly attractive to wealthy New Yorkers looking for weekend retreats.

Hitchcock's place, Broad Hollow Farm, was built around the old Quaker Meeting House, to which he added wings as time and circumstance made necessary. More important, for the atmosphere he wanted to create, were the stables and paddocks, the track and polo field in the center of it, where he bred and trained the horses—polo ponies, hunters, and steeplechasers—that even before the end of the century had made him famous.

The circle of like-minded people among whom Hitchcock lived in Westbury included the Belmonts, Whitneys, Morgans, Winthrops, Beaches, Birds, and Nicholls. Also in residence was the man who was widely believed to typify them all, for good and ill, Theodore Roosevelt. Hitchcock was an admirer and friend of his Oyster Bay neighbor, and in years to come this friendship would prove useful, decisively so, to Hitchcock's young son, Tommy, Jr. Also among his friends were the two Eustis brothers, both avid polo players and sportsmen. It was through them that he met Loulie, their sister. They were married at the beginning of the Gay Nineties, at Pride's Crossing on Boston's North Shore at the estate of a mutual friend, the banker Frederick Prince.

Thomas Hitchcock Sr. was not at all what one would expect in a man of leisure. He was more Victorian than Edwardian. Short and slim, with a wiry physique, he dressed conservatively in the English manner, and his tastes in food and drink were fastidious and simple. Like his father, his natural expression was severe. His daughter-in-law recalls that even in repose his face seemed stern and forbidding, so much so that many people who didn't know him well were quite afraid of him. Yet his voice belied his looks: it was a soft voice, with a mid-Atlantic accent, and he never raised it in anger—not with his children nor with his employees.* He was hospitable but not in the least social. He had cordial friendships, not intimate ones. He was courteous rather than friendly. One has the sense that he thought the world outside Aiken or Westbury an interesting place but excessively complicated, and on the whole better left alone. He was intelligent without being analytical; in art and music he knew what he liked, which was much the same as what his father liked, though he became an expert in Oriental rugs and knew the Bible by heart. He was nominally an Episcopalian, but not very religious, leaving spirtual matters to his wife, a devout Catholic.

As a parent, Tommy's father was more indulgent than his wife—at least with his namesake son. Tommy's sister, Helen, once remarked, "Mother used to get furious with Tommy at times. He was awfully naughty. Father was very sympathetic to him. He trusted him absolutely from the beginning. He was extraordinary with him. Anything Tommy did was all right." Perhaps the elder Hitchcock had as a parent the same great gift that he had as a horse trainer, the secret of patience. He loved the steeplechase above all other races, and he trained his steeplechasers with great care and gentleness, leading them as young animals from stable to paddock through what became known as the "Hitchcock Chute,"

---

*The latter, incidentally, were not English (the usual practice among American horse-fanciers) but Southern blacks whom he taught the arts of breeding, caring for, and training horses. Two of them, Peter Green and Lewis Martin, remained all their lives with him.

a runway across which at intervals he would place barriers of slowly increasing difficulty. In the ring, too, his constant concern was to make them unafraid. He would lead them over the tiniest obstacles, again and again, encouraging them and petting them, so that as the jumps got higher and broader the animals took them easily, naturally, fearlessly. This was his uniqueness as a trainer, that his horses seemed unacquainted with fear. It cannot be a coincidence that people used to say of his son that he too knew no fear.

Tommy's mother, whom everyone in Aiken called Miss Loulie, was a startlingly energetic, forthright, and warmhearted woman. She was in some ways the opposite of her husband: outgoing where he was reserved, charming where he was shy, animated where he was quiet. Yet like him she was strongly practical, and like him, too, she felt most at home outdoors. She was one of the first women to ride astride and abandon the sidesaddle, and the first woman to be named a master of foxhounds. She founded two schools, Aiken Prep and Fermata School for Girls. And from 1890 until 1934, the year she died, she was the principal organizer, animator, and participant in all the equestrian activities of the area, first the foxhunting, and then, after the foxes went away, the drag hunts. She was also the animating spirit behind Aiken's polo. The game had been played in Aiken before the Hitchcocks, but it was she who built the first good field and she who organized the coaching and practice sessions for young people that by the late twenties would make Aiken the preeminent training ground for polo players in America. She also encouraged girls to play the game and was probably the first to do so since the time when polo was played by court ladies in Persia.

She was a persuasive woman. When draglines had to be cut through the woods, she organized the whole community into the Axe Club, without regard to race, creed, sex, age, or ability. And each year after the clearing was done, she gave a huge lunch under the pines for everyone who had helped. Such talents led her more than once into politics. She was a mildly progressive Republican, supporting Hoover in 1932 and campaigning a year later in New York for Elliot Bacon in his race for the Senate.

Her fearlessness was legendary. Flying over jumps until well into her sixties, she took her falls, when they came, with gallantry, always getting on with the race. Perhaps, with her children, she was not as gentle or as patient as her husband, but she had an even rarer quality, an infectious gaiety that made one want to rejoice merely to look at her. She was also resourceful. Once when her husband's horse fell on him (after a collision with her brother, George, during a polo game) she was the first one on the field and gave all the orders for his care in calm, businesslike tones. This cool behavior was sufficiently extraordinary to elicit comment from the sports reporters covering the match. The implication was that she should have swooned, which is what Tantine did. And if this were not enough, Loulie Hitchcock had another quality often lacking in women of her generation: a sense of humor.

Life in any household connected to a farm, even at some distance through the hired help, is nearly as structured as in a school. The seasons bring their different demands; so do the days and the hours. There was little or no flexibility in certain key moments in the family's schedule: The children were awakened at an early hour for their daily run; all meals were served precisely on time, and everyone was expected to be there. The schedule was marked by bells that were set off in the upstairs rooms by the Hitchcocks' housekeeper, Miss May. She was a remarkable woman, hired by Tantine when Loulie's first child, Celestine, was ill as a baby, and she remained throughout her life the confidante of all the children and manager of all the details of the house. There were other servants as well, of course: the governesses Miss Skidmore and Miss Hart and black domestics, who had a separate dining room and living quarters both at Aiken and Westbury.

The couple had four children—Celestine, Helen, Thomas Jr., and Frank—and if there was anything remarkable about their upbringing, apart from the wealth that made it possible, it was an extraordinary concern with health. At the Fay School, for example, where he was sent at the age of ten, Tommy came down with a cold. He told the other boys that if he wrote his mother about it, she would send for him immediately to come home and get well. His friends didn't believe him, of course; so just to show them, he did tell his mother, and she did take him out of school. The story illustrates that he had enough distance from his mother's anxiety to take advantage of it; even so, his lifelong preoccupation with physical fitness was unusual, even for an athlete. He employed a personal trainer throughout the twenties and thirties, boxed whenever he could find a partner, played tennis and squash, skied, and ran a mile or more every day of his life. Much of this he did to keep in shape for the polo season and because he was a naturally competitive man, but his parents may well have instilled in him, as well, something like a dread of illness. His father had lost a sister when he was ten; his mother had lost both parents before she was six; his great-aunt Tantine (who lived with the Hitchcocks until she died in 1924) had lost her parents, brother, and sister-in-law. Both of his own parents had been sickly as children. In such a household it would have been natural that the conventional ideal of their class—a healthy mind in a healthy body—should acquire an exceptional urgency. He may well have assumed the unspoken corollary that any other death, especially a violent one in games or war, would be preferable.

Games, at any rate, were what he was born to. His youth at Aiken and Westbury was completely dominated by that mixed blessing of an upper-class childhood, organized activities. The principal one was riding, which all the children learned shortly after they learned to walk, if not before. At Aiken, there were drags every weekend, not the usual leisurely cross-country rides but flatout races through the woods, leaping timber fences banked with brush on either side. The Hitchcocks, father and mother, usually led these races, and in later years, when Mrs. Hitchcock's eyesight began to fail, those who caught up to them could hear her husband saying calmly to his wife, "Now, Loulie, we are coming to a jump."

There were other equestrian sports—sprints, show jumping, gymkhana. But none was half so appealing to young Tommy as polo. What he needed was an antagonist against whom he could actually feel his own strength and skill in action. A race was fun, the speed was exhilarating, but there was something hopelessly abstract about it. There was nothing abstract about polo. Nor about shooting. He had a shotgun in his hands at about the same time they gave him a polo mallet. There's a picture of him—aged six perhaps, clad in a velvet suit with knickers and white stockings, his brilliant blond hair hidden under a Fauntleroy hat—standing beside an enormous black man in a black suit who is evidently instructing him in the uses of a gun half again as tall as Fauntleroy. He became a superb shot, but he was never caught up in the ritual of shooting, the fetishism of guns, the tiny snobbish competitions over whose dog was the better. To him machines that flung clay pigeons were much more reliable than birds, and afterward there could be no argument over who had shot what or how many.

During the season, in Aiken, and throughout the Westbury summer, there was a nearly unbroken succession of social activities for the children to take part in if they wished—and sometimes when they didn't wish. In Aiken there were dances and picnics and amateur theatricals and buggy rides (where the object was to get a girl to sit on your lap) and cards and canoeing on the ponds. Nothing was missing except the abrasive excitement of a great city, and no one in the Hitchcock family missed that.

His sister, Helen, was the closest to him in age and temperament. Quite simply, she worshiped him. "When he went away to school," she told an interviewer, "I felt as though I were being divorced." She also paid him the supreme compliment of thinking him very naughty. He was, in a Tom Sawyerish sort of way, full of derring-do and mischievous pranks. Once, his parents gave a dinner party in Westbury. It was in the early days of the automobile, and Tommy was curious to try one of these contraptions. With Helen and a few other friends, he waited until the guests were seated at the table. Then he instructed his own little party to climb aboard an enormous Phaeton belonging to the Whitneys. How he managed the thing as well as he did no one knew—he'd never driven before—but after cruising about the policeless and untrafficked lanes for what seemed forever (to Helen), he chauffeured his gang safely back, only to find his mother and an agitated guest waiting in the drive.

Tommy was punished for that escapade (a fact that he jokingly blamed on the date, Friday the 13th), but there wasn't much that his mother could do when he contrived to miss his sister Celestine's wedding (to Julian Peabody, an architect) in the spring of 1912. He was singularly unimpressed by this great event: "Who did you say was getting married?" he had asked Helen on being told the news. "That girl I sometimes pass in the hall?"* And on the morning of the great day he invited Helen to

---

*His older sister, Celestine, known as "Tantine," was eight years older than he.

accompany him on a short jaunt in the buggy with their favorite pet, a donkey called Armandine. Off they went, but just where the dirt road sloped down to a ford in the Sand River, young Tommy did something to the wretched Armandine that made him upset the fly, slip the traces, and run off. Helen was overcome with terror and disappointment at the thought of missing Celestine's wedding, but Tommy reassured her that she had plenty of time to get back. He, of course, would have to retrieve the runaway donkey—a task that conveniently caused him to miss the ceremony but not the reception.

Tommy was fond of the dare. Once, hunting for frogs around a pond in Westbury, he offered a quarter to anyone—Sonny Whitney was there, Douglas Burden, some others, and Helen, of course—who would catch a tossed leech in his (or her) mouth. Sounds of retching greeted the proposal, followed by, "Well, let's see you do it!" No sooner dared than done. Tommy had swallowed the leech.

There was also the incident of the bicycle jump that only he would attempt. But with all these feats—and there were many of them, all serving to keep his friends' admiration of him on the edge of idolatry—his chums had the sense that somehow or other, like Tom Sawyer, he always knew exactly what he was doing.

The Hitchcock house was constantly full of children. This was not entirely because the Hitchcock boys and girls were so popular. It was also because Mrs. Hitchcock was genuinely fond of young people. She listened to them, paid attention to them, and encouraged them to grow up. Douglas Burden, for example, a playmate of Tommy's at both Aiken and Westbury and a lifelong friend, seems to have regarded the Hitchcock place as a haven from his own rather disorderly and heartless family. He was always welcome, and so were all the children's friends.

At the same time, everyone who knew them recognized the Hitchcocks' extraordinary sense of family solidarity. They were quite untouched by the solvents that great wealth set loose among many families of their class. They traveled little, seldom went to or gave parties, never lost themselves in buying and building, gave themselves up to no fads or fashions, rarely separated, and did not divorce. As a little boy Tommy wrote his mother from Aiken (she was ill in New York) about his approaching birthday party. He didn't want any "stranger children" at the party, he said, only his sister, parents, and Tantine. To the end of his life, he remained a cheerfully dutiful and affectionate son and a charmingly complicitous brother. He appreciated his good fortune, writing as much to Helen when he was seventeen, not an age when gratitude is often prominent among the feelings that one has for one's parents or the circumstances of one's upbringing. He seems to have known young, and never forgotten, that in family and place he'd been born lucky.

The idyll ended in the fall of 1910 when, at the age of ten, Tommy Hitchcock was sent to the Fay School, a pre-prep boarding school in Southboro, Massachusetts. Perhaps his parents felt that Tom Sawyer had to be tamed. More likely, they merely wanted him educated, for there was not yet even a reasonably satisfactory school in Aiken. Fay had been in existence for over half a century, serving precisely the same sort of families as the Hitchcocks—rural or suburban parents who wanted their boys* to go to one of the great New England prep schools such as Groton, St. Paul's, Andover, or Exeter, but who lacked any proper neighborhood "country day" to prepare them for the entrance exams.

Fay in 1910 was one big, rambling, three-story wooden building that looked just as all schools do—a cross between a small factory and a cheap hotel. Inside, surprisingly, this structure was just the sort of place that small boys like to live in—a warren of corridors, a labyrinth of cubicles, a maze of rooms and toilets and closets and other hideouts. There was also a hall for assembly, for the reading of dreaded reports, and for study space for the full complement of a hundred students. Outdoors there were broad playing fields, where boys were encouraged to work off their aggressions in games. It was bloody work, especially when the whole school was organized for a game of capture-the-flag in the snowy pine forest nearby. It was also great fun.

Tommy learned enough in his two years at Fay to win entrance at St. Paul's School (SPS). In 1912 this was not difficult; or so one may surmise from Tommy's difficulty with spelling. Yet there was a pattern to his errors for which formidable Tante Celestine must take the blame. She

---

*Girls, at least those in the Hitchcock family, were educated entirely at home. Foxcroft, where they might have gone, wasn't founded until the 1920s.

had taught him how to read and write in French. This resulted, when he turned to English, in some bizarre transpositions of French spellings for English words. For instance, in a bundle of tiny letters that Tommy wrote to his mother from Aiken when he was six or seven and she was ill in New York, French crept into his writing over and over, as when he says, "We will compte [he means count, which is compter in French] tonight how many days we will to see you." His spelling improved at Fay and St. Paul's, but he never got good at it.

As for what he left behind at Fay, apparently it was the same persistent awe that he struck in his friends at home. William Jackson, later a good friend and World War II colleague, came to Fay two years after Tommy left. He remembers standing one day looking idly at photographs of school football teams in previous years. An older boy came by, stopped, pointed a finger at the figure of Tommy Hitchcock, and said, "That's Tommy Hitchcock." Was he so good a player? Jackson wanted to know. "No," said the other in reverential tones, "but that's Tommy Hitchcock, honest to God it is."

The Second-Form dormitory at St. Paul's was a replica of the ones at Fay: the same three radiators lined up in the aisle like gymnastic equipment, the same curtained alcoves with partitions precisely seven feet high, the same master's bedroom strategically placed to facilitate his mission of eternal vigilance, the same big windows at one end, which, Tommy knew, would stay open even in the coldest nights of the year. Tommy felt perfectly at home in the dormitory. And though he was a "new boy" and a Second Former, back at the bottom of the heap, many of the fellows whom he saw that first day of school in September must have been familiar. Apart from his cousin, George Eustis, and a couple of boys from Fay, a great many of his formmates came from the same part of Long Island that he did. His parents knew their parents, he could count on that much, but he probably knew them too.

St. Paul's had always been a "New York school" (in the same sense that St. Mark's had always been a "Boston school"). In Tommy's form, for example, of sixty boys there were only seven Bostonians, eight from Philadelphia, ten from New Jersey, but twenty-three from New York.

Moreover, over one-third of the boys were from rural and semirural areas—places, in other words, just like Westbury. There was little chance that a St. Paul's boy of Tommy's day would ever encounter someone who was not quite like himself, in home setting and background, in religious and moral attitudes, and in his expectations, both social and economic. They varied only in what they expected of themselves.

But if all this were familiar—from Westbury or Fay—much about St. Paul's was new and different. There was the sheer size of the place, and the richness of its facilities. Admittedly, he must have been disappointed to be stuck in a dormitory again, but he could look forward, in two years, to getting into a decent-size room, either alone or with a roommate, in any one of the upperschool houses. These were scattered about the campus, which lay in a valley of gently rolling fields, meandering ponds and streams, and woods. If the school had any focus, metaphorically as well as visually, it was supposed to be the chapel, a Norman-revival building in brick and brownstone. In fact, however, the school focused on the playing fields, the tennis courts (twenty-four grass, nine clay), the nine-hole golf course, and, above all, the ponds—in winter for hockey, in summer for rowing.

There was a new rector at St. Paul's when Tommy went up there in the fall of 1912. His name was Samuel S. Drury and, happy and proud as Drury was to have been made head of one of the oldest and most prestigious boys' schools in the country, he was not altogether pleased that the ponds and playing fields occupied such a prominent place in the imaginations of his charges. One part of Dr. Drury's complex personality would always remain that of a missionary with New England's Puritan conscience.

When he came to St. Paul's he felt in many ways an outsider. The school in 1912 had almost four thousand living alumni, more than any private school except Andover and Exeter, and they were the essence of what privilege meant in America. They had, most of them, great wealth, social prominence, and considerable influence. They were the heirs of the merchants, industrialists, miners, railway builders, financiers, meat packers, and utility magnates who had created America's Industrial Revolution. These alumni had also created, they and their wives and children, a social stage for themselves that, in its grandiosity, was unique in the world. Viewed by the old aristocracy of Europe, this stage—really a linked panorama of Fifth Avenue chateaux, Newport cottages, and vast estates in the Eastern countryside—seemed both naive and vulgar, alluring and repulsive, but also endowed with undeniable energy. Viewed by the old, puritanical, upper classes of New England, this society seemed something much worse—a dangerously provocative display of vulgar undisciplined wealth that threatened the virtue and stability of the nation. An aristocracy of raw force and economic supremacy had been set in place. Dr. Drury's mission, as he saw it, was to forge within its heirs an aristocracy of disciplined power, responsibility, and idealism.

What Drury feared most for the boys of St. Paul's was that the material luxury they were born to would disrupt their great promise as the natural leaders of the country and the world. Luxury put them too far from reality, from stern necessity. "Most of them," he wrote, "are at least two generations removed from manual labor. They are getting soft." The boys' fathers, if not their mothers, had many of the same fears and the same expectations. They knew that there is no leadership without power. The boys were heirs to power—in resources, influence, and the respect of the less privileged. But power without a willingness to grasp a specific function in the world, without a desire to play some great role—without that, the boys would squander everything.

Yet what was this great role? Drury needed an image, a beau ideal of the type of young man whom he wanted his boys to be. It took shape in the five years that Tommy Hitchcock was at the school. He would contribute to it. So would the looming challenges of war.

To a twelve-year-old Second Former, of course, Dr. Drury was a rather strange and remote figure, an ungainly black presence that moved in and through the routine of school, but mostly above it. Tommy was in it, all the way. The boys rose early from their alcove beds and trotted, shivering, off to the communal bathrooms, then to breakfast. A chapel service began the day, the boys seated in banked pews by form, four rows on each side of the long nave that led from the porch to the altar. Behind and above them the masters sat ensconced in narrow thrones of Gothic woodwork. The service followed the Episcopal Church calendar: a reading of the Gospel or the Old Testament, a responsive reading from the Psalms, a hymn, a prayer, and then the great organ would burst into the recessional, and all the boys would file out, two by two, to their classes. Mrs. Hitchcock had been dubious about this aspect of St. Paul's. As a devout Catholic, she asked Dr. Drury whether her son's religion might not be undermined by constant immersion in a Protestant liturgy. He had replied that the boy would have to attend chapel service, but that he would be allowed to go to town for Mass on Sunday. St. Paul's posed no threat to his faith, Drury assured her.

Classes began at 8:25 a.m. There were usually six of them a day, back-to-back recitation periods of forty minutes that took the boys up to lunch and then began again, after sports, at 4:45 p.m. and lasted until supper. After supper there was study hall, then back to the dormitory and bed. There were variations in this schedule according to the season, the church calendar, and Dr. Drury's whim (it was his power and pleasure to give the boys a day off every now and then). And as the students grew older, they were given more freedom, not from the routine but from faculty supervision.

There were vacations as well, of course, generous ones at Christmas and Easter, which Tommy took at Aiken with his family: riding, shooting, playing polo, and generally venting the rebellious energies that inevitably built up in his free-spirited soul under such a regime. He "racketed around," as Drury would say, during his holidays and in the summers. But Aiken and Westbury, or at least the life that Tommy led there—an outdoor life of challenge and activity—would never have displeased the rector. It was not "soft."

Tommy's first two years at St. Paul's are, officially, a blank. His name does not appear on the roster of any team sport, even though athletics at the school had for some time been organized so that every boy, no matter what his age or skill, could participate. There were three clubs—the Isthmians, Old Hundreds, and Delphians—and each boy was assigned to one for intramural football, hockey, and baseball. There were also two clubs for crew in the spring—the Shattucks and Halcyons. Tommy was a Delphian and a Shattuck, but it wasn't until the fall of his Third-Form year, 1914, that he was mentioned in the records. He played football that season, alternating between left halfback and fullback, for a lowly Delphian team that had a bad season.

He did better on his own in the school turkey shoot. At fourteen he was already a devastating skeet and trapshooter—and a rather unorthodox one. Most people step up to the line, raise the gun to their shoulders, give the order "Pull!" and then aim and fire. Tommy, however, would usually amble up to the line, stand there rather diffidently with the gun cradled in one arm, and then call the pull, at which point he would raise the gun to his shoulder, aim, fire—and invariably destroy the clay pigeon. Douglas Burden (who was at Groton then, but still visited the Hitchcocks on vacations in Aiken) told a story about Tommy's prowess as a marksman. One afternoon Tommy announced that they were going to a shooting match. They climbed into the buggy, the beloved Armandine in the traces, but, on arriving, Burden was bewildered to note that the other contestants were all adults, including some of the most serious-minded shots in Aiken. Burden begged out and urged his friend to do likewise: he would only look foolish. Tommy smiled his quick little smile—half shy, half mischievous—and took his place. He won. Burden never forgot the image of a sturdy young boy, whipping the gun to his shoulder and firing with "the speed of lightning and the deadly accuracy of an executioner."

Hitchcock won the St. Paul's turkey shoot in 1914. Characteristically, though, he never entered it again. Even at fourteen, he was one of those people who always play to win—but seldom play at all unless there's a risk of losing.

Shooting, of course, was a skill that he'd learned at home. He'd played football at Fay. New to him at St. Paul's were hockey and crew. At St. Paul's, hockey was the great jewel in the sporting curriculum. With its good ponds and lakes, the school early decided to convert the mixed blessing of long winters into an asset. It took the Canadian sport as its own, changing the rules slightly in the process. Then as so many SPS hockey players went on to Ivy League colleges and introduced it there, the sport slowly spread from Concord all over New England and as far south as Princeton. But even well into the 1930s, SPS's dominance of the game was such that the Yale, Princeton, and Harvard hockey teams were invaribly made up of St. Paul's alumni, from the freshman squads to the varsities. Moreover, because in the early days there were no other outside teams that could compete with the school varsity, most of the major games in the season were played against college teams. And whether these men had been playing longer than the "Paulies" didn't seem to matter: SPS often won.

Everyone played, sometimes from mid-November till early March. In Tommy's time there were nine rinks on the Lower School Pond; each athletic club had twelve teams, so that on any afternoon in winter there might be as many as three hundred boys playing hockey—their shouts, the crack of pucks on sticks, and the crunch of skates on hard ice all rising in the cold air like the breath from their lungs. There was a mystique about it, too. The boys attended to the winter weather with pagan superstition. The forces that made the ice—particularly the brilliant black ice that comes with the first hard, fast freeze—were greeted with rejoicing, all the more so when the rector called a holiday to celebrate the manna that had fallen on the ponds overnight.

Tommy loved hockey. He never learned to skate well and therefore didn't make the varsity, but the speed, the wild bursting free from the boards, the bruising contact offered everything he wanted in a game at that stage in his life. Then, at the end of the afternoon, taking his equipment off in the skate house by the iron stove, there was the happy sensation of lassitude, the mind floating free, purged and serene.

In the spring of 1914, Tommy rowed, apparently for the first time, on a Halcyon four, at bow. On Anniversary Day, a reunion day celebration at St. Paul's, his boat beat the Shattuck four by five lengths, and in the excellent time of 5:25.4. The victory doubtless pleased him, but the truth is that he didn't much like rowing and never would, though he tried it again at Oxford after the war. No sport is more confining, physically and spiritually. It aims at the total integration of the individual's strength and will into a rhythmical whole. Turkey Pond, where the boys rowed, was a beautiful spot, surrounded by evergreens and birch trees. The fresh air blew strong there on some days. Yet, straining on the oars for unison and power, Tommy must have felt that he could just as well have been indoors, grunting in a gymnasium. On a crew, one races backward to the goal, with opponents invisible, on a straight line, the pace set by the coxswain, a tiny tyrant in the stern. It was a challenge of sorts, but not his sort.

Yet crew could stand as a metaphor for the changes that Dr. Drury was bringing to the school in the years before and during the First World War. He had been preceded in the rectory by a succession of weak headmasters under whom boys and faculty enjoyed a nearly savage anarchy. The masters were ill-paid, the great majority unmarried, and the strain of their duties was occasionally too much for some of them. There were instances of masters coming home from an overnight in Boston, drunk and guilt ridden. The boys in the dormitory, seizing their chance to avenge the oppressions of the past, would barricade them in their rooms and taunt them. Threats were frequent and there was a consistently high level of violence—boy on boy, master on boy. One man leapt on a student for failing to tip his hat to him on the path; another had to be forcibly dragged away from a boy whom he was energetically throttling in a corridor. Hazing was routine, even institutionalized. One day each fall, appropriately known as Bloody Sunday, was consecrated to a ritual mass beating of all new boys by the old.

It was to Samuel Drury's credit—certainly it was in his interests—to put an end to this barbarity. He told the trustees, the parents, the alumni, and the boys that the essence of school life as he saw it was "the exaltation of discipline." The keynote of the school, henceforth, would be obedience—obedience of boys to master, masters to the rector, and the rector to the will of God. This meant, in practice, a Draconian enforcement of scores of rules, against sin, of course, smoking, drinking, fagging, card-playing, but also against all unnecessary material possessions, especially money. From Drury's point of view, the rules served not only to hold the boys up to the mark of obedience but also to protect them from the enervating seductions of the luxurious world from which they came. In the interests of preventing these children of privilege from "getting soft," he preached the stern doctrine of self-denial. In one of the many cautionary tales that he wrote of school life, he put these words in the mouth of a headmaster lecturing a disobedient boy: "A stone for a pillow . . . adversity and solitude for this boy. That's it! No cushions but stones. The stone of self-control. The great stone of saying, 'No.'"

In Dr. Drury's eyes, sports provided perfect training in the exaltation of discipline. True, sports also occasioned dismaying reminders of the "country club" image of the place. Apart from a vigorous game of squash, Drury indulged in no athletics himself. But sports were changing in his early years at St. Paul's. Not long before he (and Tommy Hitchcock) came to Concord, the games favored by the boys were loosely organized, wide open: cricket, tennis, golf, cross-country running, and something that resembled rugby more than football.

By the 1910s, however, more and more boys were being caught up in tightly organized team sports: American football, hockey, and, above all, crew. Drury and his fellow instructors saw in team sports a practical as well as an ethical lesson. The practical lesson was that leadership, the great promise in these boys' future, had to be won from and in the team. Individual excellence was worthless unless nourished by a common consciousness and harnessed to a common goal. Leaders must first be followers. A boy of Tommy's day captured the St. Paul's ethos perfectly in an essay published in the *Horae*. The whole aim of the school, he wrote, was to train boys not in "the blind trust of the herd" (that was for the less privileged, presumably) but in "the thinking obedience of the pack."

As he would have done in most of the Eastern boarding schools of the time, Tommy was initiated in the literature and institutions of England as much as those of America—actually more so (which probably pleased Tommy's father). Two years of British history were offered, only one of American. "Selections" from the writings of the English classics were read year after year; of American writing they saw only Longfellow, Hawthorne, and Francis Parkman's *Oregon Trail*. Science courses—physics, chemistry, and a daring innovation called Physiology and Hygiene (read "reproductive biology")—were available, but rather looked down on as being too specialized and morally neuter. Sacred studies was required each year, a bland mixture of Bible study and the history of the Anglican and Episcopal Churches and their missions.

Instruction in these courses lay in the hands of more than forty faculty members, most of whom had a bachelor's degree from one of the better New England colleges. They taught, almost without exception, according to the well-tried system of recitation. There was no class discussion, no debate, only questions and answers, with masters doing all the questioning, pupils the answering if they could. Because this system eventually grows wearisome for teachers and a misery for students, the chief concern of all but the most gifted of the masters was keeping order in the classroom. This they did, according to a consultant whom Drury brought in to study the curriculum, mostly by yelling. The consultant was struck by "the extraordinarily loud tones" that he heard used in the Saint Paul's classrooms. Tommy must have disliked the noise; he came from a household in which the voice of authority spoke quietly and patiently.

Tommy made his way from form to form with no trouble. His grades hovered around the seventy mark—average for a school in which the top marks awarded were seldom above eighty. One year he received a testimonial for exceptional work. He joined the Scientific Association in his Fifth-Form year and later presented a paper on sound waves. He also joined the Cadmean literary society, and one year he debated the Concordian society on the merits of playing sports against other schools. His unexceptional academic performance at school (and later at Harvard, for that matter) was perfectly normal. Even as long ago as the eve of World War I, St. Paul's, in the eyes of parents and students alike, was what it is still: a specialized institution to prepare boys, and now girls as well, for college. If in the process the students acquired a distinctive manner and outlook, so much the better, but the main business of the place was to help them win entry into Harvard, Yale, Princeton, and the rest. This was not difficult. From 1909 to 1914, about 250 boys graduated from St. Paul's, of whom 235 went straight to good colleges. Nor was it difficult to graduate from college: Two hundred of this group did so. The point is that neither St. Paul's nor any other school on this chain of promotions was likely to impose challenging academic standards until the colleges did so, which didn't happen until about forty years after Tommy left. He got a good education at the school, marginally better than he would have had at most public high schools, but the fact that he didn't make more of it was as much a comment on the times as on his own capacities.

In his last two years at St. Paul's, Tommy was a hero. It was not because of his achievements as an athlete. Some of the students undoubtedly knew that he was already a first-class polo player, for polo was very much in the summer curriculum, so to speak, of the school. In 1913 five SPS graduates were among the competitors for a place on the American team that hoped to defend the Westchester Cup against England: H. W. Harriman of the form of 1897; H. S. Phipps, 1898; C. Wheeler, 1896; F. S. von Stade, 1903; L. E. Stoddard, 1885. Tommy was as good as all but the very best in this much admired sport, and in the summer of 1916 his name was in the papers as having won the Rathbone Cup.

Still, in school sports, his principal achievement was to captain the first Delphian football team in a winning season in his last year. For the rest, he was a scrappy and eager hockey player, but no star, and he only tolerated rowing.

At bottom the reason why he was a hero lay in his presence. By the age of sixteen, he was that rarity among schoolboys, someone perfectly at ease in his own skin. He was completely without pretension. He had no side to him. He was modest, not in the self-deprecating manner of people who call attention to their virtues by wittily minimizing them, but with the unthinking modesty of people who take even their best performances as challenges to carry out an even better one.

His presence had little to do with striking good looks. He lived in a time when masculine beauty was highly valued and praised without embarrassment. Tommy at sixteen had already attained his full height of five feet ten inches and he weighed a solidly muscled 152 pounds. Oddly, considering the tremendous development of his shoulders and right arm (it looked like a blacksmith's arm to one observer, the muscles standing out as if in a Michelangelo sculpture), his hands were small and delicate, his fair skin astonishingly soft. The tow-colored hair of his childhood had become darker—though it would always bleach in the summer—and a rebel lock of it seemed permanently apostrophied over his right eye. His features were bold: a long, straight nose; full, strong lips that revealed his passing amusement instantaneously and, as quickly, hid it again.

He never learned to relax in the eye of a camera: he stiffened slightly, politely giving in to the interruption. Normally, however, he was anything but stiff. He lolled, he slumped, and at any gathering of more than one he seemed somehow always to be just outside the circle. He was not shy. He positioned himself on the margin because it was the best place from which to observe. Socially, he was a spectator, not a contestant—and happily so. Even at sixteen he had a keen taste for social folly—in others. It amused him when someone made a fool of himself or outraged propriety in some way. A creature of the fresh air and action, he possessed a fine sense of the artificiality of codes of behavior. As a practical matter he always observed them, but he relished it when their fragility exploded in some wayward outbreak of idiocy, high jinks, or absurdity.

Underlying the presence of this man-boy was a quality as palpable as an electrical field. He embodied force. His schoolmates saw it displayed on the playing fields and hockey rink: his tremendous appetite to win, his relentlessness, the way that his mind worked in combat, now calculating where lay the advantage, now letting himself go in a near frenzy to achieve it. But even in repose he communicated force—except when he was bored—and then his eyes would skitter for escape. He had a way of looking at a person that could be enormously steadying, encouraging. But that was when the objective was given. Often, otherwise, there was a slight challenge in his hazel eyes, as if to say, "Ready? Okay, let's do it!" and a perfectly assured suggestion that he himself was ready for absolutely anything.

To the end of his life, there were those who would always say of Tommy Hitchcock that he was impetuous, violent, cruel. He was not. But he communicated the capacity for violent action and so inspired in his fellows a wary respect verging on awe. Later, the image that he aroused in those who knew him would settle, the edges of wariness dissolve away, leaving a fully rendered figure, compact, dynamic, resourceful.

Tommy Hitchcock was elected president of his Sixth Form, 1916–1917. Dr. Drury was delighted to report the news to the Hitchcocks, "confidentially" noting that Tommy had been his choice as well. What he didn't say, confidentially or otherwise, was that there had been more at stake in this election than a schoolboy popularity contest.

To the outside observer—the proud parent, for example—St. Paul's could seem to be a perfect theocracy, a benevolent despotism exercised by a man of God. This, until Tommy's Fifth-Form year, was an illusion. In actuality St. Paul's was governed more like a colony. At the top, directing the more important affairs such as the school's outside relations and its economy, were the rector and his assistants, the faculty. Under them were the "natives," the boys who were allowed to run the day-to-day affairs of the school much as they wished. Since the early 1880s, school politics had been in the hands of two secret societies, the oldest called the Hoi. The second was called the Bogi, in that it was originally made up of graduating Fifth Formers, or "bogus" Sixth Formers. Members enjoyed an immunity from ordinary school discipline that would have amazed their parents. At least once a year, for example, the Hoi shinnied out of their dormitories, clambered on to a waiting carriage, and went up to the Hopkinton Inn for an elaborate meal, brandy, and cigars. Bogis were given a special pin, they practiced a special handshake, and they taxed each other to subscribe to contraband issues of boys' magazines like *Puck* and *Life*.

Election to the societies followed the usual rules of school and collegiate clubs. The fifteen members—ten Sixth Formers and five Fifth Formers (the numbers changed as the school grew) —elected five members from the rising Sixth Form, who, in turn, elected five members from the rising Fifth Form. Membership was accorded high prestige, for the good reason that members wielded great power in the school, operating almost exactly as did the political machines of the cities of their day. Like the bosses, the boys' stock in trade was patronage. There were many positions of status in the school—*Horae* editorships, the Athletic Association, literary-society secretaryships, and more—and all were either held outright by members of the dominant club or in their gift. Moreover, if the office happened to be an elective one, the clubs were not above the usual forms of machine corruption—ballot-stuffing, intimidation, and bribery.

Until Dr. Drury arrived at St. Paul's, the rule of the "secret" societies was tolerated, more or less reluctantly. In some respects they made the masters' job easier: a minimal sort of order was kept by the boys themselves, and in any crisis—extreme bullying, say—they knew exactly whom to contact to get the bigger boy to stop.

Drury, however, was cut from a different cloth. He was a Progressive, a good-government man, and he loathed corruption wherever he saw it. More importantly, the Hoi and Bogi limited his own power. He vowed to get rid of them. Drury, however, was a sufficiently clever politician to realize that to abolish them by rectorial fiat risked arousing the anger of hundreds of powerful alumni who, having enjoyed the honor and power of membership in one of the societies, might see no reason to deny such honors and powers to their children. Many of these alumni, indeed, felt more immediate loyalty to their secret society than to the school: Dinners with former and present members were held at Christmas and Easter in New York, a tradition that went back thirty years; one society even owned "property" in the school, a camp at the far end of Turkey Road where members would go on suitable evenings to drink brandy and champagne, bootlegged into the woods by the driver of the Shattuck barge.

But the rector had a number of advantages in his campaign. First, times had changed after a decade of civil service reform efforts in the cities, led by men such as Theodore Roosevelt, and St. Paul's had become sensitive to the reproach of political corruption. Second, the clubs' initiation ceremonies had become increasingly grotesque, not to say sadistic. Among the Bogi, for example, a favorite "trial" of the initiate was to put him to bed mummified in coils of flypaper. The Hoi, for its part, fancied branding: a penny, heated white-hot over a gas jet, was placed on the initiate's belly. Finally, Drury had on his staff a young master who enjoyed an extraordinary degree of confidence and respect among the boys of Tommy's form, the rising Sixth Form, whom he hoped to persuade to destroy the secret societies. The young master was John Gilbert Winant.

Winant was twenty-six years old in 1915, Tommy's Fifth-Form year. He had graduated from St. Paul's in 1908. Tall, lanky, and strong, he looked not unlike one of his heroes, the young Abe Lincoln, and, like Lincoln, he was rock hard in his convictions, but easy and gentle in manner.

If Winant was the intermediary between Drury and the boys, Hitchcock was the intermediary between Winant and the secret societies. Tommy was a member, of course, but hardly a proud one. The cruelty of the initiations probably counted for less in his judgment than the childishness and pettiness of the elections, and the hocus-pocus of their meetings. He liked spontaneous outrageousness and absurdity, not the institutionalized sort. He enjoyed friendships, not clubbiness. Moreover, for two years now he had been one of Winant's circle—marginal but also impressed by the older man's character and idealism, his soft-spoken energy. Tommy would never be a reformer, but he now threw his prestige behind Winant's plan and with others persuaded the secret societies to disband as of the school year 1916–1917.

From September 1914, the opening of the new term, a few weeks after the guns of August had begun booming over Europe, the whole moral tone of St. Paul's School was colored by the consciousness of a great war—terrible and remote, yet also filled with alluring promise, as if all that the school stood for could be redeemed in this fullness of time. Drury was slow to sense the promise in the war. In time, it gave him the ideal figure for which he had been searching to dramatize the mission of his school. War was nothing if not adversity and denial. War was the perfect antidote for a generation of young men in danger of getting soft. War offered an exaltation of discipline unlike any other, certainly unlike anything that he could inspire at St. Paul's. It remained only to endow the war with a purpose, a cause, a transcendent goal that would lift the participants (his boys) to willing self-sacrifice, to an embrace of adversity.

The cause would be revealed soon enough, but in the fall of 1914, Drury could find none compatible with his sense of right. With Woodrow Wilson and with the vast majority of his countrymen, he professed neutrality toward the combatants, and providentially, the war news that he announced to the boys on opening day of 1914 was perfectly neutral as well. Two masters had chosen to serve country over school, but one had joined the British while the other had joined the Germans. As the year went on, however, the war news that kept breaking into the isolated Concord community was less balanced. The *Horae* reported in the late fall that three alumni—David King, 1911; Elliot Cowdin, 1905; and Victor Chapman, 1907—had enlisted in the foreign legion and were already fighting in the defense of Paris. About the same time, Theodore Marburg, a former U.S. minister to Belgium, gave the boys an account of Belgium's heroism in the war.

By early spring of 1915, St. Paul's was first among the Eastern boarding schools to establish a roll of honor. Both the first and second American college graduates to be killed in action in the Great War were SPS alumni: George Williamson, a lawyer and writer, who died fighting with the British near Ypres on November 8, 1914, and Andre C. Champollion, an artist and conservationist, who was killed in the French army in the Lorraine on March 25, 1915. No "old boy" from St. Paul's would ever be killed in the service of Germany, though one, a doctor, was decorated for his help to the German Red Cross. By the end of the war, however, 762 alumni out of 4,000 had served in U.S. or Allied forces, and 48 had given their lives for the cause.

Before the end of the spring term of 1915, masters and boys in Concord—as at virtually all Eastern boarding schools—had raised the money to purchase "a noble Ford" for the ambulance corps. It was driven by a 1910 Harvard graduate who wrote the school at least once a year about his adventures—and the Ford's—at the front. At the Last Night Exercises in June of 1915, the boys learned that they might soon be able to do more—indeed, ought to do more—than tamely endow an ambulance. Leonard Wood, the country's most eminent general, intimate of the school's most renowned novelist, Owen Wister, and close friend, too, of the school's favorite public man, Theodore Roosevelt, had come to talk on "preparedness."

General Wood had been campaigning up and down the Eastern Seaboard, proclaiming the inevitability of American involvement in the war and decrying the pitiful condition of the nation's military forces. By this time, the sinking of the *Lusitania*, with the loss of 1,198 lives, 114 of them American (including 2 SPS alumni), had convinced all but the most prudent of the school community that the Germans actually meant their enemies harm.

Wood's defense plan proposed setting up student military instruction camps (wriggling in this womb was the ROTC of another war); but as no such camps yet existed in the summer of 1915, the boys went off on a holiday, probably viewed by Drury as just more racketing around. Many of their fathers and older brothers, however, signed up for the first of the famed "businessmen's camps" in Plattsburgh, New York, to prepare themselves for the coming contest.

Tommy spent the summer of 1915 playing polo in Narragansett, Rhode Island, and later at Westbury. When he thought of the war it was as his parents did: They were unquestionably of the preparedness party.

His mother had been born in France, linked to it by ties of blood. Her first cousin Marie (Johnson) DuBos and her husband, Auguste, would soon lose their only son, Jean, in the grisly slaughter of Verdun. Tommy's father must have often wondered where he would be now had he chosen to live in England, as he nearly did on leaving Oxford. Colonel Roosevelt, the most stirring voice of preparedness, was a close friend of the Hitchcocks. The talk that summer must have been of war: the Allied chances of victory, American intervention, the huge loans floated by the Morgan Bank in England and France, and the terrific lift to the American economy given by Allied purchases here.

Back at school, Tommy was deep in the usual routine (old stuff now, for a Fifth Former), but rumors of war kept filtering in, suddenly charging the atmosphere with excitement. Concord had never seemed so much a part of the world. Each week brought a personal account of the war by a graduate. The *Horae* published an eloquent letter from Victor Chapman, in the Lafayette Escadrille, describing a bombing mission into Germany, and a detailed account by Julian Allen (a former roommate of Tommy's) of his work with wounded French soldiers at the American hospital at Neuilly. There was a lecture by Edward Toland on his experiences with the Ambulance Corps, and a grim report by David King of a battle at Verdun where his battalion lost fifteen hundred men in one day, then spent three days under constant bombardment trapped in a small fort "like two hundred fifty mice in a cracker tin."

More and more, Tommy felt growing in him an unfamiliar malaise. What was he to do? In late February he wrote his sister Helen a long letter:

> *It is a terrible day out; cold and raining. I suddenly realized that I have not received any letters for a deuce of a long time, and following up that train of thought, I also remembered that I have not written any. . . . Hence this.*
>
> *A great many nice people have been up here lately. Allen Ashburn stayed in my study for about three days. Bardy kept me awake all night, and some pretty girls, who were up here over February 22nd*

(Washington's Birthday, time of the traditional Mid-Winter Dance) made me forget all about my work. All the parties are over and it is raining, a cold piercing rain.

At regular intervals I think about what to do this summer and my brain gets clogged and I remain in a stupor for several days. I recover from this infantile paralysis in time to think about what courses to take at college.

When I come to, I wonder what the devil to do when I get out of college, and by that time I am too exhausted to faint, so I sit at my desk and look out of the window and watch it rain, a cold piercing rain.

Another schoolboy military-preparedness camp had been planned for the summer, a five-week course on Plum Island in Long Island Sound. The *Horae* editorialized, "No longer . . . the weak, anemic, half-hearted bluff at national defense . . . their duty will be to learn how to fight, in order that fighting will not be necessary." A St. Paul's infantry company was formed in the spring under the leadership of a master who had been at Plattsburgh. There is no record of what Tommy thought of the infantry company, but it's hard to imagine that parading, marching in close-order drill, the manual of arms, and the rest of it much appealed to him. Fifty-five of his schoolmates signed up for Plum Island, but in the end Tommy was not one of them. He tried the navy.

There was, he knew, a program called the Naval Training Cruise for Civilians, but he also knew that he was only sixteen years old and that one had to be eighteen to qualify. However, there was a small-print exception for young men with "previous nautical experience" that offered some hope, and he resolved to apply. He could sail, row; he knew the basic knots; he could swim. He was also, as anyone could see from his physical development, unlikely to embarrass the navy by collapsing under the rigors of a battleship cruise. On July 3 he was accepted and assigned to the USS *Maine*. His father went down to the dock at Newport to see him off. He found the officers pleasant, and he enjoyed learning what they had to teach him. There is a photograph of him standing with a half-dozen of his shipmates on the deck, looking slightly foolish in his oversize uniform. The experience convinced him that the navy was not what he wanted either. He must have found it claustrophobic, and he suffered from seasickness as well. At the end the Navy Department presented him with a certificate signifying his successful completion of the course. It was signed by Franklin D. Roosevelt, the acting secretary of the navy. Tommy was proud of that testimonial; it was one of the few such memorabilia that he saved.

He played polo, too, that summer of 1916, the last summer of peace—again at Narragansett. It was cooler there than at Meadow Brook, the resort being on the westward side of the bay, with Jamestown Island lying between it and Newport. The Hitchcocks rented a small house not far from the beach and adjoining the Narragansett polo field. Douglas Burden, always glad to spend whatever time he could with the Hitchcock family, came down from Groton at the beginning of the summer and stayed the season with Tommy, sharing a tiny maid's room in the attic. In the morning they rose early, went to the stables, and exercised the ponies. Tommy took care of the Hitchcock string, while Burden looked after a string owned by the great International Cup player and captain, Harry Payne Whitney. Before lunch the boys went to the beach and afterward returned to stick and ball or practice matches. In the evening, sometimes, there would be parties, and occasionally they would go over to Newport for a debutante ball—it was two ferry rides away, and they could spend the night at the Burdens.

Most of the time, however, they stayed at Narragansett, a place more tolerant than Newport of high spirits, of informality, and of the privacy that the elder Hitchcocks preferred. Some evenings they'd dine with Tommy's parents, on others they might motor to the Dunes Club to see their friends. Tommy, with one older sister and one sister so close in age that they might have been twins, had none of the typical boarding school boy's bashfulness with girls. Standing about on those deep verandas—the boys in white flannels and blue blazers, the girls in flounced layers of lace—Tommy cut a less handsome figure than Burden, who was strikingly good-looking; nonetheless, Tommy communicated a sense of barely contained animal spirits that some girls found irresistible.

He made conquests on the polo field as well. His play had never been so fast and determined; he seemed everywhere at once, checking and whirling as if he were on a broomstick, relentlessly chasing the ball, exultantly riding off his opponents. He played hard, with an unwavering concentration of purpose that sometimes alarmed knowledgeable onlookers. "Look out for that Mr. Hitchcock," his groom murmured to Burden when the two were on opposite sides. "You just watch out for him." Yet surprisingly in one so good and so young, Tommy was also a generous player. Of the Rathbone Cup finals, the junior championship that his team won that year, the *New York Times* said, "Burden was the star of the game, his plays being marked by long and perfectly straight hits." What Burden remembers about the game, however, is that Tommy, playing at three, hit pass after pass to his friend at one, while Burden had only to pick up the ball and put it through. They won the cup over a Point Judith team by a score of 15½ to 6, Burden racking up six goals and Tommy, ten (Tommy, also losing the half a point on a penalty).

That fall, he was a Sixth Former, at the pinnacle of his school career, and he threw himself into school activities and responsibilities as never before. Fear of a polio epidemic delayed opening day until October 5, but in November he led the Delphians to an undefeated season over their rivals and was rewarded with a place on the SPS varsity. It remained honorific, however, because the school was unable to arrange any outside games that year. He also took the leadership—ironically, in view of where he would find himself eighteen months hence—of a fund-raising campaign for Allied prisoners of war. They raised $5,800, $800 more than he'd expected.

He lived in the New Upper, under Gil Winant. The two talked, sometimes late into the night: Tommy about what he was going to do with himself, Winant about his pursuit of a seat in the New Hampshire State Assembly. Drury, responding positively as always to any hint of idealism in one of his subordinates, had given Winant all the time he could spare to pursue his campaign, and in the past months the young master had visited every workplace and almost every home in his district. His platform was strongly progressive, far to the left of most of his students. He was for a forty-hour workweek, for example. Most SPS boys would have deplored that limitation on the "freedom" of labor. He also supported women's suffrage, which SPS boys were forever debating and forever turning down as a threat to the sanctity of the home. If Winant's views were too radical for Tommy, he never let their disagreements come between him and his admiration of the older man. Besides, they probably talked more about the war than about electoral politics.

By early February 1917, a week before his seventeenth birthday, Tommy had evidently made up his mind to join the aviation corps. He seems to have anticipated some resistance from his parents, for in a letter to his father he felt that he had to argue the point. The navy was not a realistic option, he said, his "knowledge of naval things" was insufficient. On the face of it, this was an absurdity: He knew a good deal more about naval things than he did about aviation things. Nevertheless, there was a deeper sense in which he was right. However much Tommy knew about the navy, he knew that it was not for him; however little he knew about combat flying, he knew—and rightly—that it was for him.

His father must have known it, too. In 1917 the Hitchcocks were closer in time to the Wright brothers' feat at Kitty Hawk than those in the 1980s are to the first space flight. And flying was not a technological fantasy on TV. The elder Hitchcock had seen it done, often and from the earliest days of flight (Aiken was not far from Kitty Hawk). Anyone could do it—anyone, that is, with the necessary skill and daring. It was a form of sport, a new world game.

Moreover, as a deadly sport, flying had acquired an enormous following in America. World War I chalked up many "firsts," but one was that it became "the first press agents' war" (as the *New York Times* put it, as early as September 1914). War correspondents such as Richard Harding Davis came into their own in this static war where all battles were much alike and where, in the intervals, a curious domesticity settled over the trenches, which made "human interest" stories all the easier to report. But of all the journalism that appeared on this side of the Atlantic, the story that most caught the imaginations of families like the Hitchcocks was the story of the Lafayette Escadrille.

It began with the formation of a predominantly American fighter squadron within the French Air Service: the N-124 (N for Nieuport, the type of plane they flew). For French propagandists, however, N-124 was a less-than-catchy name for a fighting group whose career they hoped to exploit in America to win support for the French cause. They hit, instead, on the inspired "Lafayette Escadrille." In a short time it became what it has remained ever since, the most famous air-combat group in history. Its career was brief, beginning in April 1916 and ending, for all intents and purposes, some months after the United States came into the war a year later. By that time many of the original volunteers were dead or wounded, but the aims for which they'd made their sacrifice had been attained. The Lafayette's well-publicized valor had silenced the talk in European governmental circles, Allied and German, that Americans were afraid to fight. Myron T. Herrick, the longtime U.S. ambassador to France, wrote, "To many of us they seemed saviors of our national honor, giving the lie to current sneers upon the courage of the nation." At the same time, by fighting in the spotlight of publicity—and in the newest, most dangerous, and most conspicuous form of warfare—the Lafayette had dramatized the war for American public opinion in a way that a volunteer in the trenches (and there were many American volunteers in the trenches) could never do.

The imaginative appeal of aviation, of combat in the air, was compelling long before most people understood what it was. For hundreds of years warfare had been waged not by individuals but by armies. Mass warfare doesn't rule out individual heroism, of course, but heroism under such conditions is unlikely to be seen, and if seen, reported, and if reported, confirmed, and if confirmed, rewarded. Trench warfare is mass warfare industrialized, so that while the anonymity of the soldier or junior officer is somewhat dispelled by the intimacy of trench life iteself—which also makes heroism visible again—the actual agents of death are wholly impersonal, mechanical, a screaming rain. As one young Andover boy put it, after seeing artillary fire for the first time in the ambulance corps, "This war is all electric operation, explosions, death—and that is what fills you with fear—a fear of electricity, of the unknown and omnipotent."

The war in the air was just as dependent on "electricity," the weapons just as impersonal, the transport just as mysterious (few aviators had the slightest knowledge of how and why their machine managed to fly). But aerial combat was individual combat. Pilots were always being told to fly in strict formation—it was less dangerous for them and more so for the enemy. In fact, the pilots always somehow went off on their own, solitary hunters in the immensities of space. Early in the war, pilots began painting private insignia on the fuselages of their planes, like devices on a shield, so that they could be recognized by their opponents and remembered when they were shot down. Soon the various squadrons began designing insignia of their own. Finally, the combat was visible, supremely so. Flying in overcast weather was almost impossible in those days of rudimentary navigational equipment, and the optimum fighting altitude for a World War I fighter plane was never so high that one couldn't witness it from the ground or from observation balloons. When battle was joined, the combatants had an audience. Not always, not even usually, could this audience—soldiers in the trenches, support troops, civilians in back of the lines—actually distinguish much of what was going on in the sky over their heads. But they could see something, and the boys in the air knew it, and it made all the difference. It made it possible to keep score.

The French were apparently the first to conceive the notion of the "ace," and they saw in it a marvelous opportunity to stoke the fires of patriotism. The Germans adopted the idea from the French and heavily publicized their own aces, Richtoffen, Boelcke, and the rest. The British never formally endorsed the scoring system, but the Americans did, possibly because so many of their most famous fliers had fought with the French before the United States entered the war.

It was a pernicious thing, much despised by the pilots themselves. The great French ace Guynmer, for example, was approached by a woman at a reception who asked, "Ah, *mon cher* Lieutenant, what medal has France not yet pinned to your breast?" He looked at her coldly and replied, "A wooden cross, madame."

His rival, Boelcke, was retired against his will by the German air force after Richtoffen was killed, for fear that he, too, would be shot down and the population demoralized. One night he went to the opera, which he loved, and noticed that the words of an aria had been rewritten to sing his glory. He was so sickened by this idolatry that he returned immediately to the front and a few days later was shot down.

That aerial combat was in some sense personal, that journalists could keep score on the performances of individual warriors, raised air warfare to a completely different level of significance from what was happening on the ground. The great literature of World War I would come out of the trenches, out of the agony and ironies of self-regard, as men watched themselves sucked into the bloody mangle that lay between the two lines that the French called, with gross affection, *les boyaux* (the bowels). There was no literature of the air, only a rhetoric, hackneyed, comforting, and yet also inspiring, as in the words of Lloyd George. "High in the firmament . . . they fight out the eternal rivalry of right and wrong . . . Every flight is a romance, every record an epic. They are the knighthood of this war, without fear and without reproach; and they recall the legendary days of chivalry, not merely by the daring of their exploits, but by the nobility of their spirit."

When Tommy Hitchcock sailed for France in the spring of 1917, he carried with him a present from his mother, a collection of Victor Chapman's letters published by his father. Thanking her, he wrote (expansively, for him) what a wonderful man Victor must have been. By that time Chapman was dead, the first American flier to fall in the war, and his funeral precipitated an outpouring of proud grief on both sides of the Atlantic. That was in early July 1916. But another death, on October 12, had brought the war, and the Lafayette, even closer to the Hitchcock home.

Norman Prince was twenty-nine when he died. His plane, riddled with bullets, had crashed in a field in the Vosges on returning from a bombing raid. The Hitchcocks, parents and son, knew Norman well: he was the eldest son of their great friends, Frederick and Abigail Prince, from whose house in Pride's Crossing they'd been married. Norman was a short, powerfully built young man who had graduated from Groton, Harvard, and the Harvard Law School and had played a good deal of polo before becoming, in 1913, enthralled by flying. He enlisted in the French army early in the war, and in December 1915 he was already a hero in preparedness circles. Front-page articles in New York, Boston, Philadelphia, and Pittsburgh carried the news that he and two other young American aviators in the French army were returning to the States on an eight-day leave. Besides Prince there was Elliot Cowdin, son of a Tuxedo Park ribbon manufacturer and also a poloist, and William Thaw, a Yale dropout and a longtime aviation buff (he'd been the first man to fly under all four of New York's East River bridges).

The men were on a propaganda errand for the Allies; they knew it and made the most of their celebrity. The Germans knew it, too, and Ambassador von Bernstorff, after an encounter with Thaw, whom he'd known socially, called on Wilson to intern the three pilots as violators of American neutrality. (Wilson did nothing.) Cowdin deprecated the dangers of aviation, saying that the worst of it was the cold; Thaw kept up a series of pleas for preparedness; and Prince, speaking at Boston's Tavern Club and at the Yale Club in New York, praised the excellent technical instruction given French aviators.

By the time the group returned to France in January 1916, they left behind "a vivid impression of the romantic life led by a new branch of fighting man." American response to the aviators also convinced the French War Ministry that the inconvenience of setting up a special air squadron for American volunteers would be more than balanced by the propaganda benefits. Moreover, the most famous American patron of aviation, William K. Vanderbilt, had agreed to supplement the 50-franc salary normally given French airmen with a $100-a-month stipend. (Vanderbilt continued his support even after the number of Americans flying for France had jumped from a dozen or so to two hundred.)

Stories of the Lafayette, the cavalry of the air, stirred the imaginations of everyone at St. Paul's School, finally including the rector himself. Indeed, Samuel Drury had found an image of what he wanted his boys to be, an image struck of the same metal as the knighthood of the air: a youthful warrior with "a homing affinity," as he would say, "for the things that are difficult and daring and fine." The image was of David, the fair shepherd who refuses the armor of Saul because he has not yet proved his worth to wear it, then runs to meet the arrogant Goliath armed only with his sling, his smooth stone, and the bright gaiety of his conviction—and slays him so that "all the earth may know that there is a God in Israel." For the rest of his life, Drury held up this heroic ideal for St. Paul's. David belonged to the bright day, to the smooth, hard stones of a desert, and to a struggle with gross, vainglorious evil. St. Paul's School, he would say, must not become an infirmary for cripples, but an armory, full of breastplates of righteousness and swords of salvation. The armory became real only once in Drury's lifetime—just now, in Tommy Hitchcock's last year of school.

Sometime before the Easter vacation of 1917, Tommy made up his mind to go to war as a combat pilot. His parents agreed, asking only that he go down to Newport News, Virginia, where the Curtis Aircraft Company ran a flying school, to test his aptitude for the new game. This meant leaving school early and required Drury's permission. He readily gave it, writing Mr. Hitchcock, "Please tell his mother that we have high hopes for his contributing to the great cause and returning to her more fully a source of pride than ever." Shortly after Tommy went down to Newport News, the United States declared war. On April 5, at 3:00 a.m., the great moment proclaimed by the evangels of preparedness had arrived. And the elder Hitchcock was as eager to serve the Allies as his son was. Almost as soon as America declared war, the administration undertook to supply the men and machines that would soon gain the Allies supremacy in the air. The French proposed that within six months the United States begin delivery of 5,000 pilots, 4,500 planes, and 50,000 mechanics. This proposal, optimistic though it was, proved popular with the American people; and it provided the elder Hitchcock with an immediate opportunity to serve. There was no shortage of young Americans who wanted to fly; eventually more than fifty-eight thousand would volunteer for the U.S. Air Service. But there was a need for officers in the training programs and Tommy's father, despite his fifty-seven years, was commissioned a major at the Mineola Air Field.

For Tommy, however, it was not so simple. He felt, with good reason, that if he joined the American army he might never see action. The War Department was in such chaos that ordinary foot soldiers, much less trained aviators, would not be fighting in France before six months. Furthermore, he was too young for the American Aviation Corps. Years later Hitchcock would half-seriously complain that the Americans had prevented him from fighting for his country in the First World War because he was too young and in the Second because he was too old. This was true enough, but there's no evidence that in the first war he tried hard to join the American service. His heart had been set on the Lafayette Escadrille, which seemed to offer the fastest route to the front.

By the time Tommy could attempt to join the squadron, the Escadrille was, strictly speaking, no more. It had been swallowed up by the Lafayette Flying Corps. Legally the corps was a branch of the French foreign legion. This arrangement enabled France, for diplomatic purposes, to define its American pilots as mercenaries rather than as volunteers. But as the corps grew, it also became more bureaucratic, more formal and strict, and one of the criteria about which it was strict was age. Nineteen was the limit in the American aviation, but the Lafayette, from Tommy's viewpoint, was no better. The limit was eighteen, and he was still seventeen. The corps maintained an enlistment office in New York; nothing could have been more convenient. But how was he to pass the age barrier?

At this juncture, Tommy's parents spoke to the one man in America who was certain to be sympathetic to Tommy's wishes and who could, with equal certainty, do something about them, Theodore Roosevelt. Roosevelt was then desperately trying to persuade Wilson, the man whom he had vilified for three years as having no more guts than a sick dog, to give him command of a regiment. Roosevelt's sons had rushed into the service, Theodore into the army, Quentin into the air corps, with their father's fervent blessing. He could hardly refuse to help the son of his friend. Whatever Roosevelt did, it worked, and some weeks later the grateful Mr. Hitchcock received a letter from the former president:

Dear Tommy, I was more than pleased to be of even the slightest use; your Tommy is as fine an example of the best American type of soldier and gentleman as I know—he couldn't be anything else, having in view his father and mother.

Yes, you and I, and our wives, do indeed have cause to be proud of our boys.

Always yours, Theo. Roosevelt

Events moved quickly for Tommy from that moment on. Back at St. Paul's at the end of April, he found the school in turmoil. He learned that Gil Winant was making plans to join the Lafayette, too, as soon as the legislature adjourned in June. But Tommy would not wait so long. He asked Dr. Drury if he could leave before graduation. The rector asked only for a letter from his father. On May 31 he wrote Mr. Hitchcock in Westbury:

> *Tom has handed me your letter of May 25th, and on Sunday we had a pleasant breakfast together. I hope you realize how much we love and admire your boy here at St. Paul's and how prayerfully we follow his "changes and chances" during the coming months . . . It seemed to me that he had grown older during just the week of his absence.*

It was a splendid way to leave: no graduation ceremony, with its inevitable anticlimax, no sticky good-byes. It was a clean break, made all the easier by the knowledge that at St. Paul's he had indeed been "loved and admired." This was no idle compliment of Drury's. Hitchcock had achieved in his years at St. Paul's a balance of qualities—self-assurance and modesty, aggressiveness and compassion, humor and seriousness— that must have struck the rector as the summation of everything that young manhood should be.

Chapter Two

France, 1917–1918

THE *TOURAINE* WAS A BIG, FRENCH-OWNED LUXURY LINER THAT FOR three years had been ferrying volunteer ambulance drivers, nurses, French officials, and the bolder sort of tourist back and forth to the war. She was armed, carrying a monstrous sixteen-inch gun in the bow, and by June she was overcrowded. But like a once-elegant woman fallen on hard times, she made every effort to keep up appearances. The food, Tommy noticed, was excellent, and though the cabins were a bit stuffy, they weren't bad enough to keep him from sleeping ten hours a night.

U-boats were on everyone's mind. The submarines had sunk thousands of tons of Allied shipping since February alone. But worrying about matters over which one had no control was not a Hitchcock characteristic. Tommy had several friends on board, most of them headed for the ambulance service, and on one occasion he posed for a photograph with a group of them. There were "York, Winter, Guest, Rodgers and Shreiber," and others unnamed in the caption, all looking several years older than Tommy. He is sitting slightly apart from the rest, wearing his St. Paul's regulation dark suit and looking at the camera with mild seriousness, an open book in his hands, most likely the collection of Victor Chapman's letters his mother had given him.

He had expected at the beginning of the voyage to be thoroughly bored before he arrived at Bordeaux, and he was. As the liner steamed the ten miles up the Gironde on the morning of Sunday, June 10, he stood by the rail in the sunshine and watched the patterned vineyards passing by. As the ship neared the city, the narrowing river brought them closer to the shore. At one point he could look right down into the compound of a prisoner-of-war camp, which the French had provided as an attraction for incoming troops. At the quay Tommy packed his bags into a rickety old cart and clattered off for the station hotel to spend the night before going on to Paris.

That evening he had his first taste of what soldiers do when they're not fighting heroically; they fight unheroically. He was sitting in a cafe with a group of Lafayette volunteers when some French soldiers came over to inquire as to who or what they were. One of the Americans loudly began insisting that they were Germans. *"Nous sommes Boches,"* he cried, and the others took up the refrain. A huge fracas followed, which Tommy happily reported in a letter to Helen, though he felt bound to explain that the Americans had been "a bit tight." More to his taste in absurdity was the story he told of another American, a fellow who had been a stoker on a railroad before the war. He decided that the quickest way to Paris was to hop a ride on a night train, pretending to be a fireman. The trouble was, Tommy wrote, that the man hadn't the smallest clue as to where he was or where he was going and consequently spent the entire night shoveling coal, only to find himself, at dawn, still in the Bordeaux train yards.

Tommy arrived in Paris on the morning of June 12. It had been arranged that he would stay with family friends, the Frederick Allens, who had kept a house in Paris since 1908. Allen was an international lawyer who had been secretary and counsel to the Lafayette Flying Corps since 1916. His son Frederick, just out of Harvard and already a flier, had joined the American aviation back in the States; Julian, his second son, who'd been in Tommy's class at St. Paul's, was with the American ambulance corps and would soon transfer to the Coldstream Guards. His daughter, Barbara, then twenty, was with Miss Anne Morgan's American Friends of France, driving a car. She and Julian were the only family members in Paris that June, staying there with Lisa Dolan and Caroline Stevens, two friends of Barbara's who were also doing volunteer work. The older Allens were in New York.

Arriving late in the evening, Tommy spent the night in a hotel rather than disturb his hosts. The next morning, Wednesday, June 13, General Pershing was triumphantly presented to the people of Paris by the French government. With Marshall Joffre, other generals, and members of the cabinet, he rode at the head of a great parade up the Champs-Elysees. Tommy, however, never saw the parade. What caught his eye as he made his way to the Allens were the signs of war in the streets. Everywhere he looked were women dressed in black, men hobbling on crutches, the blinded, the gassed. Later he would learn to spot the deeper wounds in blanched faces, expressionless eyes, bodies held rigidly erect by sheer will. He saw what others before him had seen, that there was no gaiety in Paris in 1917. It had been replaced by a stiff fortitude that people once thought more characteristic of the English than the French.

The Allens' house was in the 16th Arrondissement, at 19 Rue Reynouard. The quartier, near the Bois, was uncrowded in those days, suburban and middle-class. The Allens' place, however, dated from the eighteenth century; it was an elegant *hôtel particulier* with a courtyard on the street. Ushered in by a servant, Tommy passed through the hall to the main drawing room with its great windows giving onto a magnificent, terraced garden that went down the Seine. This was to be his home for the next eighteen months, the place to which he returned whenever he had a permission, or leave.

For two weeks Tommy combined fun, family, and bureaucratic routine in a not unpleasant mixture. He was a young American in Paris in the spring. He was seeing old friends and making new ones. He discovered congenial and hospitable cousins, the DuBoses, who made much of him. And there was the astonishing fact—he remarked on it several times in letters home—that even under the terrible "handicap" of war, Paris could still be a wondrously charming city in which to spend a spring afternoon. It made him a bit homesick; the teahouses and cafes and restaurant terraces reminded him how much Helen would love to be there. Still, underlying all his thoughts—and undercutting his pleasure as well, to a degree—was his eagerness to get on with it, to get through his training, to get his wings (be breveted), and to get to the front where the combat was. This is why he'd come to France, and he never lost sight of it.

His first order of business was at the headquarters of the Lafayette Flying Corps, at 23 Avenue de Bois de Boulogne. It was a modest town house belonging to Dr. Edmund D. Gros, an American physician who had helped Prince, Cowdin, and Thaw to set up the Lafayette eighteen months before. Gros received each candidate, gave him a physical examination, chatted with him briefly ("a sort of moral examination"), and then set in motion the paperwork that sooner or later would result in the volunteer's being sent to the aviation school at Avord. Tommy arrived on the morning of June 14 and was greeted by Mrs. Georgia Ovington, Dr. Gros's secretary and the wife of an American business- man in Paris. (Their only son, Carter, was then in training at Avord; he would be killed in combat a year later.) She took his enlistment papers from the New York office, his letters of recommendation, and showed him into Dr. Gros's office. A bulky middle-aged man with a Prussian haircut and mustache, the doctor soon had Tommy jumping up and down a few times, balancing on one foot with his eyes closed, twirling around on a piano stool, also with his eyes closed, and walking in a straight line, with his eyes open. Pronounced fit "medically and morally," he was returned to Mrs. Ovington, who explained that next he would be summoned to the military caserne at Les Invalides, where he would be inducted into the foreign legion. Then he would receive his orders to report to Avord.

At least he hoped to go to Avord. It was reputed to be (and was) the best aviation school in the world, especially for the sort of aviator Tommy wanted to be, a *pilote de chasse*, a pursuit pilot.* But the French were eager to have pilots of every sort, bombers and aerial observers, as well as the more glamorous, and therefore more sought-after, pursuit pilots. In the- ory Hitchcock could have been sent to another school, and he admitted that the possibility worried him slightly. But for now, as he left Dr. Gros's office to lunch with the DuBoses, all he knew was that he had to wait.

Auguste DuBos had married Tommy's mother's first cousin, Marie Johnston, yet another of the Eustis family to be raised abroad. They had two children: Madeleine, a rather plain girl, younger than Tommy, and Jean, who had been killed the previous autumn, cut down by machine- gun fire, his body lost in the mud.

---

*The term "fighter pilot" belongs to the next world war.

46

Tommy wrote his mother that the family still grieved Jean's loss, a fact that seemed to puzzle him. "They should not feel so badly," he said, "because he died so well. It should be a pleasure more than sorrow to them."

But "Cousin Auguste," as Tommy called him, whatever his sorrow, was also a man of the world. A friend of Edward VII, he loved *le monde* and shared with his young cousin an appreciation of fine horses. In fact, much of Hitchcock's time in Paris was spent with horses. He spent many hours at the steeplechase in Chantilly and was impressed that such a racing scene existed at all in wartime. He wrote his mother that twelve hundred or so horses were stabled at Chantilly and that fields were run with as many as ten to fifteen horses. And this was only the steeplechases; at Anteuil and Longchamps there was flat racing as well.

Apart from the racing, there were errands to run, letters of introduction to be presented to his bankers, Monroe & Co., and a uniform to be ordered from Hill Brothers and boots from Buntings. He hadn't the right to wear the uniform yet—it would come only with the brevet—but it was very striking in appearance, with a horizon-blue tunic, broad leather belt and tan jodhpurs, and laced boots. Overseas caps were then coming into fashion, so he got one of those, too.

Hitchcock also spent a good deal of time with the group of young people who collected around the Allens: Julian and his sister Barbara, Rose Dolan, Caroline Stevens, and Chester Bassett. One Saturday they escaped the heat of the city to go swimming at Saint Cloud; another day they all went out to Fontainebleau to see the palace and lunch in a fine restaurant. He dined several times with an older couple, the Count and the Countess Wijslaw Orlowski (Aunt Mabel to the Allens). He had never met anyone quite as worldly as the count, and he was much impressed. "A most attractive and amusing man," he wrote his parents, "who has been all over the world and gambled at everything." The social life took its toll on his purse. "I've been living pretty high," he wrote his mother, asking her to be sure to send his allowance, which he hadn't received since he was at St. Paul's in May.

How preposterously far away Concord, New Hampshire, must have seemed to him then. But he had not forgotten St. Paul's or Dr. Drury. Tommy wrote the rector a cheerful letter, asking for news of school—

who had won the prizes at graduation, whether the Shattucks or Halcyons had won the boat races. But in the midst of all this activity, he never forgot why he was in France. "I have been having a fine time here," he wrote his mother on June 20, "but will not be sorry to get down to Avord, because this is neither the time or place to amuse oneself."*

The Ecole Militaire d' Aviation at Avord was not only the best flying school in the world, it was also the largest. Located 120 miles south of Paris at the western end of the chateau country, the school was spread over more than three square miles of flat farmland halfway between Bourges and Nevers. The landing fields themselves occupied the greatest part of this space, of course, but Avord was designed to house two thousand students, several hundred instructors and mechanics, and about nine hundred airplanes. The site had been laid out with an elegant geometry, unmistakably French: barracks, bathhouses, messes, offices, and the enormous white canvas-covered hangars were all like plantings in a formal garden, knit together by paths of white gravel.

Hitchcock arrived July 1 and remained there for the next four months, alternately fretting at the delays in his progress through the school and exulting in the actual flying. At the commissariat, he was told at what barracks to report and handed an innocent-looking straw mattress to serve as bedding. His smart new uniform from Hill Brothers would have to wait until he'd earned his brevet, but he'd brought down with him a light khaki uniform for everyday wear. In addition he then received from the French the standard-issue leathers and the teddy-bear suit, plus Meyrowitz goggles. Burdened with this gear, he made his way to his new quarters, which he found to be "not all that bad." It was a high-ceilinged wooden shed, lighted by windows at either end and by electricity at night, and it had hot-water sinks and showers a few steps away. At first glance the accommodations were not very different from the dormitories at Fay or SPS, and Hitchcock, despite having just come from the comparative luxury of the Allens', probably felt on fairly familiar ground.

Many of his twenty-two barrack mates probably seemed familiar, too. It was commonplace to divide Lafayette volunteers into two groups, the

---

*Six days later his papers arrived. He was to go to Avord. On Thursday, June 28, he was gone.

"university men" and the "adventurers," the former overwhelmingly from Ivy League schools and in their mid to late twenties, the adventurers a more diverse group. Tommy said of his new acquaintances that they are a "pretty nice lot, on the whole."* There was Billy Tailer, a friend from Roslyn, Long Island, who was actually training at Tours but whom Tommy would visit occasionally and see in Paris when they were en permission.

Assigned later that fall to the famous Cigonges (Stork) group, Spad 67, Tailer was killed over Verdun on February 5, 1918. Robert Hanford, another friend and a great football player in the States, didn't live to reach the front: he was killed in a midair collision during his last flight before being breveted.

His two closest companions, with whom he later shared quarters off the base, were Upton Sullivan, a big, handsome Harvard man from Philadelphia who later flew for the Lafayette over Nancy and still later for the Americans in naval aviation, and Sidney R. Drew Jr. Almost ten years older than Hitchcock, Drew was the son of an actor, a nephew of the famous John Drew. He had already made a promising start in films, having starred in the romantic comedy *A Girl Named Philippa*. Drew gave up a good deal more than most men when he volunteered, first for the ambulance corps and then for aviation. Though not a naturally gifted pilot, he stuck to it and was assigned to the front in March 1918. A few weeks later he was dead, shot down in flames in a furious battle with four German Albatross fighters.

One other name came up in Tommy's correspondence, that of Julian Biddle, this time in connection with one of the less dangerous occupational hazards of Avord: the fleas and bedbugs. As Tommy wrote his mother, "The only real exercise I get, besides walking 3 or 4 miles every day, is scratching." There was a large nest of insects in his innocent-looking mattress, and he described how he amused himself one evening by flipping the straw bag, thus causing the beasts to "lose their sense of direction." The trick worked for only a few days, however, and he was then rescued by some insect powder provided by Julian Biddle. The Hitchcocks had known Biddle as a cross-country rider and an athlete from the Main

---

*All quotations are from T. H.'s letters home, unless otherwise noted.

Line, and he appears to have been kind to their son. He left Avord soon after Tommy arrived and was killed only a few weeks later when his plane fell into the sea near Dunkirk.

There were two courses of training given at Avord, the Caudron and the Bleriot, so called for the planes on which one learned. There were other aircraft: the big, clumsy Voisins and Farmans, with their engines in the rear; the huge, three-engine Italian machines called Caperoni; the lovely two-man Schmitts; and most dazzling of all to Hitchcock, the swift, strong Nieuport fighters. But these were either obsolete or reserved for "graduates" of the Caudron or Bleriot classes. The Caudron was a big plane, quite fast, and used mostly for directing artillery fire; men who chose to learn on Caudrons almost inevitably ended up doing bomb runs or photoreconnaissance work; they also tended to live longer than *pilotes de chasse*. Nevertheless, a *pilote de chasse* was what Hitchcock intended to become, and this meant taking Bleriot training.

The Bleriot course was unique to French aviation. It consisted of five classes of increasing difficulty, followed by a test. The first was called the Penguin, this because the student practiced in a clipped-wing Bleriot that was unable to fly; the aim was to master the foot rudder and to keep the engine from stalling. The *rolleur* class came next: the wings of the plane were full-length now, but the engine had a governor to prevent takeoff. The object was to perfect one's handling of the rudder (all these planes had a tendency to fishtail, a comical but alarming failing); the test added the stick to the other things that one had to do with one's hands. In the third class the student was finally airborne, though only for a minute or two, taking off and landing, taking off and landing. Here the difficulties were to maintain the line of flight, tail up, the fuselage parallel to the ground.

In the fourth class, the *tour de piste* (around the field), the student learned the rudiments of turning, a basic lesson in how to make the invisible air as supportive as a banked roadway. For the first time he felt the exultation and perils of true flight, for he was high enough to see the curvature of the earth, high enough to be torn to pieces if he crashed. In the fifth class, the student was taught the rest of the basic vocabulary of flight: diving and pulling up (called by everyone piqueing and redressing);

a zooming turn to the right or left; the serpentine descent and the spiral descent, each of these with a dead motor, to give practice for the inevitable moment when one's engine would conk out and force a landing.

The final stage of the training came with graduation from Bleriots to Caudrons, preparatory to the final test for the brevet. The difference between the two planes was like the difference between a single scull and a dory; the Caudron was bigger, heavier, slower, and less sensitive; it could also go farther; and this was the point of the brevet test. First came the petit voyage to Chateauroux and back, then the grand voyage, a triangular course—Avord, Chateauroux, Ramrantin, and back—then an altitude test. That was it: the briefest of ceremonies, an indifferent Gallic handshake from an officier *moniteur*, and the brevet, a little gold and silver wreath with wings, along with two gold winged collar pins, was won.

What made this program unique was what it did not contain. There was no aeronautical theory, no study of how planes were built, or how their engines worked, no preliminary flights with an instructor, and no military drill. Every other air service insisted on one or more of these. The Americans insisted on all of them. Critics pointed out that the Bleriot system was terribly wasteful of machines and men, and it was true that the accident rate was higher at Avord than at the flying schools of Britain or America. The pilots' letters home, including Hitchcock's, were seldom without an account of the latest disaster to befall them or their friends. Some accidents were hilarious, as when one flier crashed through the roof of the camp bakery, only to emerge a few minutes later covered with flour, smiling idiotically but unhurt. But sometimes the letters paint a tableau of horror: a whole class—officers, men, and mechanics—stand transfixed, jaws agape, eyes squinting upward as one of their companions, unable to pull out of a dive, plunges down to a self-made grave.

Economically, too, the system was wasteful. James Norman Hall went through the program before Hitchcock (and later became a good friend). He remembered a day at Avord when eleven planes were wrecked; not a day went by, he said, without two or three accidents that would not have occurred under the British system.

Nevertheless, from the pilot's point of view, learning by doing the Bleriot way was indisputably the best preparation for combat. Not only was it more thorough and rigorous, but the Bleriots, tricky and sensitive to the touch, were the best machines on which to learn. As Hitchcock wrote his father, "If you can fly a Bleriot you can fly anything." And if, for some reason one couldn't learn to fly a Bleriot, one could certainly learn to fly a Caudron; those who failed in the Bleriot were put into Caudrons, whereas those who failed in the Caudrons had nowhere to go but out.

His first sortie in a Penguin came ten days after his arrival. It was not at all easy to manipulate the foot pedals while at the same time feeding the engine just the right amount of gas. Consequently, the Penguin field was the funniest show at Avord; everyone gathered around to watch the ludicrous little planes roaring and skidding around like crazed bull calves in a pasture. Hitchcock, however, gave them no laughs.

He had observed that the students who performed the best at keeping the machine in a straight line were the ones who, contrary to the *moniteur*'s advice to go slowly, actually gave it the most gas.

His progress from class to class was almost as smooth as his first sortie. On August 6 he made his first ascent—a trip of about two hundred yards across a ravine. He was not thrilled by the experience. It reminded him of being on a pulling polo pony and also of sitting on a stick between two chairs. A week later, however, he was in the *tour de piste* class and really flying for the first time. It was the greatest joy that he'd ever known. Aloft, flying over the neatly scissored rectangles of the Cher valley, he could see for the first time that the great earth really is a globe, a quilted ball in an infinitude of space. He loved the sheer elevation of it, the speed, the maneuverability, and he loved the solitude. It was like skating all by himself on the clear black ice of Turkey Pond at St. Paul's, like riding at Aiken early in the morning before anyone else was awake.

A month later, however, his confidence was badly shaken by a series of accidents. The first came at the end of a piste when, having tried to gun the Bleriot around with the motor, instead of waiting for a mechanic to drag it around, he ran into a ditch and broke a wheel. The second accident was more embarrassing because it occurred in front of his class. He landed and again tried to turn around without the mechanic, this time gunning the engine so hard that he ran into a tree and knocked off a wing. Then on September 20 he almost broke another wing when a puff of wind caught him as he was landing.

A few days later he bungled another landing, causing the plane to upend on its nose, hang there for a few sickening seconds, then slowly fall over on its back. This was the last avoidable accident he was ever to have in a plane.

A month later, in mid-October, he earned his brevet. Before setting out on their voyages, the students were summoned by one of the officers and given precise orders with respect to a number of contingencies: how much to indemnify a farmer for frightening his sheep to death, for example, or what to do if one strayed into German territory. In addition, each pilot received his flying orders: "The bearer is ordered to report, by air, at the cities of Chateauroux and Ramrantin, flying a Caudron, and leaving the Ecole Militaire d' Aviation at Avord on the 18th of October, 1917, without passenger on board."

Frightening sheep to death was hardly as unlikely an event as might appear. Virtually no one at Avord seems to have completed his voyages without making a forced landing somewhere. Anything could go wrong, and did. Novice pilots were always losing themselves in the clouds and having to come down to ask an awestruck peasant the direction to Chateauroux, or a terrifying thunderstorm would come rolling out of the west and press down the plane as if by the the hand of God. To the pilots' advantage, their planes, even the Caudrons, had wonderfully short takeoff and landing capacities and could bounce about safely enough on any moderately unobstructed field. By far the most preferred forced landings were made on the lawns of one of the many chateaux in the area. The counts and barons who owned the chateaux, all of whom were reputed to have beautiful daughters, showed the grounded aviators the most cordial hospitality—so much so that as their reputations spread from class to class, forced landings became more and more frequent and less and less forced.

There was no *pause de chateau* for Hitchcock when he was forced to land on the first leg of his petit voyage. Clouds and pelting rain sent him down into a field not far from Chateauroux. No grateful nobleman or humble farmer greeted him, however. He huddled in the shelter of his plane, waiting for the storm to blow over, then climbed back into the cockpit and took off again, arriving at Chateauroux so late that he had to spend the night. The next morning he flew back to Avord and landed just minutes before another storm hit. The following day he managed to complete the test—a rare feat inasmuch as it usually took two or three days. Hitchcock passed the altitude test in the early morning and the triangular course in the late afternoon. He wrote later that the tension of flying so much in a single day had somewhat spoiled the delights of "riding over pretty country." But nothing dampened his joy at the breveting ceremony. At last he was a *pilote*, and a full-fledged corporal in the French army.

His pleasure was short-lived. That evening he learned of Bob Hanford's midair collison over Chateauroux and of an accident at the Plessy training field that killed another friend, Sam Skinner. Tommy never tried to ignore his sadness at such losses; but to a marked degree, he possessed an equilibrium that allowed him to be deeply moved but also to rebound from any grief. He could also be brutally humorous. He wrote to Helen during September, "The last few days have been pretty bad on the mentalite at the school; some eight men have been turned into daisy food: one who got his head mixed up with a propeller and lost it in the confusion, and the seven others (all Frenchmen) who fell in machines."

Yet there was a special poignancy about these losses. None of those who died had been killed in combat. More than once in his letters, Tommy notes the death of a friend—Hanford, Biddle, Meeker—and comments on how terrible it is to be killed without even reaching the front. What was important to Hitchcock was the honor, the reputation, the memory that one creates. Soldiers fight. They do not serve who stand and wait. This view of the nature of war and his role in it decisively colored Tommy's experience at Avord. Every minute of his stay there was measured by whether it advanced or delayed his progress to the front. Primarily the seventeen-year-old saw nothing but delay. It was ten days before he attended his first Penguin class, and ten days of waiting before someone assigned him to a machine, and then there was the inevitable wait for the weather to improve or the wait in line for a meal or a shower or mail.

Tommy was under considerable pressure at Avord. Flying was exhausting work even for those who most relished its freedom. Elliot

Springs wrote that after every flight he would have to crawl under his plane for a while to recuperate. Hitchcock himself echoed those feelings, saying that sometimes he felt weak-kneed and drained after a flight.

This was a normal and common reaction among many of the pilots, but Hitchcock also brought a certain competitiveness to learning to fly that made him harder on himself. Intellectually, he was convinced that the Bleriot system was the best training there was, even though the training took longer than any other program. Still, he was often mildly annoyed to learn that a friend in the American aviation, Gil Winant, for one, had learned to fly before he had, and that his father had done it in six days. In that mood he could be childishly impatient with the French, angrily declaring in letters home that he wanted to transfer forthwith to the American service. His parents encouraged him. In fact, much of the correspondence between them—both at Avord and later, at the front, when Tommy was again in despair at the lack of action—concerned the question of when and how the boy could join the U.S. air arm. The Hitchcocks were very well placed to help him if he decided to do so. Trubee Davison, their friend and neighbor on Long Island, was the Assistant Secretary of War for Air. At times, indeed, it seemed as if a whole host of Hitchcock friends and relatives were anxiously peering over the horizon to see how young Tommy was getting on in France. Unfortunately, they could never be sure. One week he would be utterly determined to transfer; the next, inspired by the imminent prospect of his brevet or by clearing skies over the front, he would declare that nothing could tempt him to leave the French—not even, as was later the case, a promise of thirty days' leave.

Tommy was not alone in his temptation to go over to his own country's forces; the Lafayette talked of little else—especially after July 1917 when Congress appropriated the unheard-of sum of $640 million "to darken the skies of Germany with clouds of planes." For men like him, however, men who wanted above all to get into the fight, there were very good reasons to hesitate. The Americans might turn out pilots more rapidly than the French, but they were not being sent to the front and in all likelihood would not be until the spring of 1918. Moreover, so long as Colonel Billy Mitchell, the only high-ranking American officer to have flown an airplane, remained embattled with superiors, his partisans among the Americans in the French army would remain skeptical of the quality of American leadership in the air. Finally, there was the fact that no U.S. plane could equal the combat performance of even the oldest French planes in service over the front.

Tommy was alone in his youth, however: He would be the youngest American to be breveted in the war. This more than anything accounted for his vacillation, his wild swings between elation and despair, and his impatience. Even as he was complaining bitterly about the slowness of the Avord training, for example, he was proceeding through the course faster than most of his fellows. Not as fast as the record book of the Lafayette would have it—two and a half months, from June 29 to September 17, when it was actually three and a half, to October 17. Even so he earned his wings a full month ahead of the average student. His youth also explains the occasional note of boastfulness in his letters to his father. Once, for instance, he seems to be saying that while his father may have learned to fly more rapidly than he has been able to do, the father can't have been prepared to fight, as he, Tommy, has been. "The French have good machines," he says, "and they know what they are about. But the Americans may have to learn some things by trial and error, and I don't intend to be part of the experiment." By and large, however, this whisper of Oedipal rivalry is rare; more common is a delighted appreciation of the fact that he and his father are engaged in a shared adventure, thousands of miles apart for the moment, but one day, not inconceivably, together. "I am always anxious to hear from you, Father," he wrote in mid-September. "Your work, you know, is my work, and therefore very interesting to me." And soon he began to change the ending of his letters: "Best love to all" becomes "Best luck."

In the end, after all the string pulling his family was prepared to do for him, the only help they gave him in France was material.

Like other Lafayette men whose parents could afford it, Hitchcock received an allowance. At first it amounted to $250 a month, transferred from the elder Hitchcock's bankers to H. Monroe & Co., their agents in Paris. By September, however, this was proving insufficient. Tommy suggested that his father give him whatever he'd planned to give him at college. "Things are very expensive over here," he wrote, "and aviators en permission live pretty high." Both statements were quite true. The cost of living in France had shot upward because of the war, and around this time Hitchcock and his closest friends, Sullivan and Drew, were asked to move out of the barracks at Avord as an emergency measure. They went to a small hotel in the village of Sauvigny, three and a half miles away, and commuted to "work," Tommy on a motorcycle, Sully and Sidney on bicycles.

On October 29 Tommy learned of an opening for ten volunteers to go to the aerial combat school at Pau. Though it meant giving up a week's permission in Paris, he didn't hesitate. All day he traveled back and forth between Avord and Sauvigny, packing his gear and collecting his papers, the most important of which he promptly lost. He was not at all sorry to leave. The whole four months, he wrote his mother, had been a "terrible waste of precious time," but he hated breaking up "the nice little home that the friendship of Sully and Sidney Drew" had made for him.

At 5:30 p.m. the three of them sat down for Hitchcock's last supper at the Hotel du Centre. It ended picturesquely with the arrival of a donkey cart drawn by the village washerwoman and her daughter. Hitchcock threw his luggage in the back, shook hands with M. le patron and the rest of the staff, and climbed up on top of the luggage. The donkey immediately broke into a gallop, yanking his cart over the cobblestones at a terrifying rate. Sully and Sidney laughed and set off for the station on foot, arriving in good time to put their friend on the train. Hitchcock would meet Sully several months later at Nancy, near the front; Drew he never saw again.

At Avord he had learned to fly; at Pau he learned to fight in the air, and he loved every minute of his training there. Pau was in the foothills of the Pyrenees, about 125 miles east of Biarritz, a resort popular with the English and Americans who came for the shooting and riding. The Princes had a house there and so did the Huttons, other friends of the Hitchcocks. At the invitation of Miss Anne Hutton, Tommy occasionally went for dinner, a bath, and a sound sleep. Early in the morning he would ride one of their horses back to the field. At Avord he might have appreciated these luxuries: they might have compensated for not being able to fly as often as he wanted. At Pau he flew every day, and the comforts were largely wasted on him.

Four grades of proficiency were called for, each to be learned in three or four days. *Vol de groupe* was the first exercise, a form of "follow the leader" in which each pilot stayed fifty meters behind and slightly above the one before him. Next came training in the basic maneuvers of aerial combat, in which the students learned among other things the *vrille* (a vertical descent, the plane turning on its own axis), the *tournant* (or barrel roll), *la montagne Russe* (a dive with dead engine, redress with engine back on, followed by a steep ascent), the *renversement* (a loop with a barrel roll at the apex), and the *virage* (a swooping vertical turn). Third came the *vol de precision*, a deadly game of quoits in which the pilot, from three thousand feet, attempted to hit a sixty-meter target painted on the ground. Finally came the *vol de combat*, either one-on-one or in dogfights of three to four planes on a side with the instructors in captured German planes playing the part of the Bosches.

"I am having the time of my life," Hitchcock wrote his father in early November, soon after he arrived at Pau. Indeed, he worried that flying was becoming too easy for him. He asked whether his father, too, didn't sometimes lose concentration in the air. The lapse in the Nieuport plane that he was then flying was potentially fatal. Its 110-horsepower engine and short wings gave it great climbing power and maneuverability at high altitudes, but it could drop out of the sky like a plumb bob.

The French instructors were convinced that Americans were reckless pilots. "You Americans," one of them told James Norman Hall, "when you get to the front you will get the Boche; but let me tell you, they will kill many of you. Not one or two; very many." The Frenchman was probably right. In the early years of the war, the Americans were volunteers: Almost by definition they would have been less cautious than other Allied aviators. Then, after the United States entered the war, the Americans were fresh, while everyone else was tired. Finally, there was the basic difference in the way that Americans and Frenchmen look at war. *C'est la guerre* is a cliche that the French take quite literally: war is war. The Americans, on the other hand, and the British, too, though less and less as the killing went on, saw warfare as a game, a sport—the greatest on earth. Half a century separated the Americans from the Civil War, the last hideous conflict that America endured; they had fresh in their minds—indeed in their midst—living memories of the romantic toy-soldier conflict in Cuba, of the charge up San Juan Hill, and all the rest of it. War was a form of deadly play. Tommy Hitchcock was utterly American in his view of war. The "game" was the controlling metaphor of almost every endeavor of his life, but in his mind the "game" had a tremendous seriousness that lifted it far above play.

His letters from Pau, and later from the front, became detached, even theoretical. On November 19, for example, he wrote to his father about how he would be killed if he were killed: "I shall have made too wide a turn and become separated from my patrol, and in my anxiety to rejoin it I will make a straight line with full motor, giving the waiting Bosche a clear shot at me." At times he seems the jaded professional. He invariably describes his training as "work" and flying as a "business." It is something that he does "pretty well" but that he must work at constantly in order to perfect it. His teachers think so highly of his skill that they ask him to do two extra days of *vol de combat* with them; but Tommy writes only that he needs more practice in gunnery.

He was not always so serious. Once or twice at Pau, he was carried away by the joyous freedom of the air. Flying west one day he soared so high that he could see the blue of the Atlantic beyond Biarritz; higher and higher still, if only he could do it, he knew he could see Long Island. On the way back he swooped by an enormous, gaily-colored balloon. He passed so close he could see the passengers smile, no doubt apprehensively. Another day he went out with two other fellows and flew up the river for fifty miles.

Clouds forced them to fly close over the water between the tall banks of the stream. On the way back they pretended that all the creeping things they saw on earth—cows, pigs, people—were Germans, and they dived on them. That was a good day, and Hitchcock ended his letter, "Am very sleepy and so will say good night. Best love, Tommy."

"Quiet" was the word Hitchcock used to describe the sector of the front where he arrived late in the evening of December 12, 1917. He meant to reassure his parents, no doubt, but he was disappointed. A few weeks before, writing his uncle Frank, Tommy had said that wherever he was assigned he hoped that he could make it "dangerous, interesting and exciting." The tedium of military life had gotten to him again. Pau had been a bracing interlude but an atypical one. His subsequent two weeks outside Paris at Plessy Belleville, the enormous staging area for all French aviation, had been as excruciating as Avord. It was "the most desolate place on earth," muddy, bleak, and bureaucratic. There was little flying and little machine-gun practice. By the time Tommy arrived at his squadron, he was not pleased to find himself on a "quiet" front.

Luneville was in the Lorraine, in the northeast of France, a smallish town on the road between Nancy and Bar-le-Due. The trenches were eight miles away. From the air one could almost see the whole 350-mile extent of them, cutting across Europe from Ostend to the Vosges, like a scar on an old tree trunk. Only a few miles north of Luneville was Verdun, a stretch of *boyau* where nearly a million men (including Jean DeBos) had died in a ten-month battle the year before. At Chemin des Dames, the French had once more attempted to breach the German lines, but after 180,000 casualties they stopped—to wait for the Americans. The Germans were as exhausted as the French, and since the Americans did not arrive until the end of February, two and a half months after Hitchcock reported to his escadrille, he was absolutely right, the front was quiet.

The twelve men of Escadrille N-87 (later Sp-44) were quartered in a modest *maison particuliere* on the outskirts of Luneville. Three stories high, with little iron balconies outside the French windows, the house was set in a small garden surrounded by a stucco wall ten feet high. The bedrooms were on the top two floors, and on the ground floor were the living room, dining room, and kitchen. All were modestly furnished and painted a dull gray. When Tommy arrived, on a cold evening in early December, the commanding officer introduced him to his squadron-mates. All were French except one: William Wellman.

Hitchcock was always somewhat indifferent to strangers; a man's personality or family background, his autobiography, so to speak, seldom aroused his curiosity. People to him were what they did, in the here and now, not who they were. As a result, he hadn't much to say about his squadronmates, except for two. Both were flamboyant men, reckless, dashing, and carefree, sometimes violent. One was an aristocratic Frenchman named Charles d'Estainville, who told Tommy that he had been a slacker at the outset of the war but was making up for it. Hitchcock would go on patrol with him many times—including his last patrol—and remained friends with him until the end of his life. The other was William Wellman, age twenty-one. He came from Cambridge, Massachusetts, and in his own eyes he was quite a lad. At Newton High, he wrote in his memoirs, he had "fought, boxed, played football, hockey and every kind of mad prank." Like many volunteers he came to France prepared to give his life for the cause, but not before he'd had a few escapades of his own. In Paris, en route to Avord, he saved a beautiful girl from suicide, diving into the Seine seconds after seeing her slim, white figure falling through the darkness. Days later he saved a family from their burning apartment house, which had been bombed by German planes only minutes before. Wellman had a melodramatic imagination perfectly suited to the movie director he would become after the war—and fine instincts that brought him out ahead whenever the circumstances were right. Both men, in short, were of the sort who usually amused Hitchcock: outrageous, anarchic, and brave.

All December the weather was foul—cold, with low clouds and frequent snowstorms. Flying under such conditions was out of the question, and Hitchcock languished unhappily. At first he thought that Luneville was not a bad place to spend the winter. He slept as late as he could, usually until ten o'clock. Then he dressed warmly, just in case there was a chance of clearing skies. A breakfast of bread and chocolate or a hard-boiled egg waited for Hitchcock in the hangar. But he never ate. The remainder of the morning he spent gazing at his machine, chatting with his mechanic, called Noodles, and his squadronmates. Lunch was at noon, *a la maison*. Afterward he returned to the hangars for more gazing at his plane, more chat, and more longing for the weather to break. Darkness fell at four o'clock, so he would return to his quarters by way of the streets, which he said were "like rivers of ink along which everyone walks with foolish little electric lights, flashing them on and off, so as not to run into one another."

Back in his room he wrote letters or read until suppertime. His mother and Cousin Marie kept him supplied with books and magazines, even the Sunday edition of the *New York Herald*, which took a month or two to arrive. Supper, served at seven o'clock, was a substantial meal, consisting of soup, meat, vegetables, and wine or beer. The pilots paid seventy francs a fortnight for the privilege of eating well, and though they sometimes felt guilty about the luxury of their accommodations, compared to the trenches, they also knew the morbid significance of being asked to advance their seventy francs for only two weeks at a time; statistically, they hadn't much chance of living any longer than that. The *popotier*, or cook, had been hired away from Maxim's by the resourceful Charles d'Estainville, who also supplied the wines. Fighting and women were the sole topics of conversation around the table.

Hitchcock was never completely comfortable in this company. Even if his experience of fighting and women had been greater than it was, his code forbade talking about such matters. His letters of December indicate a return of the same boyish impatience and disdain that cropped up at Avord. He began to think he was in a "punk" escadrille. In one letter he lashed out at his comrades: "With the exception of two or three, none of them want to work. What is more, they do not know their job." He wondered about changing to a better escadrille, where he could "learn from good men." He was right about learning from good men; there was a real apprenticeship to be followed by those who wanted to do more than merely survive the war. But he was wrong about there being no one from whom to learn at Luneville. There were fine aviators in N-87, but in the first month there was simply no action. Until December 23 he went on patrol no more than once or twice. If the weather weren't bad, his machine gun was, and he stayed on the ground until a new one, a Vickers, was installed in its place.

On December 23 there was a bit of excitement, enough at least to write home about. In the morning he and Wellman and a few others were standing around the hangars as usual, when out of the clouds over their heads came the droning of a German Albatross engine. The pilot evidently thought he was safely behind his own lines: he had already begun his approach for a landing when he spotted something amiss and wheeled like a swallow back to the safety of the clouds. The men of N-87 raced to their machines and took off after him. But after nearly getting lost themselves, they returned to the field with nothing to show for their ardor. The following day, Christmas Eve, Tommy went out again but became separated from his patrol because of some dirt lodged in his fuel line. He took advantage of the precious hour aloft to practice target shooting with his Vickers. He missed seeing Wellman attack—and miss—a German Aviatik on a photoreconnaissance patrol. But a half hour later, he did see his friend crash on the field at Luneville and emerge happily unhurt.

Christmas was a day like any other. The Great War myth that hostilities were suspended on the Lord's birthday, while the troops exchanged presents in no-man's-land, was true of the first Christmas of the war, when there was some fraternization with the enemy. But officers on both sides were ordered to make sure that it never happened again, and it didn't. On Christmas Day, 1917, in Luneville the morning sky was again overcast, and Tommy went to high mass in the town church. The service seemed alien to him, though, disorienting, and he crept out before it was over. Back in his room at the house, he was acutely homesick. He imagined every detail of Christmas at Aiken: the simple, lovely service in the small church, the bracing ride home in the cold air, the stockings hung from the dining room mantel, the hominy and liver that they always had for breakfast. He wrote a short, sad note home.

After lunch the weather cleared somewhat, and to shake off his melancholy he suggested to Wellman that they go over to the field and do a little hunting. The cloud cover kept them at 2,500 feet, but they crossed the lines into Germany, hoping to provoke someone to come up and fight them. All that happened was that they were shot at from the ground, a first for Hitchcock, and he didn't like it. There was a peculiar unreality about these puffs of smoke in the great depths of space; they seemed as inconsequential as a cloud. In fact, antiaircraft artillery was notoriously inaccurate, even at 2,500 feet, and Hitchcock had little to worry about. But a snowstorm was something else again. They saw one coming and raced back to the field just before it broke over them. Even so, Wellman again crashed on landing, losing his second plane in two days.

After Christmas Hitchcock had more flying and more target practice, and his morale improved considerably. He saw that his companions were still "not exactly balls of fire" when it came to fighting, but Tommy admitted that it was not for him to criticize men who had been so often in combat that they had grown sick of it. He had found a pair of skates somehow or other, and a stream nearby to skate on; it amused him to think that he'd come this far to do what he had been doing a year before at St. Paul's. Once, as a favor to Cousin Marie, he looked up an old woman in the area who had been kind to Jean shortly before he was killed. On another occasion he attended the funeral of a squadron gunner who had been killed in an accident.

He thought often during these slow, bleak days of transferring to the Americans, but the option was even less realistic than it had been at Avord. Not only was he still too young; he was more convinced than ever that America was never going to get her forces into battle. He also had a real incentive to stay with the French. Because he had taken no permission between Avord and Pau, after six months at Luneville he would be eligible for a thirty-day leave, plenty of time for him to go home. Thereafter, whenever he felt renewed pressure from his family or in himself to go over to the Americans, he thought of the glorious times awaiting him on Long Island in the spring if he stuck it out in his quiet sector for just a while longer.

More important, however, was his quickening sense that soon, any day he would at last see the face of battle. Toward the end of December he wrote Aunt Celestine, "I have not had combat yet, but hope to meet up with a Bosche soon." On January 4 one of his squadronmates brought down a German two-seater, a triumph that made Hitchcock long for a chance of his own. The following day Tommy went out on patrol but encountered no Bosche. Then came the morning of January 6.

He was up, as usual on good days, at dawn, awakened by the orderly. But it wasn't until 10:15 a.m. that Captain Agire gave him his orders. With two other Nieuports he was to escort an aerial-reconnaissance mission to photograph German troop movements.

Clumsy in his teddybear suit, Tommy walked ·to his machine and swung himself into it, left foot on a step built into the fuselage, left hand on one of the struts between the wings, right hand on the padded rim of the cockpit; then slowly he eased into the narrow opening, as if lowering himself into a hot bath. Inside the cockpit he was hit by the strong but not unpleasant smell of dope and castor oil. Fastening the wide belt tightly around his waist, he tentatively kicked the rudder pedals, looking back to see if the rudder moved properly on its ninety-degree arc. He tested the stick next, hauling it forward and back, watching carefully to see whether the elevators on the wings responded. These mechanisms were responsible for sending the plane into the swooping dive that ideally was the beginning of a good surprise attack. The plane's wires made a satisfactory squealing noise as they moved through the pulleys and cleats. Having checked out the controls, Hitchcock turned to the motor. Noodles, on cue, stepped up to the huge propeller and placed both hands on the upper blade as if he were going to clamber onto the engine cowling. He yelled at Hitchcock, *"Coupe! Plein gas!"* Tommy checked to see that the ignition switch was off and that the fuel cock was open. Noodles threw his weight on the propeller, rotating it two or three times, to suck gas through the hollow crankshaft and into the engine. "Contact!" he shouted. "Contact!" Tommy shouted back. He turned on the ignition.

Two mechanics appeared from inside the hangar and braced themselves against the Nieuport's lower wing. Noodles looked around one last time, then flung himself on the propeller as though to wrench it off. The engine burst into life, belching blue-white smoke back over the cowling into Hitchcock's face. Noodles pulled the wooden blocks from the wheels and signaled his assistants to duck out of the way. The machine was free.

With his gloved left hand Hitchcock wiped the eisenglas windshield and headed into the icy wind blowing off the Alps. Forward he could see nothing but throbbing metal and stretched fabric and the blue blur of his propeller. He kept the stick well forward until the tail lifted, then, easing back on it, he felt the heart-stopping liberation of the plane from the ground as it soared up and over the trees at the end of the grass field. At a thousand feet he joined the other Nieuports and began circling the aerodrome waiting for the heavier reconnaissance plane to gain altitude.

Riding escort on an aerial reconnaissance flight (AR) was difficult and frustrating work. The ARs were much slower than the Nieuports (one of the reasons why they needed escorting), which meant that the pursuit pilot had to fly continually in an S pattern to remain abreast of his ward. Added to this was, the difficulty of keeping the things in sight. Camouflaged to make them invisible to an attacker from above, they all too easily disappeared from the view of their protectors. This is what happened to Hitchcock; he got up too high and lost his patrol.

Perhaps he thought then of what he'd been told at Pau, that for most novice *pilotes de chasse*, losing their patrol was the beginning of a sequence that ended with their being destroyed by a German patrol. More likely he was happy to be free of the entangling alliance that he had contracted on the ground. He was not opposed to teamwork, but flying was freedom and solitude or it wasn't quite flying.

Suddenly, far to the south, Hitchcock saw puffs of French antiaircraft fire and, well above them, a dark speck that he knew was an enemy plane. His heart quickened. He veered to the right and began clawing his way upward to gain precious altitude on his target. Absurdly Tommy found himself spurring the machine with his heels, but the Rhone engine just hummed along in mechanical oblivion. After an eternity he found that he had reached the altitude he wanted, fifty-two hundred meters, but was still too far away to attack. The sun wasn't behind him either, nor was there any cloud cover conveniently at hand.

Still the German hadn't seen him. If he had, he would not have made a sudden break for home that drastically shortened the distance between him and Hitchcock. At the same time, however, Tommy saw that he was up against a two-seater, the most tempting and most dangerous of targets—tempting because they were heavier and less maneuverable than single-seaters, more dangerous because the gunner in the rear seat had an unobstructed shot at anyone attacking him. His only blind spot was a small cone of approach below and to the rear. This, of course, was the approach Hitchcock planned to make. The German's change of direction had placed him two hundred meters away and slightly below Tommy. Seconds later the gunner saw his peril, whirled his gun around and opened fire. At the edge of awareness Hitchcock heard the rat-tat-tat of the enemy gun. He took it as a signal to begin. He shoved the Nieuport into a steep dive, hoping to get under the German's tail before the pilot could evade him. It didn't work. The German did just what he was supposed to and turned sharply to give his gunner a clear shot at Hitchcock.

What happened next Tommy attributed to luck. He was in a position to shoot, and he shot. The gun hadn't gone off six times before the German plane went into a spinning dive. For a moment Tommy couldn't believe what he'd done, yet he'd seen a tracer enter the fuselage just under the pilot's cockpit. Like a tiny flaming arrow it had gone home and the plane had spun toward the earth. He had a kill! Then he remembered that time and again planes would play the stricken bird, only to pull out just before hitting the ground and fly off to safety. Hitchcock dived after him. It seemed later as if he had never flown so fast. The engine screamed, the wind shrieked through the wires, and still the German was out of reach of his gun. Then, at about two thousand meters, the Bosche went into a spiral, falling more slowly then. Catching up, Hitchcock fired a few more shots. "Wasted," he wrote that afternoon to his mother, "he spiraled right into the slope of a hill in the Vosges Mountains, nose down."

Stunned, caught between jubilation and awe, he circled the smoking wreckage of his first kill. He saw a peasant woman come running out of a nearby house and returned her wave. But his sense of triumph did not last long.

"I thought it was the Fourth of July," he wrote afterward. "But instead of being on the ground watching the fireworks go off, I was the goat. A white swarm of luminous bullets went tearing past me." He realized to his terror that this was not a bit of friendly France over which he was idly circling, but Germany. He took a careful look at the area so that he would be able to identify it later, to confirm his kill, and made for home.

He was running low on fuel; his maps didn't include this sector, and a low cloud cover blanketed the ground ahead. More nervous than he had been in his fight minutes before, he could see, right in front of his nose, the precious gas flowing through a tube to the engine. But then he spotted white hangars and a few French Sopwiths circling about a field a mile or so away, and simultaneously his last dribble of gas disappeared down the tube. He landed in a pasture just short of the aerodrome. It was a small place to put down his plane, and he bounced onto a road and then, nose down, into a ditch.

The comedy of the ending did nothing to spoil his day. He was in Luxeuil-les-Bains, the first station of the Lafayette Escadrille, where Prince, Thaw, and Chapman had fought. After being extricated from his plane and told that it couldn't be fixed for several days, Hitchcock went to the Grande Hotel de la Pomme d'Or, bathed, and ordered a fine victory dinner for himself. He ate and wrote home at the same time—"because I want to give you my first impression." It was a long letter, detached and self-critical. At the end, after excusing himself for the grease spots he'd made on the stationery, he let his hopes for himself show. "If the kill is confirmed," he wrote, "I get a Croix de Guerre with a palm; if not, I get the reputation of being a big bluffer." (In the end he did get the Croix de Guere, with palm.) Back at Luneville the next evening his squadronmates made much of him, although his subsequent letters were even more modest in stressing his good luck than the first had been.

To replace the banged-up Nieuport left at Luxeuil-les-Bains he was given a newer model of the same plane with a better motor and a gun with telescopic sight. In the French aviation service, nothing succeeded like success. He discovered that with a few more Germans to his credit he would be given a Spad. Meanwhile he continued his practice sessions with the new machine gun, remembering perhaps stories of the peerless Canadian ace Billy Bishop (seventy-two kills), who practiced his marksmanship early in the war by throwing tin cans out of his cockpit and shooting them as they fell. Hitchcock was forever badgering someone at the base to take up the sleeve (as the towed target was called) and let him have a go at it.

The morning of January 12 offered the first flying that he had since his victory on January 6. With d'Estainville he went up for a little *chasse* over the lines before lunch. At 4,500 meters, still on their side of the trenches, they spotted a German two-seater coming toward them. D'Estainville, who was leading, instantly began to climb, spiraling up a winding staircase to attain the conventional attack position. Hitchcock followed, somewhat hampered by an inferior engine. At the apex of their ascent, everything appeared set for a textbook kill. The Black Cat pair had the coveted altitude, the German hadn't seen them, and they had the sun at their backs. D'Estainville dived first—he had the seniority and Hitchcock saw him go, the last he would see of him until they headed back to the aerodrome.

Tommy couldn't see the German either, but as he sent his plane nose down, he knew, or thought he knew, where the enemy lay. The wind howled past and Hitchcock was inwardly congratulating old Noodles for tuning up the engine so splendidly when he suddenly realized that he had miscalculated. Instead of passing behind his opponent with enough margin to redress and come up under his tail in the gunner's blind spot, he found himself flying head-on into him. Stomping the rudder pedal, he whirled out of the way. On his second pass he managed to position himself properly. The instant the two-seater came in sight, Hitchcock opened fire. Working the Vickers in short bursts, closing in from two hundred meters, he saw that most of the tracers were missing the target, passing too far to the right. Then to his surprise and delight, the German began to fall in a spinning nosedive. "There goes number 2, I thought," as he put it later, "and how easy it seemed!" He went after him, attempting to follow him to the ground and mark the spot of his victory, but at that moment his engine began to fail, and he had to dive off on another tangent in order to catch it and bring it to life again. Still he had reason to believe that d'Estainville was nearby and would record his kill.

There was no kill. Back at Luneville d'Estainville told him that the enemy fluttered almost to the ground, redressed, and flew serenely off toward Germany. That evening, writing home, Hitchcock mercilessly criticized his mistakes; on his first attack he had failed to wait until d'Estainville had completed his pass before he himself dived; moreover, he had compounded the error of bad timing with a failure to locate his target before going after it. Then, having made a correct second approach, he had thrown away his chance by opening fire from too great a distance. He had let the excitement of battle overcome his judgment. He promised himself that the next time he would wait until his gun "was in the enemy's collar" before pulling the trigger.

Hitchcock's third combat took place early in the afternoon of January 19. Bad weather had kept him grounded for five days, which was particularly annoying because he had just been assigned a new and better Nieuport. It was not the Spad that he coveted but an improvement just the same, and Tommy was keen to try it out. He got up early that morning and went over to the firing range, where he and Noodles worked on sighting his machine gun until shortly after eleven o'clock. Wellman sauntered over and announced that he and a staff officer were preparing a surprise for the Bosche two-seater that had taken to flying over Luneville around noon. He invited Tommy to join them. There was still some work to do on the gun, however, so they didn't leave until after lunch, and by that time Wellman had been ordered on another mission.

Hitchcock and the staff officer took off at about 12:30 p.m., eyes scanning the quarter from which they knew the Bosche would come, if he came. At about a thousand meters Hitchcock saw the staff officer's Spad peel away and return to the aerodrome with an overheated engine. Then a few seconds later he spotted the German two-seater coming over the lines into France. He headed for greater altitude and noted with satisfaction that the fellow was flying with unusual boldness. The wind was blowing strongly from the west, which gave his opponent an advantage should he have to turn and make a run for it.

At the apex of his climb, Hitchcock peered out of the cockpit and was dismayed to see a Nieuport diving straight down, close to "his" target. There was no break in the dive; the French plane wobbled slightly, then instantly went into a *vrille* and crashed. The German gunner had hit him neatly as he passed. Tommy was above, by just a hundred meters. He dived and turned at the same time, coming up under the German plane's tail. He waited and, as he had said he would, "put the gun in his collar" before firing. He could see the tracers pumping into the fuselage near the pilot's cockpit.

"He didn't fall," Hitchcock later wrote, "but kept going [in a] descending serpentine line. I shot and shot and shot but he was a very bad target, diving, redressing and diving again, and I could not make him fall. Finally I noticed that his [the German's] propeller was dead and so I got a little distance off and watched. I knew he had to come down and did not relish the idea of getting killed by his gunner who had been merrily shooting at me all this while."

The German two-seater crashed in a field only a few hundred yards on their side of the lines. It was Hitchcock's second official "kill," a more gratifying one, perhaps, in that there had been no killing. He felt merry himself, in fact, when he saw the two Germans crawl out of the wreckage and wave at him.

Back at the aerodrome, however, he was saddened to learn that it was Lieutenant Miot whom his Germans had sent plummeting to earth. "Poor Miot," Tommy wrote that evening. "We all feel very badly about it. He was a very nice fellow. His place at table will be empty tonight." Miot's was the first and last death in the squadron in the three months that Tommy was with it. His letters show little anger over the loss, but on January 20 he did something so foolhardy that only a vindictive rage can account tor it.

Flying on patrol over Nancy in bitterly cold but clear weather, he and Wellman spotted a German two-seater poking its way into France. They fell on the plane instantly, Wellman firing from above, Hitchcock from below. Unhurt, the Germans whirled back toward their own lines. Again and again the two Americans dived on the German plane, wheeling under and over it in great circles like hawks with a pigeon. But the enemy was no pigeon, and in retrospect Hitchcock was awed by their skill. Each time they attacked, the German pilot managed to elude the fire and at the same time disclose them to his gunner, all the while doggedly pushing eastward to the German side of the line. The fight went on for a long time. Their tracers, fired in short bursts to conserve ammunition, always went wide of the mark or passed harmlessly through the two-seater's fuselage. It would not fall. Then, abandoning all evasive maneuvers, it went into a steep dive, redressed, and landed at a German aerodrome.

For a moment the two Americans were stunned. Fifteen miles inside enemy territory, ammunition and gas nearly exhausted, their prey tauntingly alive and safe on the ground, at high noon with no cloud cover to shelter them, the only prudent thing to do was to give up and go home. But Hitchcock and Wellman couldn't do it, couldn't bear to have beaten their foe but failed to destroy him. And so this time they followed him down, Tommy in the lead. On the first pass, Wellman wrote later, they killed the pilot. On the second and a third they shot up the hangars. On the way out, they paused to ring the bell of a nearby village church with their bullets.

They both returned safely to Luneville, though Wellman once again wrecked his plane on landing. The weather turned ugly, and Hitchcock came down with a cold. He was, as he wrote his father, "laying low for a while." As far as the war was concerned, it didn't matter what he did. The Germans seemed to have disappeared.

Loafing around, waiting for the next round to begin, was frustrating. "It is very boring of the Germans," he wrote his mother in Aiken on January 28, "to make us hunt and hunt and not find anything."

In a letter of February 6 to Uncle Frank he expressed his complaint briskly. "I have landed in what is considered a chic escadrille. That means we have a nice captain, the food and lodging are good, and there is not much work to do. But from my point of view, as all captains are more or less the same to me, as I sleep just as well on a hard bed as a soft one, and as I live for the flying and the flying alone, it is not overly satisfactory." Moreover, he was aware that, for him at least, the enforced idleness was actually dangerous. "I enjoy the fights very much," he told his uncle, "but they are so rare it tempts me to take unnecessary chances." Twice in the week he had done just that, once going up after a German without bothering to put on his helmet or gloves, a senseless thing to do in the cold. And a few days later he was nearly trapped in a fight miles inside Germany with two enemy two-seaters.

He resolved once again to transfer to American aviation. He had a ten-day permission coming up on February 12, and he planned to make the most of it by engaging the proper bureaucratic gears. On his arrival in Paris, he went straight to Dr. Gros and signed the necessary papers.

Yet, no sooner had he set the process in motion than he began to feel that he had betrayed his group. And from this grew a feeling that it was, after all, a good squadron, or at least no worse than any other that he was likely to join. "Good news from the escadrille!" he wrote his mother from the Hotel de Castiglione. "One of our fellows got a Hun and now there are plenty to get. I go back Sunday and am looking forward to some good fun." He did what was expected of him in the city. He saw the DuBoses and thanked them for the stream of food packages, warm clothing, and reading material that they had been sending him. He saw the Allens; Uncle Willie Eustis was in town, on his way to Pau to recover from a bout with pneumonia. He also ran into Gil Winant, and the two went to dinner and the opera. The American temptation waned, and then with news that Luneville had warmed up in his absence, disappeared altogether.

Back with his escadrille he was soon as active as he could wish. One day he and a few others flew escort for a new arrival to the squadron, a French pilot specially trained to take pictures of enemy troop movements inside Germany. The new arrival was the brightest man in the group, Tommy wrote his father, and when that morning he was shot down by five Bosche, Hitchcock was sadder and angrier than he had been since the death of Lieutenant Miot. The next day he pulled himself out of bed at what he called the "unearthly" hour of 5:30 a.m., hoping to catch a German plane that flew over Luneville around six o'clock every morning. The German never showed up for the rendezvous, but Hitchcock spotted another plane heading back to Germany, and he went after it. The pilot could not have seen him, for he suddenly veered and came back into France, heading straight for Hitchcock, who immediately climbed to the altitude that he wanted and then plummeted down on his unwary target. But just as he was pulling up under the two-seater's tail, his motor quit. "The damned thing just wouldn't move," as he told his father. It caught again after a sickening few seconds of free fall, but by then the German had disappeared into the clouds. Hitchcock returned to the aerodrome, furious with himself at missing the kill.

Soon after, on the last day of February, a French officer came to Luneville carrying authorization for Hitchcock to take a home leave of thirty days. Hitchcock had only to hand over the document to Captain Agire to be on his way back to Westbury. But he tore it up and then wrote his father, "On thinking things over, however, I have decided that this is not the time to take a rest." The next two months, he believed, were going to be crucial, and he simply did not feel at all right with himself "scheming to get off." He said he wanted to wait until next winter, if the opportunity came up again.

Les chasses in the first few days of March were not "overly satisfactory"; there were bad days of no flying, alternating with good days without opponents to fight. Tommy remained in high spirits nonetheless. The whole squadron was eagerly anticipating new planes, single-wing Moronnes, which, though less powerful than Nieuports at high altitude, were far more maneuverable in fights at less than three thousand meters.

Moreover, on March 4 he was promoted. He was thrilled, not only by this token of official respect for his work but also at the marvelous rank that he had attained. He was a *marechal de logis*, the equivalent of sergeant in the cavalry or artillery. On March 5 he sent the news to his mother: "So now I am known as marechal de logis Hitchcock. That sounds pretty slick, don't you think? Something like Marechal de France Joffre." The next day, March 6, 1918, he was shot down.

CHAPTER THREE

Germany, 1918

As usual, the orders of the day were posted on the bulletin board when Hitchcock and Wellman arrived at the hangars for their morning coffee. They saw that they were to be separated, Wellman flying with Ruamp, Bouisset, and Discours; Hitchcock with d'Estainville and Captain Agire.

It was good flying weather, a few clouds above and a light mist on the ground, but at fifteen hundred meters the bright sunlight carried a suggestion of spring and made for almost perfect visibility. As they swung north toward Nancy, the focus of their patrol that day, Hitchcock felt again the exhilarating harmony of his own energy and the vibrant wood and wire, the shellacked fiber and roaring engine of his plane. The only discordant note was the engine's perversity in spitting back a thin spray of oil, which slowly obscured the view through the windshield. It was annoying to have to keep wiping it off.

Presently, two black specks appeared in the sky over Nancy—two Albatrosses. To this point Hitchcock had been maintaining formation with Agire and d'Estainville, but at the sight of two enemy planes he gave full throttle to the plane. The Albatrosses, for their part, retreated the ten kilometers or so that separated them from German territory and then began circling, evidently deciding to give fight.

From the Germans' point of view, the decision was a more than acceptable risk: their opponent was alone, far from his base—indeed, far from France. For Hitchcock the contest was chancy. And if he had known all the facts, he probably would have gone back. He knew that he was over the lines, and he believed that he had the advantage of superior altitude. What he didn't know, however, was that he had no support, and that there was a third Albatross above and behind him, hiding in the sun. This was the plane that shot him down. As Hitchcock dived steeply on his circling prey, the third plane followed and opened fire. Later he remembered only the sound of the gun, his astonishment, and then oblivion.

He was unconscious for only a few seconds, but when he came to, it was to see the earth spinning crazily beneath him, swamping his vision. Instinctively, he pulled back on the stick and headed west for France, still bewildered by what had happened. It was inconceivable that the two Albatrosses could have fired on him before he had come anywhere near them. Just then he saw a terrific burst of tracers pass between his right wings. He looked around, straight into the masked face of a German pilot. He never forgot his sickening fascination at the sight of that man. He could not see his face—it was hidden behind goggles—but the enemy pilot had a long streamer flying from his helmet, and Tommy could see the movement of his head as he took aim. Soaring and diving, he twisted away from the pulsing tracers; even as he felt bullets ripping through the fuselage, he kept edging toward France, where he hoped the Bosche would leave him alone.

Then, after another burst of bullets, he heard something give in the rear of the plane, which then, of its own accord, turned back into Germany. He stamped hard on the left rudder—nothing. He looked down. Slowly he realized what he'd felt dimly from the first: his right leg was numb, slightly twitching, altogether useless. Desperate, he wing-slipped down to the left and nearly crashed in a forest. He was that close to the ground. He managed to redress and wheeled away from the trees. The plane, now flying more or less by itself, slowly settled onto a field and crashed, ripping away its undercarriage, tearing off a wing. Barely conscious, he looked up and saw the three Albatrosses diving on him one by one. They did not fire. He passed out then, but not before he saw German soldiers emerging from the woods.

For the next six months, Tommy Hitchcock's mind was dominated by two obsessions: food and escape. The first requires little explanation.

The Germans in World War I generally treated their prisoners well, but after four years of war on three fronts, the German nation, landlocked and bleeding, was close to starvation. There was little food for the soldiers, less for the prisoners.

Hitchcock knew this and never reproached his captors with starving the prisoners. But food—the food that the Red Cross would bring, food sent from home, ideal dinners, real dinners, any sort of food at all—were the stuff of his dreams day and night. He was embarrassed, but he couldn't help himself. "You probably think me an awful glutton," he wrote the DuBoses, "but I assure you that it is with a watering mouth that I write you all these good things. My only fear is that you will not appreciate how much of this food I want and how much I want it. I could go on all day suggesting eatables and drinkables [he had already written three tightly spaced pages] but I will leave it to you . . . to use your imagination. I am sure that Madeleine will have some valuable suggestions," he concluded with hope.

During his captivity, Hitchcock met several men whose desire to be free had nearly driven them mad. At one camp he met a Lieutenant Crampel, who had been captured two years before during the first German attack on Verdun. They were introduced by Herschel McKee, a Lafayette man from Indiana whom Tommy had known slightly at Camp Avord. "McKee led me into the crowded barracks," Hitchcock recalled a year later, "through groups of men, playing cards or lounging about on straw mattresses doing nothing, down to the very end of the room where a good-looking slim man with blond hair that curled a little at the ends sat on a pile of mattresses playing solitaire. . . . He attracted me from the first. . . . Although his appearance was still that of a young man his face plainly showed the unmistakable signs of suffering and hunger."

For weeks thereafter Tommy sat at Crampel's feet, soaking up everything the older man had to tell of the dangerous "game" of escape. "Escaping had become a monomania with him. His only diversion was solitaire, and even that he played superstitiously: 'If it comes out, I shall get away.' . . . Crampel had evaded his captors six different times, only to be caught again and brought back to prison."

Hitchcock's obsession with escape was healthier than Crampel's; much of it stemmed from youthful high spirits. But there was another factor: he was a pilot. Flying provides, for those who love it, the most exquisite, stirring sensation of freedom they could know. Hitchcock had been explicit about this in his letters from Luneville, often mentioning his dread of being made prisoner. It was not that he feared mistreatment. He knew that the stories of Germans torturing POWs were largely propaganda to discourage desertion. Rather, he feared the loss of freedom itself, the freedom, above all, of flying.

A few days after his capture, he wrote, lying on a hospital bed near a window, "I was startled from my day-dreams by the old familiar rat-tat-tat of machine guns. Way up in the sky two small specks were darting at a larger one. As they came lower they disengaged themselves and turned back westward. A large two-seated plane glided down over our heads and disappeared behind a clump of trees. It was glorious." Prison was ignominious; it was to be grounded in the most humiliating fashion, cut off from all that was glorious in life. For the first time in his eighteen years he became seriously depressed.

It hit him immediately after his capture. Four soldiers had placed him on a stretcher and carried him a few miles to a dressing station that smelled powerfully of bad cigars. He fainted again as his wound was being dressed but awoke to learn that he'd been lucky: the bullet had passed through his right buttock and out the thigh without touching bone. Still, he recalled later, "I have never before felt more depressed. . . . I could not look forward. . . . I had to content myself with . . . the good times and fun that I had had before." But the past was filled with reproach: "What a fool I was not to have been more careful. Why had I not waited for my two comrades? If I had only seen that third machine. Then I thought out a thousand different possibilities that might have happened, how I might have landed in France."

For the next few weeks, the thought of escape lay dormant, obscured by the pain of his wound, which became infected and would not heal, and by sporadic, unaccountable moves from one place to another. Often he was made to walk, which was agony. He had crashed near Chateau Salins, due north of Luneville and west of Nancy. From there he was taken, by every conceivable mode of transport from oxcart to trolley, to St. Avoid, a town in what is now France but was then, by conquest in the 1870 war, in Germany. Walking painfully through the streets from one conveyance to another, he was astonished to find himself and his guards surrounded by dozens of small children all screaming insults at him in German.

There were two prison hospitals at St. Avord, and Hitchcock spent about ten days in each. His wound healed slowly and he was feverish, but most of all he suffered from loneliness. For a brief period there was an English-speaking orderly to talk to, and later a British RFC lieutenant. For long days and nights, however, he was alone in an empty dormitory, accompanied only by a young French infantryman so absorbed in his pain that he could only cry softly.

On April 1 he was moved to a prison hospital in Saarbriicken, a large industrial city fifty miles from the front, which had been the original objective of Pershing's "independent" push for victory. That April, however, it was the Germans who were pushing. The Bolshevik revolution in Russia had made it possible for the Kaiser to concentrate all his forces in the West, and in the spring of 1918 he staked everything on a last counteroffensive. For a time the German armies were unstoppable, driving back the French and British and American lines sometimes for as much as thirty-five miles. At one moment they were within fifty-five miles of Paris. The victories exhausted them, however, and when they were halted—as they were all along the front by the end of April—it was evident to everyone that the Central Powers had lost the war. They had no more blood to shed. Neither had the British and the French. But the Americans did, more than enough to tip the balance of despair against the Germans.

Hitchcock, lying on his cot, knew none of this. He found himself among Russian prisoners captured on the Eastern Front and sent to Western Germany to work in the coal mines of the Saarland. One, he noticed, rubbed salt in his wound rather than return to the pits.

In the Saarbriicken hospital, however, Tommy's fever vanished. He had written home on Easter Sunday a bare-bones account of his last fight, the crash, and his capture. The note was meant to be reassuring to the people in Westbury, and no doubt it was. All they had heard up to that point was by a form letter from Captain Agire. Within the limits of the formula phrases employed on such occasions by officers—*"son magnifique courage, son sang froid, son intelligenceet son energie"* —the letter was a sincere expression of grief over the loss of an excellent pilot and a charming comrade. But the Hitchcocks must have been left in anguish over what actually had happened to their boy, for Agire was none too clear. "It seems very likely," the captain said, in French, "that in the course of his steep dive his motor must have faltered under the sudden cooling and loss of pressure, and not caught again, with the result that the marechal de logis Hitchcock, at the moment very close to the ground and far from our lines, would have been forced to land . . . and was then made prisoner."

Agire's letter was posted on March 8 and arrived at the Hitchcocks' a month or so later. Cables would have been sent, but they could hardly have been reassuring. Then came a letter from Dr. G. E. Brewer, a family friend and a medical officer attached to the American army, who had lunched with Tommy at Luneville a week before he was lost. Brewer reported that there had been a fight—with three enemy planes—and that Tommy was last seen "heading downward very fast as if his engine had stopped, almost perpendicularly." He ended, moreover, on a note that could have sounded like an obituary: "I have been greatly impressed," he wrote, "with the expression of sorrow and devotion and admiration of Tom's courage and skill and the high esteem in which he was held by all the officers and men of his unit."

Not until early May did the Hitchcocks receive positive assurance that their son was alive.

Two weeks after his arrival at the prison hospital at Saarbriicken, Tommy hatched his first escape plot. He had noticed that in good weather the skies over the city were patrolled by Albatross fighters, which took off and landed at a field some distance behind the hospital. The plan, which he conceived with an RFC pilot named Smith, who had been sent to the hospital for a minor operation, was to climb out of their third-story barracks at night onto an adjoining roof and from there make their way to the aerodrome, where they would steal a plane and fly for France. Smith in the end refused to go along with this scheme, and before Tommy could persuade him to take a chance, he was transferred back to prison.

About May 1, Hitchcock was considered well enough to be transferred from the hospital to a camp called Giessen, near Frankfurt. The trip from Saarbriicken was a delight after nearly two months of incarceration among suffering and hungry men. They went by train—he and seven Frenchmen and their guards—and the way north took them to Koblenz through the serpentine valley of the Moselle River. It was full spring and perfect weather, and for long moments Tommy could imagine that he was neither hurt nor captive but a well and free man, an American tourist looking out at a passing landscape of rural tranquility. From Koblenz they went down the Rhine to Frankfurt, then, after changing trains, to the camp at Giessen, where they arrived at 10:30 p.m., too late to be admitted to the barracks. Hitchcock collapsed on a bench in the guard room only to be awakened a few hours later by an overpowering stench, which he recognized as the smell of putrifying flesh. He found himself sitting next to a man cradling his foot and moaning softly in a brogue, "Oh, my toe, my toe." He was an Irishman who'd been invalided out of a chalk mine after a cart ran over his foot, and for the rest of the night, until dawn came and Tommy was taken away to the camp, he comforted the suffering man, listening to his stories and telling his own.

He wasn't long at Giessen, but his stay was memorable: he was given a bath. Actually he got more than a bath. With a few dozen fellow prisoners, he was marched into a large shower room with a furnacelike machine at one end of it. They were told to strip, and when they did, their clothes were placed in the furnace and baked. Then an attendant marched into the room holding two hair clippers. "Barber?" he growled, looking inquiringly about the room. There being no former barbers in the group, he shoved the clippers into the hands of the two nearest men, made clipping motions with his hand, and left. Despite the delousing, the shaved head and the rest of it, Hitchcock was glad of the cleaning that he and his clothes got—the corpses of the bugs baked into the material like little signs of a good job well done.

From Giessen he was sent south to Darmstadt, where he spent ten days or so waiting to be assigned a "permanent" prison. Early on the morning of May 15, with two English sergeants and under the eyes of an intelligent but "vicious-looking" German corporal, he boarded a train headed eastward—where exactly the corporal would not say. They spent a day and a night uncomfortably perched on the wooden benches of a third-class carriage before the train pulled into Munich, where Tommy was separated from his English companions and escorted to another train. Several hours later he disembarked in a town called Landshut, which, even as a prisoner, he thought one of the most beautiful places that he'd ever seen.

With dozens of medieval and baroque churches, Landshut was set in rich farmland on the banks of the Isar some sixty kilometers from the Danube. The prison itself was a landmark, Trousnitz Castle, built in the early thirteenth century. It stood at the top of a steep hill, surrounded by an ancient masonry wall, which was also the outer wall of the stables and grainery, the keep, and the lodgings proper. The entrance was a huge wooden door, a door of fairy tales and dreams, and when it opened and he stepped inside, Tommy thought for a long moment that there must have been some mistake. All around him were gardens of fruit and vegetables and flowers. The warden seemed a figure from Grimm; he greeted Tommy in good English and told him that he would be confined there until another camp was completed nearby. He said that Castle Trousnitz was exclusively for English-speaking non-commissioned officers and that he, marechal de logis Hitchcock, was the first, and so far the only, inmate.

The feeling of enchantment lasted only a few days, after which he grew lonely and restless again. This passed when other men, English RFC officers and Americans from the Lafayette, began slowly to fill up the old castle. But with them came the old longing to escape, more powerful now than ever. It was like sexual hunger, he wrote later, like the sight of a pretty girl after one has been in the woods or at school for a long time, "[she sets] your pulses pounding and your temples throbbing. The thought of freedom arouses even a greater, more enveloping sensation in a prisoner. On a perfectly cool evening in bed I have broken out in a profuse sweat and only with difficulty restrained my mad impulses to dash out and run away anywhere, regardless of direction, just to be free."

Though he was working hard to regain his strength—at least once a day the whole camp would do calisthenics—his hip was still painful when he put too much weight on it or walked for long. And walking—a lot of it—was what he would have to do if he wanted to escape from Landshut. Getting out of the castle was one thing, but the castle was at least seventy kilometers from the Austrian border. Throughout June, then, Hitchcock bided his time. The routine never varied: late rising, light lunch ("unusually" light, he wrote home), some exercise in the afternoon, a shower, dinner, a walk around the grounds, cards, or reading until sleep came. Everyone talked of food, he reported, but soon regretted it. For as their imaginations leaped to culinary delights, mouths would begin to water, and suddenly there would be a halt in the reveries, as all with one mind became horribly aware of where they were.

Thomas Buffam, a stocky, dark-haired young man from New York, a former ambulance corpsman and Lafayette *pilote de chasse* who had been shot down only three weeks after joining his escadrille, was as mad to escape as Hitchcock, and a good deal better able to walk. He and two Englishmen conceived a plan that, in its basics, would serve as the plot of countless movies and plays and TV dramas of the next world war. The plan was this. Over the showers was a loft, and in this loft on the designated evening the three men would hide themselves just at dark. Food would have been stocked there bit by bit, far in advance. Three dummies would then be placed in their cots to deceive Sergeant Papp on his nightly rounds. Then, sometime in the early morning, when the guards were at their drowsiest, the three men would descend from their shower loft and make their way across the fifty yards of open space that separated them from a barbed-wire fence, the wall, and freedom.

The plan worked. Roll call the next morning was, as Hitchcock said, "great fun." The sergeant counted off his charges—one, two, three, etc.—came to the end, did a double take, and asked, "Who's missing?" No answer. The sergeant grew angry. Captain Hollis spoke for the group, all repressing snickers: "Perhaps some men are still sleeping, sir." Search and hullabaloo followed, and then restrictions and bad temper all around.

Ten days later, however, on July 13, the three men were brought back to camp and the fun was over. Tommy never forgot the expression he saw on one man's face; he'd been the strongest of the three and now his eyes stared out blankly, as if the inward vision of hunger and hardship were so terrible that he would be compelled to see it for the rest of his life. Another blow fell that morning. He and Herman Whitmore, a big, heavyset Lafayette man from Haverhill, Massachusetts, were told to pack their gear and get ready to leave for the NCO camp at Lechfeld.

In a sense Hitchcock was glad to leave Castle Trousnitz. His letters from there were more than usually self-reproachful for the idle, "stupid" life he was leading "when so much [was] going on outside." But the huge unlovely camp at Lechfeld supplied the necessary corrective. From the moment he arrived, Tommy was plotting his escape.

Lechfeld was divided into two compounds, one for NCOs and the other for enlisted men. The camp was surrounded by three concentric fences of barbed wire and a broad plain that stretched, totally without cover, to the Lech River. The one virtue of the place, from a potential escaper's point of view, was that one had only to follow the river, a fairly straight one in its northerly stretches, for about 125 miles and then be on the way to Switzerland. Otherwise the camp had the strictest security of any that Hitchcock had yet seen, wrapped day and night in a tight cordon of guards, and with arc lights battering the whole area from dusk to dawn. Roll calls of the twelve hundred NCOs were exceptionally strict and prompt, at seven o'clock each morning and evening. The food was virtually inedible; most of the men, including Tommy, got by on Red Cross packages and other food sent by their families. Finally, the French prisoners, of whom Hitchcock was one, were forbidden shoes. Hitchcock had to give up his solid field boots for sabots.

Though he was classified as French, Hitchcock messed with the British, a favor for which he was grateful in the early days of his internment when his food supplies had not yet started coming through. He spent most of his time, however, in a barracks reserved for "les evades," men who had attempted escape one or more times or who were suspected of wanting to do so. As a matter of course, all French aviators were locked up in the "evades" barracks, whether they had tried to get away or not.

Hitchcock's own account of his imprisonment at Lechfeld follows. The time was midsummer 1918.

One day, Crampel introduced me to a small well-built man with bright, piercing eyes. "This is Monsieur le sergeant Schneider, President of the Committee d'Evasion. Schneider, my friend Hitchcock." Schneider explained that in a big camp, where there were so many people trying to escape all the time, it was necessary to have some organization among the prisoners; first to prevent one escape attempt from spoiling another; second, to provide maps and compasses for those who were not able to get them for themselves. He promised to order a good map for me through a German sentry who was in the pay of the committee. In return I gave him my word to let him know twenty-four hours before I planned to leave. It was not necessary, he told me, for me to tell him how I planned to leave as long as I told him when. Crampel gave me an extra compass of his own, and I spent all that afternoon building a stool with a cavity in one of its legs, where I hid the much-prized compass.

It took me several weeks of work and maneuvering to get my kit together. I sacrificed my overcoat for a sack and a pair of braces provided the shoulder straps. The shoes, however, were the hardest of all to get hold of. Not only were they very scarce, but I had little to offer for them. I did not want to part with my watch, for it might be very valuable on the road to the frontier. The gold identification, that I had once wanted to trade for a toothbrush, did the trick. After much searching I found an Englishman who had two pair of shoes, but both pairs were too small for me. He was, however, willing to part with one pair for the gold disk. I then found another Englishman who had a pair of shoes that were too large for him, so I traded my pair for his, and he was delighted. The pair I got were brand new, and although they were a bit too large for me, they were lots better than the sabots.

In the meantime I had been talking with Crampel every day. He had found a place in the wires where he thought there would be a good chance for us to cut our way through just at dusk, before the double guard of the night took up their posts. The plan looked feasible; everything was made ready to leave at an early date. Six of us were to go, Crampel, Pauli, and Ottavi, all old veterans, Glenisson, my bunkie,

McKee and I made up the whole party. If we got scattered getting out of the camp we were to meet in a woods about two miles away.

Our attempt to break away had been postponed a week in order to give Pauli, a lieutenant in the Foreign Legion, an opportunity to recover from the prison term that he had just been serving for his last attempt to escape. Pauli was a very small man, not more than five feet two inches tall, but as strong as an ox. Fatigue, hunger, exposure, meant nothing to him, for he had served a hard apprenticeship with the legion in Morocco. In my opinion Pauli was the ablest escaper of the lot, for not only had he actually got away more times than the rest, but his departures had been quicker to take place after he had planned them. Then, too, his subsequent capture had always resulted through very bad luck rather than some blunder on his part.

Ottavi, Pauli's best friend, was impetuosity itself. His escapes had been brilliantly planned and well-executed up to a certain point, then Ottavi had taken chances and relied upon his strong arms and fleet legs to get him out of difficulties. He had, for example, walked through large towns when the wiser course would have been to trudge around them. He had spent many months in prison for having lost his temper at German guards and told them, often with physical demonstrations, what he thought of them. A thoroughly delightful and enviable character, Ottavi too often allowed his heart to overpower his head and consequently was not so successful at escaping as Pauli. Crampel supplied the caution, Pauli supplied the wisdom, Ottavi supplied the dash for the party.

Glenisson had the next mattress to me. He was a heavyset fellow with a serious face that suggested that he would be a mean man in a fight. He took prison life very hard, and was determined to get back to France that summer, no matter what happened. Poor fellow, he was going to be married on his next leave, only ten days after he was shot down. He had heard no word from his fiancee for four months.

I was very well pleased with the character of the men I was about to set out with; they all seemed to know what they were about and every one of them was determined to succeed.

However, things did not work out as we had planned. After everyone was ready to leave, the cordon of sentinels was shifted so that a guard was posted directly opposite the place that we had selected to cut through, and our plans to escape en masse had to be postponed until we could find some other suitable scheme.

Meanwhile I made the acquaintance of a French sergeant who spoke English fairly well. His name was Henri Bavoux. He was the most unselfish and kind hearted man that I have ever met, but he lacked the qualities of nerve and decision that are essential to success of every kind. During the four years that he had been prisoner he had made only one attempt to escape, and he was then waiting to be repatriated as a non-combatant. [Crampel abhorred the idea of ever returning to France in any other way than on his two feet; he would far rather have stayed in prison with the meager hope of escaping and being able to fight again then be repatriated as a noncombatant. Ottavi, Pauli and many others in the barracks of the evades felt the same way as Crampel.] Henri on the other hand, was not of the same type as these other men. He was very nice to me—why I don't know. Perhaps he wished to get the American point of view. At any rate, he introduced me to a man called Galganni, a small athletic man of undeterminable age. His skin, browned by the sun, stretched over bone and muscle. His face looked as if it was chiseled out of rock; however, a pair of bright smiling eyes gave him an expression of alertness and a gaiety that spoke of good quick nerves and a sense of humor. He walked with a springy easy step without any apparent effort. He offered me his hand with a pleasant smile.

"Enchante de faire votre connaissance."

"Et moi aussi," *I replied.*

He spoke no English but his French was easy to understand.

"Henri tells me that you wish to make an escape," he began after we had selected a quiet spot in the middle of the athletic field. "If you will promise me to do just as I tell you, I guarantee that you will get to the frontier safely, but whether you get across then or not is a matter of luck. But if once you get out of this camp and you follow my

*instructions to the letter, you will undoubtedly see Switzerland. If you
will not promise to follow my instructions to the letter, I shall not give
them to you. Do you promise?"*

I hesitated a moment to think it over. I liked the way this man
talked, his manner and bearing, his appearance, and what I knew of
his past life all argued in favor of the accuracy of the information that
he was about to give me. I had heard many arguments over ways of
reaching the Swiss frontier, but here I had an opportunity of getting
some specific detailed information.

"Yes," I said, "I promise to follow your itinerary exactly as you
give it."

He made a few scratches in the ground where we were sitting, as
if he were trying to unroot the grass. He dug a little hole and pulled
out of the dirt a long metal tube such as one might use for a toothbrush. He wiped if off carefully, removed the top and extracted a roll
of paper that proved to be an excellent map of southern Bavaria. He
then began to give me such detailed information of how I should go,
where I should sleep each day, what towns I should go around and on
which side I should leave them—that I despaired of remembering it
all in my head, so I took down everything that he said in a note book.

I went over all the details of the trip with him very carefully
several times, discussing every point of doubt and connecting my notes
accurately with the map. I could find no flaw in what he said as I
followed his statements on the map, and after a little study I knew
my lesson perfectly. He was just as nice as he could be in giving me
the information, for it took several hours and must have been rather
dull for him.

Galganni's itinerary gave me a great deal of confidence. I no longer felt that I would have to depend upon some old veteran to direct
me to the frontier, but I was confident that if I followed accurately
the information that I had, I stood a very good chance of reaching the
promised land in safety.

One night I received word from the office that I was to leave for
another camp early the next morning. Whitmore and McKee received
the same word. We were going to be sent to a camp for Americans,

probably Rastadt in Baden. This news hit me as a thunderbolt. Here I had everything ready to leave; in two or three days more I would be on my way to France. It was appalling. I knew that my things would be searched as I left the camp and I saw no way of concealing my elaborate maps and compass. I decided not to be beaten by just bad luck. I could always cut the wires and take my chances. All that I lacked was wire cutters. Crampel had a beautiful pair that he had often shown me. I packed my sack, tied my compass about my neck with a string, and put my maps in my breast pocket. Everything was ready.

I found Crampel in his barracks. I explained to him everything and finished by asking him for his clippers. I promised him to throw them back as soon as I had cut the last wire. He refused me. At first I could not believe him, but he was insistent and nothing that I could say would persuade him to let me have those clippers. I was too disappointed to be really mad at him, but from what letters he sent me I know that shortly after I left he felt very ashamed of himself. There was nothing I could do. I went back to my barracks the most dejected boy in the world. There was no use keeping the maps and compass so I gave them away to some friends. My nerves had been strung up to a very high pitch for the last two weeks; that Tuesday they seemed to give way completely for I sobbed like a child as I lay on my mattress and contemplated my great bad luck.

My night's rest did me much good and I awoke with new energy and ambition. The day was fine and my spirits arose with the sun; there was always a chance of escaping Rastadt, and even the train trip might afford a possible way of getting to Switzerland, I thought. Accordingly I decided to smuggle my compass past the inspection. The friend whom I had given it to the night before kindly returned the compass, and I concealed it carefully in a large loaf of bread. I did not dare to try to take my maps, as they were large, and I could always copy some other map in the next camp.

Although we were forced to undress completely before the German guards, their search of our clothes revealed nothing, and about eleven, under the surveillance of an old German private, Whitmore, McKee and I marched off with all our worldly goods to the railroad station.

An hour's ride took us as far as Augsburg where we had to wait several hours for another train to take us to Ulm. The day was fine; we had seen very little of the world lately, and we all enjoyed the trip through acres and acres of beautiful farmland.

At Augsburg, Dame Fortune, whose face for the past few days had been turned away from me, now smiled with a warm and beautiful smile that transported me to the land of promise. At Augsburg the guard, Whitmore, McKee and I entered a compartment of our own that was not occupied by any other German.

Our guard was a good-natured old fellow who had probably spent most of his time before the war hoeing potatoes on some rich German's estate. We all talked with him as best we could in our improvised German.

He told us quite frankly that we were going to Rastadt, an American camp. It would take us all night to get there, he explained, because we only traveled on local trains that stopped everywhere. He had a large guide book, containing the timetables of all the trains of Germany, as well as a large map. "Bitte, kann ich das sehen?" I asked him in my best German.

"Ya, Ya," he replied.

The timetable showed that we arrived in Ulm at 11:20 p.m., when we had to change trains again. I unfolded the map as if it was the most natural thing in the world to do, and tried not to look at it too eagerly as I studied our position and our relation to Switzerland. The map was not nearly as good as the ones that I had left behind me in Lechfeld. It was primarily a railroad map; a few of the larger roads were shown, and of course the rivers were all there, but the railroads were its chief interest and they were delineated with great exactness; each ten kilometers were marked off in different colors. However, the map had one serious defect; it went no further west than the western shore of Lake Constance. The city of Zitzenhausen, where Galganni had said I was to turn off the railroad track, was included in the map; but as soon as one walked west of Zitzenhausen, one walked off the map. However, it showed one important thing: Ulm was the nearest point we would get to Switzerland on our train trip.

I folded the map up carefully, replaced it in the book and returned it to the guard.

"Whit," I said, "with that map we can easily get as far as Zitzenhausen. From then on I think I can take you to the frontier by memory. Do you and McKee want to have a go at it with me? How about it, McKee?"

They were both very anxious to accompany me. An inventory of our food disclosed that we had enough to last us ten days; by fooling about with our sacks we managed to get the right items in the right sack, and also to get the sacks in a convenient place so that we could grab them quickly.

We were due at Ulm at 11:20. Between 10:30 and 11:20, we figured, the guard would probably doze off to sleep long enough to allow me to take the map. Then we should only have to wait until the train was not going too fast to drop off and be enveloped by the night. Accordingly at about 10 o'clock I sat down beside the guard and we all pretended with all our might to go to sleep. All, I should say, but the guard. He really went to sleep.

It did not take a great deal of skill as a pickpocket for me to get possession of the map, for the guard had laid the guidebook down on the seat between us, so that all I had to do was to locate the map, slip it out of the book and transfer it to my coat pocket. Still I was scared to death that as soon as I got the map out in the open the guard would wake up and all would be lost, so I made several feeble attempts to pull the book nearer to me as if my hand were unconsciously moving in my sleep. I very nearly woke the guard when the book brushed his hand as I was easing it over nearer to me. He grunted in his sleep and with a lazy motion swept the book back to his side. There was nothing left but to open the book where it lay and trust to good fortune. My new tactics proved thoroughly successful and in a short time I had the map safely buttoned in my pocket.

In addition to the railroad book, the guard had two large envelopes on the seat beside him. He had told us previously that one contained our dossiers and the other our money. There was about 212 marks of mine in one of those envelopes, and it occurred to me that with this money I might manage to bribe someone if I was held up on the road. So I reached over and carefully picked up the envelope with the money in it.

The train rumbled on slowly through the night. The guard slept quietly at my side; everything was in readiness for a quick get-away.

Then with a few spasmodic jerks and jumps, the train pulled up at a little station. The guard awoke, stretched himself and peered out of the window. I pretended to sleep on but as a matter of fact my nerves were strung to such a high pitch that I could hardly manage to keep my eyes even partly closed. What if he should glance down and miss the map and envelope? The guard sat down in his seat again, and for a moment I thought he would drop off to sleep again, but no, some evil genius prompted him to pick up the guidebook. There was still a chance that he might not miss the map, but as he turned over leaf after leaf in a searching manner, my hopes sank lower and lower. Finally he looked down beside him. There was only one envelope instead of two.

There was no time to discuss matters with the others. I either had to leave right away by myself or wait around until he searched us all and found the map on me. There was no question which was the best course. I got up, walked to the door, opened it, grabbed my pack, jumped out into the darkness and ran just as fast as I could.

I stumbled over a hedge and as I sped across a lawn I heard the guard's voice bellowing after me, "Halt! Halt! Halt!" I plunged into some thickets at the end of the lawn and all but fell into the Danube River, a beautifully moonlit strip of water, that lay directly in front of me. As I paused to catch my breath and get my bearings I heard the train pull off on its way to Ulm. For the present at least I was safe.

I walked along a wooded road that ran down to the river bank, and drank in all the beauties of a lovely summer night. For the first time in six months I was free. Free to turn this way or that, free to go or stay still, free to enjoy all the pleasures of nature. What a joy it was to be walking about once again in the open country.

After I had recovered from the first ecstasies of freedom I realized that my work had only just begun. By my map I was 160 kilo-

*meters from Schaffhausen and the only way I had of getting there
was to walk. I cut myself a big stick and set off up the Danube in
the direction of Ulm.*

*I soon found that the road wound about too much so I decided to
take the railroad and stick by it until I finally had to leave at Aitzenhausen. Towards morning I came in sight of the lights of Ulm. I
turned off the track to the south as that was the best way to go around
Ulm and at dawn started looking for a suitable hiding place. There
seemed to be no forest at all. I made for every dark clump that might
prove to be trees, but when I reached them they seemed to dissolve into
hedges or a few trees about a house.*

*I finally located some little fir trees planted quite close together. A
few trenches and cannon implacements suggested that in the daytime
soldiers might be drilled thereabouts, but the woods were very thick
and promised good cover. I decided to stay there.*

*The moon had been shining brightly, so that when I stepped into
the woods, the sudden darkness blinded me. Then as I worked further
in, the land sloped down and I saw before me a small lake entirely
surrounded by firs, and in the middle of it a windowless sandstone
building palely gleaming in the moonlight. My reverie was inter-
rupted when a twig snapped a few feet to my left. Whirling about I
saw a tall German soldier, or rather I saw his spiked helmet sticking
up among the branches. For a moment I thought that my imagination, excited by the gloomy surroundings, was deceiving me, but as I
looked the man pulled back the branches to have a better look at me.
He was not ten yards away. For a moment I stood petrified, unable
to collect my thoughts, then before I knew what I was doing I was
running as fast as I could out of the woods and across the fields. When
I hit the open I ran in a zig-zag to avoid possible shots, but nothing
happened and I saw no more of my lonely sentinel.*

*Day was about to break, so I hurried on, looking for cover. The
light of the moon was eclipsed by the bright rays of the sun. I could not
be seen walking about the fields in my blue French uniform. A row
of trees and bushes that looked as if it might serve my purpose proved
to conceal a stagnant brook. I went up to my waist in water before*

I discovered that I could not spend the day there with any degree of comfort. Eventually I came upon a sort of wilderness of bushes and trees. In the most sheltered spot that I could find I lay down exhausted and was soon fast asleep.

I could not have slept long, for when I awoke the sun was barely up. I was terribly cold in my wet clothes and the ground that I lay on was damp. For several hours I lay still and shivered until the sun's rays grew strong enough to warm me and dry my clothes. I ate a biscuit and some bacon, which did me lots of good. In the afternoon the sound of chopping nearby woke me again. The man could not have been more than 30 yards away. Towards evening he finished his work and went off.

I got very thirsty toward the end of the afternoon, but there was nothing to do but wait until dark to get a drink. I was bothered quite a lot during the rest of my trip by thirst, but as I got nearer Switzerland, brooks became more frequent and I managed to find quite a few green apples.

I had some difficulty getting out of the wilderness when finally it got dark enough for me to continue my journey. A marshy strip of land lay directly in my path and I could find no bridge to cross it. I ended by wading straight through the whole mess and managed to go into water and slime way up to my middle. This was a bad beginning for a night's walk. My shoes, already too large, filled up with water. Then the leather hardened and blistered my feet almost instantly. Towards morning I took off my shoes entirely, they hurt me so much, and put on a pair of slippers in their place. I could not get across the Danube to join the railroad because the only bridge that I saw was occupied by two lovers and I did not wish to wait until they went home, but decided to go down to Nuncingen by road and join the railroad there where it came again to the east of the river.

Few incidents of any interest happened during the following days of waiting and nights of walking. I scrupulously avoided all towns and houses, often having to go far out of my way. For a few days the weather held good. Two days of rain reduced my vitality, but fortunately I had more food than I had originally planned upon so I ate very nearly as much as I wanted the last few days.

The memory of those eight nights of exposure and hardship is not very distinct. I was continually strengthened by the hope of success and then let down by the thought of recapture. If I had not been alone it would have been a rather pleasant outing but as it was, at times I became tremendously lonely and discouraged. At Aitzenhausen where I turned off the railroad track I took the wrong road and had to retrace my steps about four miles before I finally got straightened out.

Galganni's information was remarkably accurate, and I had little difficulty in reaching the frontier as he had directed. Just before I reached the road where the guards were stationed I started crawling on my hands and knees. I saw no one and after a little search to the southwest I found the town of Thayngen, Switzerland, nestled among the foothills of the Alps.

I arrived there at about three in the morning, after eight nights walking.

The town policemen put me up for the night in a comfortable bed in the jail. I thanked God for my good fortune that night before I dropped off to sleep.

News of Hitchcock's escape traveled fast over the wires. His old St. Paul's roommate H. S. Henriques, serving with the Ambulance Corps near Verdun, heard it over a special telegraph that kept track of the kills chalked up by Allied flying aces. All information about *les evades* originally came from the Red Cross in Switzerland, but from there it was disseminated widely to the military authorities, to the various arms of propaganda, and to the wire services. An escape was news, "hot" news and good news (for morale purposes), and the Hitchcock family back in Westbury undoubtedly heard it first not from official quarters but from the newspaper accounts. Then a wire came from Auguste DuBos saying that Tommy was "perfectly well." The Hitchcocks took their triumphs, like their tragedies, with composure. Scores of congratulatory telegrams poured in from all over the country, from friends and relatives mostly but also from strangers thrilled by the story of the young pilot who had outsmarted the Germans and stood as a dramatic rebuke to everyone who said—or secretly feared—that Americans were "softies."

As for Tommy, he was frankly exultant. "I am free!" he saluted his mother in the letter he wrote just after crossing the border. "I am free!"

He was in Bern staying with friends of friends, the conductor Thomas Schelling and his wife. Their house, an elegant hotel in the mountains with a rather bare formal garden, seemed to him "a paradise." He did not tarry, however. Within a few days he set out by train for Paris and the Allens' house at 19 Rue Reynouard. There Henriques found him early one evening, sound asleep.

Henriques remembered chiefly his friend's modesty. Asked what had been the hardest thing that he had to endure, Hitchcock got up from the bed, went to the closet, and produced the boots that he'd traded for his gold ID tag at Lechfeld. "These," he said, with his quick smile.

But there was another reason for his reticence that evening, the irrational sense of shame felt by all men who have ever been imprisoned. Such feelings had to be sharp in an eighteen-year-old, one who was high spirited, restless in the best of times, proud, with a high sense of duty, and eager for glory. Escaping was for him a form of penance. This feeling—that somehow he'd been wrong in allowing himself to be captured and imprisoned—emerged more than a year later. He was at Harvard then, rooming with Douglas Burden, his childhood friend. In his memoirs Burden recalled that every so often he'd be awakened in the middle of the night by Hitchcock's sleep-slurred voice crying out, "But I escaped . . . but I escaped . . . but I escaped!"

In Paris, however, Hitchcock quickly pulled himself together. The first problem he had to face was the troublesome question of his military status. "Awaiting permission to leave for home in September," Cousin Auguste had wired the Hitchcocks, and his parents were overjoyed. Tommy had done enough; it was time he came back, and the surest way of getting him back was to have him tranferred from the French to the American forces, after which he could be transferred to the States as an instructor.

Tommy first heard of this plan when he presented himself to the French authorities and learned that some "big bug in Washington," as he later put it, had on Hitchcock's behalf refused his promotion to *sous-lieutenant* in the French army and instead had granted him a commission as first lieutenant in the American army. He wrote an angry letter to his parents: "All the American generals in the world can't force me to resign," he said, adding that he considered it "degrading" to find these things going on behind his back through "pull." He was also embarrassed by the French army's promoting him to *sous-lieutenant*, because he felt that it had been to gain better treatment for him in prison camp rather than to acknowledge his actual achievements as a pilot. (Actually, he had been promoted for both reasons.)

But this was small matter compared to being obliged to join the Americans and return to a "soft job behind the lines." Everything that he had heard from people in the American Air Service, he told his parents, suggested that the French was still the preferable army to fight with. Moreover, he thought, it wouldn't be right for him to go home at this point. "I have not done enough at the front," he wrote. "I would hate myself ever after if I gave in. I am afraid that if I once get home under U.S. orders I will stay there. I am more afraid of myself than anything else. Home would look awfully good now, and the front—it is good sport while it lasts, but it doesn't last long."

Then, too, his appetite for challenge was being whetted almost daily while he waited for reassignment to the front. He went often to the bar at the Hotel Meurice, an elegant rendezvous of French *pilotes en permission*. Because it was French army policy to grant three days' permission for each kill, the great aces turned up there with some regularity, so long as they lived. Guynmere was dead now, of course, buried under the cross that he had predicted would be his last award from his nation. Dead too were Lufberry, Prince, Chapman, McConnell. But Nungesser was still alive, his wounded face stitched together like a Cubist portrait, gold teeth flashing behind a demure grin, and Coiffard, and the methodical Fock, who shot down German planes with the dry precision of a merchant counting his gains. For Henriques, meeting these heroes through Hitchcock was one of the most memorable events of his life. For Tommy, it was an inspiration to return to the front.

At the same time, however, the character of the air war had changed, and the pilots stirring around the bar at the Meurice knew it. In the fall of 1918, the spotlight of publicity was falling for the first time on all-American "aces"—Americans flying in American units, such as Rickenbacker and his Flying Circus, Frank "Balloon Buster" Luke, and the rest. But the chivalry of the air, the plumed knight going forth to battle alone and unaided, like David against Goliath—those images were slowly fading. The future of aviation lay not in individual prowess in single combat but in the mass organization of men and planes. The airplane at the beginning of World War I had inspired an image of a winged horse, a living vehicle of a living man, a warrior. Similarly the combat front was a theater where women and children sent forth their champions to fight battles of elegant and brave maneuver. By the end of the war, however, the spell was breaking. Airplanes and pilots were no longer seen as the fair and fearless cavalry of the skies but as men and machines, nothing more than a novel form of artillery.

Toward the end of September, as the Franco-American forces began their attack on the Hindenberg Line, Tommy's military status was still hopelessly muddled. "All the American generals in the world" might not be able to force him to resign his rank of *sous lieutenant*, but "pull" had made a bueaucratic mess of his actual position. Was he with the French, as he claimed and wished? Or was he with the Americans, as his parents and "the big bug" in Washington wished? No one knew.

In late September he was still under great pressure from his parents to come home, but he was now more than ever convinced that he had to get back to the front. In a letter dated September 28, explaining why he had turned down the chance to go home, he put it as gently and firmly as he could: "It would be too wonderful to be with you all again and to work with Father. But, Mother, dear, don't you see how cowardly it would be to take a soft job after God had delivered me from that place? I must show myself worthy of the confidence He placed in me in letting me get out and do my very best now that I am here." Then, as if ashamed, he breaks off with "Well, enough of that."

Though he was exploring Parisian life with increasing relish and amusement, Hitchcock's last weeks in France were frustrating. The realities that he craved were not to be found going from one entertainment to another, on into the night. The realities that he needed were all at the front, and he couldn't seem to get there. So dwindled down his war: on November 11, 1918, he was still trying to be assigned to a new French squadron at the front when the fighting ended. After the armistice he took the first boat that he could get back to the States, to New York and Westbury.

Chapter Four

Freedom, 1918–1922

When Tommy Hitchcock returned to the United States in November 1918, he went directly from the boat to Westbury. Eighteen months before, Broad Hollow Farm had been his home. As he looked around at the land and the house, the frost-nipped fields, the stables and paddocks—all those images that he had carried around him at the front and in prison camp—nothing seemed real. Even his parents and his brother and sister seemed alien.

Everyone, of course, wanted to know what the war had been like: what it felt like to kill someone, for instance. And so, like most combatants, he never talked about "his" war, then or later. But he thought about it constantly. There seemed to be so much more that he could have done—if he had been at a more active front, if the weather had not been so bad, if he had gotten there earlier in the war, if he had not been so impetuous, if he had not been shot down, if the war had only gone on longer.

As 1918 petered out, Tommy told his parents that all he wanted to do was to pack up and go back to Europe. The Poles were fighting the Bolsheviks in Russia and needed pilots. To his parents he seemed badly confused. He had nightmares, and they thought he was drinking more than was good for him. They became seriously alarmed in the weeks before Christmas. He seemed like a bird in a net. There was only one solution: Tommy must complete his education at Harvard; he must take up where he had left off eighteen months before. He resisted, and early in December they sought help from Dr. Drury.

It was Mrs. Hitchcock who wrote the rector:

I am hoping that Tommy will soon go up to school, and that you will get a chance to have a nice talk with him, for he seems so dreadfully unsettled. I suppose that it is only natural after all he has been through one way or another. Nothing seems real to him on this side of the water, family, friends, or his own future. I feel that it is just a time to go through and he will be his own dear self again, but [to me] it seems very necessary for him to remain in this country now and not go back, which he is most anxious to do. I have great hopes that a visit to you and the old school may make him feel like going to Harvard. He should settle down to something soon.

He did not, not for several years. But between December 18 and the New Year, there was a flurry of correspondence between Dr. Drury and the Harvard admissions office, and at the end of it Hitchcock found himself enrolled. He lived in a suite on the third floor of Claverly Hall, on the so-called Gold Coast, which inevitably tagged him as one of the more privileged students at Harvard. The suite had two bedrooms, a sitting room, and a private bath, which he shared with Louis McCagg, an enormous, Newport-born, New York City–raised graduate of St. Paul's, and Douglas Burden. McCagg had been an ensign in the navy, and he spent most of his four years at Harvard on the water, rowing on the university crew. McCagg was in all things conscientious, considerate, and conservative. He lived by the watchword "Don't rock the boat!"

Hitchcock, on the other hand, was always rocking the boat, or at least messing it up. He was incorrigibly sloppy. All through the suite, from the door to the closet in his room, there was a deep carpet of suits, shirts, ties, socks, and underclothes that Tommy had dropped on his way to and from the outside world. It was a habit that deeply offended the oarsman's shipshape sensibilities, and Douglas Burden was forever making peace between McCagg and Hitchcock.

Burden was tall and dark haired, with an expression that women liked to call "sensitive." He was sensitive, too, at least to some aspects of life that Tommy was indifferent to at that time. He loved English and

French literature, was a member of the "intellectual" Signet Society, and acted in student productions. He appreciated good writing and worked hard to write well. It was he who realized that if Tommy could bring himself to tell his story of imprisonment and escape, Tommy might work out whatever obscure hurt it was that still woke him in the middle of the night. It did that perhaps, and it pulled him through English A, as well.

Hitchcock had never been more than an average student, even at St. Paul's, where a boy's every hour was planned for him. Harvard's haughty "sink or swim" policy made it more difficult to work. Added to this was the fact that the veterans' return had caused a bureaucratic muddle, bewildering even for those who knew what they wanted to study. Before his first year and a half was over, Hitchcock settled down to study chemical engineering, but he was never happy with the academic side of Harvard and did not do well at it. He felt apologetic about this later, saying to his wife in the thirties that he regreted wasting his time in college.

However, Tommy's college career was not out of the ordinary. The twenties marked the first time that thousands of young people went to college for no other reason than "the experience." It was a peculiar sort of experience, however, in that for most students it was purely social. They went to college to learn how to get along, how to dress and speak properly, how to be "popular." And the people they learned from, at schools like Harvard anyway, were of the same milieu as Tommy Hitchcock, that is, people who seemed to have always known how to dress, how to speak, how to give and take offense—men who (someone was always saying) never seemed to *sweat*.

But if the deepest purpose of the college experience was purely social, Hitchcock was hardly to blame for being restless and unhappy there. He didn't need to learn how to be popular: he already was popular. In fact he was a hero, an authentic one, a "newspaper" hero, as F. Scott Fitzgerald put it, even though the distinction sometimes made him uncomfortable. He played hockey occasionally, went to classes, did his work, but for the most part he tried to have fun.

A rather conventional—not to say boring—sort of fun could be had in Boston, even during Prohibition. Socially, Harvard belonged to the city, to Beacon Hill, the Back Bay and the Copley Plaza Hotel, where the big dances and debutante parties were given. Tommy was invited to all of them. Once, he and two friends dressed up in white gowns and went off to a debutante ball in Boston. They took their places in the receiving line like proper young ladies and then bolted, leaving behind them gratifying echoes of scandal. Far more dangerous form of amusement was to motor out to Dedham or the North Shore in someone's car, get systematically drunk, and then return to Cambridge. One of the people with whom Hitchcock drove around was Jerry Preston, a curly-haired fellow three years older than he was, who spent his money as though it could banish death itself. Perhaps this was in fact his purpose—he had fought in the battle of Verdun—for it was a proposition that he was always putting to the test, driving around in a huge phaeton car with a jug of bathtub gin handy in the back seat.

Another of Tommy's Harvard friends, John Gaston, became a lifelong companion. Like Hitchcock, Preston, Edward Weeks, Harry Crosby, and a few others, Gaston belonged to the brotherhood of those who had seen action in the war, having been a second lieutenant in the marines. A prankster, sometimes violent, always reckless, he had a penchant for other men's wives and a taste for "manliness and merriment" that fell wide of what Dr. Drury meant by that phrase. At Harvard he played both football and varsity hockey in 1920. Thereafter he gave himself up to less disciplined pursuits, mischief, and good times. Tommy often went with him.

The consequences were predictable: his academic work fell off badly. He also began to drink heavily—so much so that his mother wrote Burden an almost tearful letter begging his help. But Tommy, apparently, had no need of it. One day as they were walking through the yard, Hitchcock turned to Burden and said, solemnly, "You know, I've decided to quit drinking. No more liquor, just wine." And that was that. So far as anyone remembers, he seldom thereafter touched a glass of whiskey or gin.

During his summer vacation in 1919, Tommy Hitchcock started playing polo again, and in the next twenty years he set new standards of prowess for the sport that no one has yet equaled. Much of his excellence he owed to the accident of birth. His body, for example, seemed designed to play polo, the short powerful legs for gripping a horse's back, the long, muscular torso for reaching and striking the ball. It was an accident as well that he was born in a family where it was customary to learn how to play polo at an age when most children were just learning how to ride bicycles. But polo and Tommy Hitchcock, the nature of the sport and the character of the man, had deeper affinities. He played it so well because in the last analysis no sport on earth mimes so well the game he'd never been able to finish in the skies over Europe. Tommy, as William Wellman said of him many years later, was a *pilote de chasse* first, last, and always. Polo, then, was quite literally his moral equivalent of war.

In recent years, someone is always saying (usually in an effort to sell something, like polo shirts) that polo is "The Sport of Kings." It is not: A king is a chief of state, bound by the most solemn obligations to preserve his person and his dignity from harm. Polo is a game for warrior aristocrats, that is, for people whose calling inures them to difficulty and danger, and whose status lifts them above the possibility of ridicule.

The sport that Tommy went back to in 1919 traced its descent to a long line of warlike castes, most immediately to the British Army of India, behind them the Rajput, behind them the Moguls, behind them the Persian noblemen (and women) of the Empire, and behind them hordes of Afghani and Mongol tribesmen from the steppes of Asia. Americans were introduced to polo in the 1870s by James Gordon Bennett, heir to the *New York Herald*, prankster, publicist, and conspicuous consumer, who first saw it played at Burlingham, a former shooting club outside London, in 1875. The game was new then to England but all the rage and fast becoming part of the romance of India and the Empire. Bennett saw it and appropriated it—as other Americans were appropriating golf, crew, lawn tennis, yacht racing—and took it home with him, along with some equipment and a rather flexible interpretation of the rules. By the following year, the centennial of the Revolution, he had introduced enough players to the game so that with the addition of a few genuine aristocrats he could put on an exhibition match for the public. The game was featured in the *Tribune* and soon became a popular spectator sport. Only the rich, or at least the fairly well off, actually played it, but within three years ten thousand people were on hand to see the first interclub polo matches held in Prospect Park, Brooklyn, on June 21, 1879. By that time there were many clubs: Bennett's own Westchester Club (which, somewhat confusingly, moved to Newport, Rhode Island, in 1880), the Queens County Polo Club, the Buffalo Polo Club, the Brighton (New Jersey) Polo Club, and Meadow Brook.

Meadow Brook deserves more than a passing reference. What Newport was to yacht racing and the America's Cup, Meadow Brook was to polo and the Westchester Cup. It was founded in 1881—by the senior Hitchcock, among others—"to support and hunt a pack of fox hounds in the proper seasons and to promote other outdoor sports." But as the years went by, population pressure quashed the hunt, leaving Meadow Brook its 318 acres for "other outdoor sports." A polo field had been built there in 1884; forty years later there were eight of them, with stabling for at least a hundred horses. Moreover, within a thirty-mile radius of the club, there were ten other "private" fields: the Schiffs's two at Roslyn, Jay Phipps's two at Old Westbury, the W. R. Grace field, Sand's Point's field, Jock Whitney's Greentree field, Bostwick's field, the field at Piping Rock, and the one at Mitchell Air Force Base.

In the 1880s polo enthusiasts founded clubs all up and down the Eastern Seaboard, either on the grounds of older shooting clubs or at country clubs, or, *ex nihilo*, like the Polo Grounds in New York City. Bennett himself set up polo clubs at Essex and Morris Counties in New Jersey, at the Rockaway Hunt Club on the South Shore of Long Island, and at Narragansett, Rhode Island. In the Boston area were three clubs where Tommy Hitchcock played when he was at Harvard: The Country Club, so called because its founders believed themselves the first to create such a thing; the Myopia Hunt Club, so called because all its founders happened to suffer from this malady; and the Dedham Country and Polo Club. Some of these facilities were fairly rudimentary. Myopia's field, for example, had a pronounced dip at the clubhouse end, so that when the players were down there, spectators had a disconcerting view of disembodied human heads bobbling and scampering over the grass.

When Tommy Hitchcock began to play polo again after the First World War, the organizational base of the game was already established. The circuit system, or tournament play organized by region—Eastern, Southeastern, New England, Southern, Central, Rocky Mountain, Southwestern, Pacific Coast, Northwestern, Far Eastern, and Hawaiian—was established only in 1925, but even by the summer of 1919, there were, besides Meadow Brook, three principal centers of polo, each of which would impinge in one way or another on Tommy's career. The most important was California.

The English took a direct hand in establishing polo in California, both in the north and the south. In 1906 John D. Spreckels, son of the San Francisco sugar tycoon, built fields, barns, and other polo facilities on the grounds of the Coronado Country Club and soon put up a $5,000-challenge cup. As Bennett had done before him, Spreckels invited the one sort of team that could make polo instantly attractive to Californians— a team of English lords. Their names were curiously reminiscent of those preposterous noblemen who traipse through Mark Twain's stories: Lord Tweedsmouth, Lord Jones-Ker, Lord Reginald Herbert, Viscount Lucien Gower. What these lords left behind, however, was just what Spreckels had hoped they would—a new fashionable game. Southern California produced the better players, at least by Tommy Hitchcock's time. His closest rival, Eric Pedley, played at Midwick, an elaborate facility founded in 1911 midway between Pasadena and Los Angeles. (Like Hitchcock, Pedley was a "second-generation" player, having learned the game from his father, an English officer.) Santa Barbara boasted Elmer Boeseke, a gigantic man and formidable opponent. By 1928 there were 101 rated players in California, of whom perhaps 20 were respectable (i.e., with handicaps between two and six) and 5 or 6 high-goalers. (New York had the most registered players in that year, 183, but Ohio, with 132, and Illinois, with 104, were ahead of California in numbers, though not in skill.) Long before then, however—and long before Florida, where polo began only in 1925—California had been recognized as a blissful refuge from the snows and fogs of the East and of England, its climate matched by the hardness and speed of its polo fields and the hospitality of the natives.

Culturally, if not geographically, Texas was far from England, farther than California, farther than Hawaii, farther even than the other New World home of polo, Argentina, where the earliest players were English (or Anglo-Irish) and where the first polo club was called Hurlingham. Texans, mostly ranchers and their cowboy employees, played a polo all their own. It was a weekend affair. The ranchers would meet, with their wives and children, their chuck wagons and servants, at some appointed field—usually a stretch of pasture—and play a whole day through. The regalia they wore—high-heeled cowboy boots with long-roweled spurs, chaps, and sombreros—was as different from the English uniform as the Western saddle, which they also used, was different from the English. And, at least to Eastern observers, their tournaments seemed devoid of technique, rules, or time limits. But what Texas polo lacked in these respects it more than made up for in enthusiasm, aggressiveness, and horsemanship, so much so that at least one writer in the early twenties predicted, correctly, that the future of the sport lay in Texas. By the thirties polo was almost as popular a spectator sport in Texas as the rodeo. There were clubs at Abilene, Dallas, Fredericksburg, and Wichita Falls; and in the great triangle made by Austin, El Paso, and Sweetwater, there were fifteen or more small towns with teams. Twenty teams congregated each year at San Antonio before huge crowds in which the fashionable element was lost in vast numbers of cowboys, farmhands, and assorted riffraff.

Hawaii was another polo center in Hitchcock's era. He played there only once, but he found the sport thriving and popular. A hard-fought interisland tournament had been played since the foundation of the Wickman Cup in 1902. Honolulu, Maui, Kauai, Oahu, and the Fifth Cavalry at Schofield Barracks all fielded teams of fairly high caliber and with superb horses. For many years the Baldwin family team—father Frank and sons Edward, Asa, and Lawrence—won the honors. George Patton played polo in Hawaii and became the sport's most passionate advocate. In defense of taxpayer support for army polo, Patton once argued, "No man can stay cool in battle unless he is habituated to the exhilarating sense of physical peril. And no sport . . . is as good a school in this respect as polo." Patton led a Fifth Cavalry team to victory in the Wickman Cup in 1926; it gave him greater satisfaction than anything that he did until the invasion of Italy in World War II.

The history of high-goal polo in America can be broken down into four neat periods: The First Internationals, 1886–1914, The Hitchcock Era, 1919–1939, and two others that need not concern us, The Doldrums, 1945–1975, and a contemporary epoch that could be characterized as

"Democratic" or "Consumerist." The most innovative period, technically speaking, came in the thirty years before World War I, and Americans could take credit for most of the innovations. The first was the handicap system, by which players were rated on a scale from zero to ten according to ability. The rationale for handicapping was clear enough. Polo, once again, is a formidably difficult game to play. A poloist needs years of practice to avoid looking foolish ("You'd think he was killin' snakes out there!" is the way Texans put it), perhaps five to become more than just proficient. It is also, for most people, prohibitively expensive. This means that at any given time and place there will be wild discrepancies of skill among those available to play. The handicap system awards "goals" beforehand to a weaker team–weaker, that is, in the sum of the players' handicaps–and thus gives the benefit of a statistical doubt to the game's outcome.

But handicapping had another, unforeseen effect. Like the "ace" system in the air war, it provided a numerical rank for each player, a kind of stardom to which individuals could aspire by the single-minded pursuit of goal-scoring. And this changed the character of the game completely. Among the British it had become something like croquet on horseback; the Americans transformed it into something like an engagement of cavalry. Tactics changed accordingly. American teams began attacking in column formation rather than line: No. 1 on point, No. 2 doubling for him as the play permitted, No. 3 in support of No. 1 and No. 2, feeding them the ball; the Back most often on defense, but occasionally galloping free to attack on his own. From above, the action seems to unfold like the motion of a gigantic locomotive, the players now wheeling in great circles about the ball, now driving straight up and down the field like pistons.

One British observer noticed the difference brought about by the handicap system as early as 1910. He might have been discussing the difference between the British and American national character. "We used to think sometimes," said T. F. Dale, "that a goal handicap was only a useful convention and that a player could not really be expressed accurately in terms of goals. That was partly because we cared so little for goals. So close and cramped was the game, so pertinacious the defense in [English] polo, that most of the scoring was done out of the scrimmage in front of the goal. We did not trouble ourselves overmuch to record the names of those players who scored. A goal was like a fox hunt, in which the death of the fox is of little interest compared to the run which leads up to it . . . It may be a matter of wonder that some of us who had seen the best players in India, native and English, of twenty years ago, did not perceive earlier the truth that underlies the goal handicap, that a man's power of adding to the score is the true measure of his value to the team, provided that he can always combine with others."

Another development in which Americans took the lead, with Harry Payne Whitney at the head of them, was the introduction of Thoroughbred stock into the polo pony gene pool. Strictly speaking, polo ponies have been horses–i. e., more than fifteen hands high–at least since 1915. One result was a marked improvement in the aesthetics of the game: a tall man on a pony is more apt to evoke Don Quixote than a dashing dragoon. But it was Thoroughbred speed that brought the more substantive change. On ponies, polo seemed a succession of wild scuffles in front of one goal, then the other. But on a fast horse, a man could play the whole field, all three hundred yards of it. The game opened up, and at the same time demanded tactical teamwork: positioning and accurate passing, often at enormous distances.

Thoroughbred speed had one ambiguous consequence, however. More than ever before, polo became a rich man's sport. The price of polo "ponies" increased until, by the thirties, a good one could fetch at auction upwards of $10,000. The new ponies, moreover, hadn't the stamina of the old; they couldn't be expected to at the speed they were being ridden. Even after the game was restructured from three periods of twenty minutes to eight chukkers of seven and a half minutes, it was dangerous (or at least uncompetitive) to use a horse more than twice. Thus, to qualify for high-goal polo, a player had to have at his disposal, either on loan or by ownership, not only faster, more expensive horses but more of them. In this way, with some local exceptions, as in Texas, polo slipped out of reach of the moderately well-to-do and into the hands of the very rich.

But on the whole these changes made polo far more exciting to watch. The play making, the opening up of the whole field, the breathtaking speed—all transformed the game into a spectacle at once beautiful, suspenseful, and perilous, especially perilous. High-goal polo is an appallingly dangerous sport. The worst accident (or "wreck," as poloists today would call it) comes when the forelegs of one horse (galloping, one should remember, at thirty miles an hour) tangle up in the rear legs of another. When that happens, the overtaking animal trips, pitchpoling over on its back, its whole massive weight crushing down on the helpless rider. Lesser accidents are more common: concussions, broken collarbones, legs, and arms. The danger, naturally, only adds to the thrill of the game—for the players of course, but even more so for the spectators.

Rules were instituted, or more strictly enforced, to minimize the hazards. Paradoxically, though, these only added to the heart-stopping beauty of the spectacle. The rule against riding into an opponent at a right angle, for instance, forces the player to approach from the side and rear (rather as, in three dimensions, a fighter pilot must attack), and the maneuver results in one of polo's most thrilling moments: the ride-off, when horse and man are pitted directly against horse and man, flank to flank, each straining at flat-out speed to gain or block a shot.

And the penalty shot in polo is one of the most sublimely beautiful moments in sports. The referee places the ball a given number of yards out in front of the offending team's goal (the distance determined by the gravity of the offense). They take their positions, one man in the goal, the others poised to counterattack if the shot is blocked. Two men from the opposing team then ride forward, the champion, as it were, and his page, to where the little white ball lies in the grass. The audience is now hushed. Mallet upright, hand on hip, the champion holds his mount perfectly still as his partner smoothes the grass around the ball and then rides off to the side. The scene is perfectly composed, the vast expanse of green a rich fabric into which the players seem woven, like figures in a medieval tapestry. Abruptly the champion wheels his horse and canters slowly and deliberately away from the ball. His path describes a great arc like the blade of a sickle until, heading back toward the goal, he breaks the arc, comes straight down on the ball, cantering and rising high in the saddle, mallet lifted high over his head until, right over the ball now, he whips it down and forward, lofting the ball for what seems an eternity of flight toward the goal.

In the twenties and thirties, because it was so beautiful and thrilling, polo became a mass spectator sport. And this, too, was largely an American development, somewhat resented by the English. It was not foreordained that the sport should attract the attention of great newspapers, still less that matches should be opened to huge anonymous crowds. American poloists might well have done as the French did: kept the game strictly private, a not-very-strenuous pastime of the exceedingly rich. "We played selfishly for ourselves," Elie de Rothschild once recalled disgustedly, "and consigned the public to a few rows of bleachers with an icecream cart parked alongside. We were a 'confidential' sport." Confidential sports are not, however, in the American grain. As polo and poloists got better, more fun to watch, the natural American tendency was to "take it public"—not to make money, not for many years anyway, but simply because to all Americans, regardless of class, no form of excellence is considered quite complete unless and until it has been confirmed by the cheers of the people.

Polo might have gone public in the twenties and thirties without Tommy Hitchcock. There were other players very nearly as good as he; obviously so, for every great athlete needs great opponents. Still, those two decades of polo belong to him as decisively as golf in the same era belongs to Bobby Jones, or as baseball belongs to Babe Ruth. In his performances the game achieved a kind of classic perfection for which the pre–World War I period had been striving. He covered more ground than anyone else, he hit the ball more often, harder, and more accurately than anyone else, and even though it often seemed to his opponents that he was on top of each of them, all at the same time, no one ever accused him of being a prima donna; on the contrary, among all his other assets as a poloist, he was also a generous and spirited team player. As Pete Bostwick, a high-goal player himself, once said of Hitchcock, "Sometimes he did things on the field that simply made you wonder. . . ."

Yet for him, polo was never an accomplishment in which he felt he could take pride (as he did sometimes with flying, and later in his work as an investment banker). Douglas Burden recalls that Hitchcock and he lunched together just before the opening match of one of the most important series Hitchcock would ever play in, the Argentine challenge of 1928. Driving over to Meadow Brook, Burden was astonished to find himself engaged in a serious discussion of the merits of Nietzsche. "My God," he said to Hitchcock. "Aren't you nervous? How can you sit there and talk about philosophy on a day like this?" Hitchcock seemed astonished at the question. "Why not?" he said. "It's just a game." To him polo was like an heirloom: he worked at it as he might have done on a house that had been in his family for a long time, to preserve and perfect it.

He was gifted. He simply took very good care of his gifts.

In June 1919, as the first postwar polo season began, Hitchcock was especially interested in the possibility of winning a spot on the American team that would try to bring back the Westchester Cup, ensconced in England since 1914. The great pre-war captain, Harry Payne Whitney, had taken himself out of the lineup; the Waterbury brothers were retired. This left Devereux Milburn at Back as the only member of the so-called Big Four still playing—as superbly as ever. With three places open, Hitchcock thought he had a good shot at one of them.

He played in test matches that summer, trying out for the No. 2 slot against J. Watson Webb, a tall, left-handed player. They alternated, playing first for a "blue" and then for a "white" team. In the end no selection had to be made. The British cabled in mid-August that they would be unable to field a team in 1920 to defend the cup. There was little doubt, however, that if there had been a challenge team, Tommy Hitchcock Jr. would have been on it. His playing, despite a self-indulgent Cambridge winter, was all it had promised to be in the summer of 1916—breathtakingly fast and fearless, almost ferocious.

Hitchcock's all-out competitiveness alarmed some of the elders of the game. But there were others who played as he did, Westerners mostly, and that summer he met a few of them. Like a small band of outlaws let loose in the manicured gardens of the East, a Santa Barbara polo team had been taking on all comers during the 1919 season and doing quite well, mostly thanks to the incredible reach and power of its Back, Elmer J. Boeseke Jr. The captain of these outlaws was an old man by Hitchcock's standards, already in his forties. His name was George Gordon Moore.

Their first meeting took place on the field, in the finals for the Monmouth Cup at Rumson, New Jersey. Hitchcock was playing at No. 2 for a Meadow Brook team made up of Sonny Whitney, Roddy Wanamaker, and J. A. Stahl. The Santa Barbara team had Moore, W. S. Tevis, G. A. Galen, and Boeseke. From the first throw-in, Hitchcock knew it was going to be a brutal game—and that as the most dangerous man on his side he would bear the brunt of it. For four chukkers it seemed to him as if Santa Barbara could imagine nothing better to do with their afternoon than harass him. Particularly rough, whenever he got the chance, was Moore, the Santa Barbara No. 1, who seemed less interested in scoring, which was what he was supposed to be doing at that position, than in preventing Tommy from doing so. Time and again Tommy found himself being ridden off, bracketed between the enormous figure of Boeseke and the violently explosive Moore, who dug his shoulders into Hitchcock's ribs as if to suck the breath of life from him. Hitchcock loved every second of it. He reveled in the struggle, pitching into Boeseke, then Moore, stopping short, then wheeling about under their horses' tails and careening off after the skittering white willow. Boeseke was a fine player, but Moore was something else—far over the line of prudence that even Hitchcock drew for himself. Moreover, he was left-handed, which made him doubly dangerous.

At the end of the fourth chukker, squeezed once again between Boeseke and Moore, Hitchcock felt himself about to slip through when he heard Moore scream, "You son of a bitch!" Moore raised his mallet and whacked him on the side of the head. Hitchcock rode on until he heard the whistle blowing, saw Wanamaker riding over to him, and looked down to see his shoulder glistening with blood. There is usually a doctor at hand in a polo match, whose principal job is to persuade injured players that they must not return to the game. They almost always fail. True to form, this doctor failed with Hitchcock. He was back on the field in five minutes, his ear bandaged, not angry at Moore but resolved to give him the roughest three chukkers of polo the older man would ever see.

It was just what George Gordon Moore wanted. It was why he played polo—to hurt and be hurt. It was why he boxed—to hit and be hit. It was why he was in the mining game—to win and lose, either way as big as possible. When Hitchcock sat down for drinks with George Gordon Moore after losing the game to him that afternoon, he probably was aware of only three things: that the man had nearly torn his ear off; that, for reasons he couldn't yet fathom, Moore admired him; and that he was fascinated by Moore. It cost him about seven years, a good deal of money, and several illusions before he understood why Moore was so attracted to him, but he understood instantly why he was so drawn to Moore. The man was a perfect type of the reckless adventurer who had always fascinated Tommy. For the moment, however, the only influence that Moore appears to have had on him was to intrigue him with the prospect of a career in mining. Two years later Tommy would be working for Moore and living with him.

Back at Harvard in the fall of 1919, Hitchcock found himself more than ever caught up in the social life of the college. He was constantly in demand for polo at the Country Club in Brookline, the Dedham Country and Polo Club, or at Myopia on the North Shore. The polo wasn't nearly as good as at Meadow Brook. It was convenient, though, and took up some of the slack time he felt was suffocating him at Harvard. He was by far the best polo player Boston had ever seen, and a mount was always available from Common Forbes, who was especially generous to Harvard boys, or from Frederick Prince, his parents' friend down at Pride's Crossing on the North Shore.

The Princes lived in a colossal house on an estate that ran for several miles on both sides of the shore road between Beverly and Gloucester. It was a pretentious establishment by Boston Brahmin standards, surrounded as it was by a formidable iron-and-cement fence; but Prince was far from being a proper Bostonian. His wealth was inherited, but only at one remove from the source; and, though he was as ruthless in business as Bostonians often are, he had none of their pinched aloofness or their squeamish gentility.

Tommy Hitchcock filled a special need in Frederick Prince's life. He was the son whom Prince had lost in the war. Norman Prince's memory was hallowed in that household—excessively so, for everyone knew that he and his father had fought almost constantly since the boy had grown out of his sailor suit, most violently over young Norman's desire to fly. Norman had taken his pilot's license at a well-known school in Marblehead, just across Salem Harbor from Pride's Crossing, but under an assumed name, lest his father find out about it.

There was a second son, Frederick Jr., who had also flown for the Lafayette. But Freddy was a disappointment. Limp and soft-willed where his older brother had been intense and dynamic, Freddy had few qualities to feed his father's possessive vanity. Tommy Hitchcock, however, must have seemed almost a reincarnation of the idealized Norman, like him a splendid horseman, like him a *pilote de chasse*, like him a strong competitor, but, unlike him, safely the son of another man. Thus Tommy, that winter of 1919–1920, had a standing invitation to come down to Pride's Crossing. There was polo at nearby Myopia, parties and dances there or at the Essex Country Club, swimming off the rocks at Princemere, and lavish hospitality. Occasionally he went down during the week after classes to exercise Prince's ponies and to stick and ball on his private field. The invitations were hard to resist.

In February he was invited to join the Porcellian Club. Naturally he accepted. A good many of his friends from St. Paul's and New York were members—Burden and McCagg, for example—and there were few places at Harvard in those days where friends could gather to relax over a served meal and unlimited drink. The old barn, as the clubhouse was called, occupied three stories of an undistinguished brick building on Massachusetts Avenue, a minute's stroll from Claverly and the Yard. A haberdashery occupied the ground floor; on either side were the Bay State Fuel Corporation and Leavitt and Pierce, Tobacconists. The club rooms were just as unprepossessing. Only the dining room had any pretensions to elegance; the other rooms were all dark-paneled, cluttered with club mementos (chiefly in the form of pigs, the club totem) and furnished with the usual leather armchairs and horsehair sofas. It was a cozy and agreeable place, half Victorian gentleman's study, half officer's mess.

The singularity of the Porcellian Club was not just a matter of atmosphere or good fellowship or convenient food and drink. What made it preeminent above all other Harvard clubs was its antiquity (it had been founded, oddly enough, by a future clergyman in 1796) and the peculiar genius of the members over the years in maintaining a happy mix of New York éclat and New England tradition, of New York energy and New

England probity. Among the "brothers" in Hitchcock's time were Cass Canfield, William C. Charles, Washington Allston Flagg, Lloyd K. Garrison, Robert E. Strawbridge Jr., Chase Mellen, Richard Saltonstall, Paul Codman Cabot, Charles F. Havemeyer, Mason Sears, Elliot Perkins, and Robert M. Sedgwick. In the roster of Porcellian members going back to the founding, none of their accomplishments are listed, whether artistic, scholarly, or athletic. The only "success" acknowledged in the Porcellian roster is service—either to the government (elected and appointed officers), to the life of higher learning (university office or chair-holders), or to the higher life of the law (judges, public prosecutors) and to the nation (military service). Of the forty "brothers in P.C." when Hitchcock was at Harvard—all members of the classes of 1919, 1920, 1921, and 1922—twenty-nine, or three of four, served in World War I, and fifteen of these served in World War II as well.

Hitchcock used the club for the next three terms he was at Harvard; chiefly to eat but perhaps to study in the club library. He was not at all what is called a "clubable" man. Later in New York he joined clubs only when they had facilities, like the Racquet Club, that were otherwise unavailable; and the "social" aspects of these institutions made no impression on him whatsoever. After polo at the Meadow Brook Club he never even returned to the men's grill to talk over the game.

He was studying chemistry, but it was proving difficult. He liked the lab work; then at least he was doing something. But he found it painful to concentrate on the basic theory of the science, which was what the introductory courses emphasized. Moreover, most of his fellow students knew exactly what they were doing in the course: taking a step on the ladder to medical school. Hitchcock thought chemistry might be useful in the mining business, but he wasn't sure. He knew for a dead certainty that he did not want to be a doctor. His last brush with doctoring, looking at slides of wound surgery at the American Hospital in Paris, en permission one day, had made him throw up.

He was treading water at Harvard. He knew it and didn't like it. As winter turned to spring, heaving Harvard's brick sidewalks into streams of broken ice and dirty snow, his dilemma turned to misery. He felt he was getting nowhere. Why not go somewhere else? He longed to return to France. Perhaps he fancied that in France he could forget it all, especially the loving expectations of his parents. But there was the rub. Their expectations most emphatically did not include a return to Paris.

Oxford was something else again. What Luneville and the Lafayette had been for him, Oxford had been for his father. A year at Oxford, Tommy knew, would win his father's approval. Moreover, the British were ready at last to accept the American challenge for the Westchester Cup. The time would be June 1921; at Burlingham in London. If Tommy were to try to win a position on the team, he could not do better than to be in England when the practice matches began in April.

The SS *Olympic* sailed September 18, 1920, bound for Southampton and Le Havre. Percy R. Pyne Jr. was with him, an old St. Paul's friend who remained close to Tommy throughout the twenties. The son of the president of the First National Bank of New York, Toughy Pyne grew up in the New Jersey countryside around Morristown. A good polo player, though not a brilliant one, he loved hunting and riding to hounds. At SPS he wrote detailed accounts of quail shooting in the South and of hunting in England. He also wrote melancholy poems, pastorals set in the landscapes where he'd grown up. At Oxford he would fall under the spell of the great Irish poets of the time: Yeats, Synge, "H. D.," Oliver St. John Garrity, and others. He also became a convert to the cause of Irish independence.

Since Oxford did not open until October, they went first to Paris, where they stayed at the Meurice. They were there for a week, visiting the cafes and restaurants, conjuring up the shades of the war's great aces. They looked up d'Estainville, whom Hitchcock had last seen climbing into his Spad the day he was shot down, and celebrated their reunion at Maxim's. Tommy also called on the Allens and his sister Tantine, who was living in Paris with her husband, Julian Peabody, and their young child. With Cousin Auguste he went to the races and managed to lose a few francs.

London, after this jaunt, was mortally depressing. After only a few days there, he admitted to his parents that he wished he were in Paris, where "the weather is fine and everyone is in gay spirits." This was quite true: by 1920, France had grieved and shaken it off, while England was still in mourning—stoic but inconsolable.

Hitchcock went up to Oxford with Pyne and the fast-driving Jerry Preston in the early days of October. Among the students—most of them younger than Hitchcock in every sense—there was sadness and bravado. They were boys who had been too young to fight when their brothers and fathers were being killed, but they masked these feelings with a childish silliness that Tommy must have found puzzling and offensive.

Nonetheless, he was at first charmed by Oxford. The ancient colleges offered a mix of cloistered serenity and country-house luxury that was extremely agreeable. He wrote his parents, "I am more contented than I have ever been since the war ended. I could live on here with the greatest of ease for years and years with never a serious thought turning through my head." For some weeks Hitchcock gave himself over to Oxford's notion of the good life. With Preston and Pyne he had lunch parties in their rooms, smoked salmon followed by fresh fruit, heavy cream, and champagne, prepared and discreetly served by their obsequious "scout." He also joined the Breister, the hunt club his father had belonged to. At first he had been reluctant even to keep a horse. His father loved equestrian sports with the passion of a convert; his son, born to the faith, was somewhat indifferent to them all: hunting, steeplechasing, breeding and training horses, racing, whatever. Eventually he did acquire a horse and hunted with the Breister on at least a few occasions, if only to get out into the country. He couldn't take it seriously, however. "I have just come in from a very good day's hunt with the Breister," he wrote his parents in March. "As you know, I know very little about hunting, and all I tried to do was to keep out of the jam (there were about 200 out) and not jump on anyone. I had really very good luck because the only person I jumped on—I was in a bad place when the hounds got away and I followed a man very close over a bridge; his horse fell and my horse's nose hit him in the back just above the saddle—turned out to be the only friend that I had in the field, bar a few Oxford students."

He took up crew only to keep fit, and then found himself in a social tug-of-war between the Blues people, who rowed, and the Breister people, who hunted. In one letter he told of a conversation with the captain of the Brasenose crew when he tried to quit. Did Hitchcock realize the social consequences of what he was doing? the captain asked. Didn't he know that in the Vincents (an undergraduate club) hunting men were not highly regarded? If he didn't go out for the "tuggers" in the spring, he would never get his Blue and never make it into the Vincents. Tommy said that he wasn't sure of what he thought of "the hunting people" but that the rowing people, as far as he could see, were "a lot of bores." Nevertheless, he did not quit, and on the morning of the last race, he wrote his parents, wryly, "As I have had a slight pain in the lower part of my abdomen, I am thinking of getting a doctor to examine me for a rupture. But upon trying to produce the same pain this morning, no matter what position I get into, I cannot find it. I am afraid that I shall be out of luck in this respect." He did his bit for good old Brasenose that afternoon but never set foot in a shell again.

As far as chemistry was concerned, he found it still difficult to see the connection between what he was required to study and what he planned for the future. On the one hand were the laboratories where he conducted his assigned experiments; on the other, rumors of an El Dorado in the oilfields of North Africa. New wells were being dug every day, and he yearned to be on the scene, at one time even planning to go down to Morocco over Christmas. His letters reflect cycles of gloom and satisfaction. "I wrote you that I have taken up studying . . . I am hoping to be able to knock this stuff in the eye so that in a few years I shall feel independent." Later comes the letdown: "I must be very dumb and find myself very handicapped by not having studied it this way before . . . What progress I make is very little." Nonetheless, by the time Hitchcock had pretty well decided to give up Oxford and return to Harvard, he felt that he had made some headway and that the experience had been worthwhile. "Strangely enough, I have done more work here than anywhere else I have been . . . I am just beginning to get a hold on the chemistry. I shall try to leave my situation here as good as I can when I leave, so that I can come back if I want. Also I shall write to Harvard to see if I can go back there. For the first time in my life I have a real desire for knowledge that is backed up, I hope, by enough willpower to study and read." These sentiments, the cliches of filial reassurance, actually held true. At Harvard the following year, he did find in himself "a real desire for knowledge."

On the whole, despite the diversions of hunting with the Breister, despite his nascent interest in his studies, Oxford was a big disappointment to Hitchcock. In November he wrote "A dismal fog enshrouds everything; the days are very short. So little seems to take place here that a large fire, or war, to jog these people up, would be a great relief." Around Christmastime he wrote, from Paris, "I have taken a violent dislike to all English people and all things English. I hope to get over it soon." In late January: "I seem to feel much more homesick now than I did during the war. There was so much more point to being away then." Later he said flatly, "Oxford is a cozy morgue. It is void of all life." Behind his disappointment is "France," his France, the France of his vanishing youth: "There are only two countries I care a damn about now, the United States and France. Of course, the U.S. has a particular place in my heart as do all mother countries for everyone. France however enters partially if not wholly into that inner circle of country-love." Then, as if asking for understanding, he tries to connect this sentiment with his father: "You, I imagine, have the same feeling for England . . . because you lived here for four of the most susceptible years of your life."

The Oxford Christmas "vac" was a three-week holiday, long enough for Hitchcock to return to his second country. He went to Pau, ostensibly to play polo with Freddy Prince and Laddy Sanford, a young man with a bottomless bank account, much of which he used to make himself into a good polo player. In fact, however, he wanted to see once again the mountains over which he had flown for a glimpse of the sea, the river valleys where he had buzzed the livestock, and the aerodrome itself. It was garrisoned against vandals but otherwise lifeless. The planes had vanished. He felt terribly sad. Abruptly changing plans, he left Pau and went to Switzerland—another pilgrimage to the past. It too saddened him. He stayed there only a few days before taking the train to Paris.

In Paris, at last, he felt he could let the dead bury the dead, his youth bury his youth. There he could get on with his life. Appetite returned; and not just for French cooking—though he could not refrain from telling his father that English food had spoiled his stay in England. For the first time since going abroad, his letters are full of polo. If he ever had any reason to be grateful to polo it was at this critical juncture in his life. When he could have drowned in nostalgia, polo was there to hold him back, to attach him to the present, and make a place for him in the future.

The 1921 Westchester Cup matches promised to be a glittering event of the international sporting season, but there was a good deal of pessimism on the English side. Many of the country's best players had been killed in the war: Captain Jack Atkinson, Captain Noel Edwards, the famous Grenfell brothers (one a banker, the other a cavalry officer), Captain Herbert Wilson. Most critical had been the loss of Captain Leslie Cheape, the man whom many experts (including Tommy Hitchcock) considered one of the greatest players who ever lived. He had been killed in a Turkish ambush in the Sinai in 1916. England could still field excellent players, however, and in Lord Wodehouse she had a patron of the game wealthy and enthusiastic enough to mount them well.

On the American side in 1921, authority was divided between the captain, Devereux Milburn, the only man absolutely assured of a place on the team, and the logistical commander of the U.S. efforts, Robert E. Strawbridge, the Philadelphia department store heir. Strawbridge (father of Hitchcock's friend Rob) was responsible for shipping and stabling the forty-six American horses that would be used in the trial and final matches. Throughout the late winter and early spring, he guarded them as if they were made of jade. It wasn't until Milburn, a busy corporation lawyer, arrived in England in late April that the American contenders for a spot on the team were allowed to play on the horses.

Besides Hitchcock, there was Louis Stoddard, who had had international experience in 1913 and 1914; Charles E. Rumsey, younger than Stoddard but not as able; J. Watson Webb, an immensely tall man, who in photographs always looks as though he were standing beside the grave of his best friend; Earle W. Hopping, son of a former Long Island player; Roddy Wanamaker, Laddy Sanford, and Freddy Prince—these three rather far down on the list. Malcolm Stevenson, who in the 1920 season had bid fair to be chosen for the team, was unable to be in

England. His absence improved Hitchcock's chances of a position on the team, but did not guarantee it.

In fact, when Tommy arrived back at Brasenose following his emotionally painful trip to the Continent over Christmas, he found waiting for him a letter from Dev Milburn that was as much a warning as an encouragement. The American captain was counting on him, but by the same token he expected that when practice matches began in the spring, Tommy would be in peak physical condition. He added that he did not believe that Tommy could do full justice to his work at Oxford (Milburn had studied there himself) and at the same time win a place on the U.S. team. He would have to choose.

The choice was not all that easy. Hitchcock never supposed that he would give his life to polo. The world held too many other appealing risks and challenges. So he probably resented it that he should have to give up Oxford, or anything else for that matter, to play polo. However, by the middle of February he admitted that the only thing for him to do was to withdraw from the university on the most favorable terms he could arrange: a leave of absence from Brasenose, with an option of returning in the summer, or going back to Harvard credited with one satisfactory term of study.

Serious practice, Milburn had written, would begin April 15 at Tidworth, where Strawbridge had stabled the American ponies. Hitchcock went down there in mid-February to see what sort of shape they were in and found one, Benny Catchum, going blind. The rest were in fine form. If he had hoped for some practice himself, he was disappointed: the fields at Tidworth, poorly drained, were like a bog. It was the same all over England. If he were going to play any polo in the next eight weeks, it would have to be in a different climate. Spain offered the best polo on the Continent, but because virtually the only players came from the highest nobility, including the king himself, and because Hitchcock, for the moment at least, lacked entree to those exalted ranks, he would have to be content with Cannes.

He went with Jerry Preston, traveling in a style that his parents thought extravagant. They retained the services of a "man" to look after their gear (a great deal of it in Tommy's case, because he fully equipped himself for the polo before leaving London), traveled first class on le train bleu, and then stayed at the best hotel in the resort. All in all, the trip cost his parents 350 pounds ($1,347.50).

As practice for the Internationals, polo at Cannes was less than successful. Hitchcock laughed about it in letters home:

> *They had me playing polo yesterday for the first time in a made-up match. I was riding borrowed ponies, as they all come for hire here, and I all but fell off in the first play. I could not hit the ball at all and was altogether a blank failure. However, I enjoyed it very much and hope that after a few more games I shall improve. I am playing again this afternoon. There are a few good players . . . the others are very bad, but take themselves very seriously and consider that they are great dogs to be playing the old Persian game . . .*

Still his spirits began to lift higher than they had been in many months. Polo was the principal reason, of course. He needed a direct, concrete challenge to his mettle. But he was also much amused by Cannes—the Englishmen walking stiffly in their wool suits along the boardwalk, the ruined Russian aristocrats clustered here and there talking of past glories and counterrevolution. In Paris on his way back to England at the end of March, he greatly impressed his uncle Frank, who had last seen him at Christmastime, despondent and purposeless. "I found him much improved in looks," Frank Hitchcock wrote his brother, "and in good temper. . . . To my surprise, Tommy is very punctual with his engagements. He seems to be leading a rational life here. He and Roddy Wanamaker expect to fly back to England next week. All the ponies are to be moved to Hampton Court soon and Tommy expects to live there and help fit the ponies."

Milburn arrived at the end of April, and the American challenge effort went smoothly into gear. Since at least 1909, Devereux Milburn had been recognized as the greatest American polo player. Coarse-featured and crinkly-haired, he hardly fit the public's image of a polo player— which then, as now, flickers between a Leslie Howard and a Rudolph

Valentino. He was a plain man, but strong and authoritative. He always inspired Tommy, who wrote his parents that he hoped to be in top form in a few weeks after Milburn's arrival. His letters show no anxiety about whether he would be chosen for the team. He noted that Milburn's knee was giving him trouble and that young Earle Hopping was playing as well as Webb, if not better. He was also pleased to report that he had reserved for his parents "the best five-pound seats" that he could find.

On June 8, nine days before the first match, Milburn gave the lineup to the papers: Louis Stoddard at No. 1; Thomas Hitchcock Jr. at No. 2; J. Watson Webb at No. 3; and Devereux Milburn at Back. The British team was, on the average, considerably older, though also more experienced. At No. 1 was Lieutenant Colonel H. A. Timkinson, a member of the victorious 1914 quartet; at No. 2 was Major F. W. Barrett; at No. 3 was Lord Wodehouse, whose last International was in 1909, when he went down before the first assault of Harry Payne Whitney's Big Four; and at Back was Major Vivian Lockett, who had played in two previous Internationals.

On the afternoon of June 15, the Americans played their last practice game—very, very carefully. The horses had to be protected, naturally; but Milburn was also in precarious shape, having acquired lumbago as well as a bad knee. They played at Burlingham in a practice field. The main one was being saved for the first match of the tournament in two days. It seemed in beautiful condition, and the stands were properly tricked out in white paint and bunting. King George V and Queen Mary were expected, as was the polo-playing King Alfonso of Spain and a large section of what the *New York Times* called "celebrities and notables." The military would be represented by Admiral Lord Beatty and Field Marshall Earl Haig. The controversial politician and former polo player Winston Churchill would be there, as would the duke of Northern Ireland, Lord and Lady Birkenhead, and, from Spain, the duke of Feneranda. On the English social calendar that spring the International ranked even higher than Ascot. Though both events were "by invitation only," Burlingham was notably more stingy awarding invitations, much to the annoyance of American tourists and the press.

Miraculously, June 18 dawned fair and full of promise to remain so. Hitchcock was still staying at Roddy Wanamaker's mother's place near Hampton Court. He had dined alone with his friend the evening before and went to bed with a novel by Anatole France. Rising late, he ran an extra mile that morning through a nearby park to bring his metabolism down to normal. After a light lunch, he and Wanamaker eased themselves into the cozy back seats of a Rolls and made their way to Burlingham, arriving at about two o'clock.

At the far end of the field, between two high masts flying the Union Jack (two others on the near corners carried the Stars and Stripes), he saw the massed bands of the Brigade of Guards forming up in striated blocks of black, scarlet, and gold behind their towering drum majors. Spectators—the men in morning clothes, gloves, and top hats, standard racing attire, the women in their prettiest dresses—were milling about as if at some enormous garden party. At polo there were always two spectacles going on at the same time—the drama of the game and the theater of society.

At precisely 2:30 p.m. flashes of sunlight leapt from the huge silver batons of the drum majors at the far end of the field. The spectators fell silent. Down came the batons and the band crashed out the opening bars of the march from Meyerbeer's "Les Huguenots." In slow time the guards marched down the field, turned in on themselves, and marched back, faced about again at the far end, and, as the great batons flashed down, closed short and froze.

At that moment the small, lithe figure of the Prince of Wales took his place in the gallery. Top hat rakishly tipped over one eye, in the mode made chic by Admiral Beatty, his handsome face frankly delighted, Edward in 1921 was unquestionably the most popular man in the English-speaking world. He was the first royal celebrity, a figure of fantasy for millions of middle-class women, and a dream subject for the mass media.

As soon as the prince took his place in the royal box, the gates to the club were flung wide, announcing the arrival of the king and queen. Preceded by two scarlet-uniformed outriders, two vast horse-drawn carriages slowly drew up before the stands and discharged their royal passengers. They were followed by the Spanish king, the Portuguese king and queen (these two deposed), and various ladies and gentlemen in waiting. More music from the band then—the British and American anthems— followed by a presentation of the teams to King George, who had, according to custom, a few words for both. With that, the game could begin.

Without question the proudest man at Burlingham at the end of the U.S.-British International tournament of 1921 was Thomas Hitchcock Sr. Thirty-five years and six tournaments before, he had played in the first International, and his team had lost. He had just seen his son play a leading part in a resounding victory, which returned the cup to his country in two straight games, 11–4 and 10–6. He must have relished this satisfaction of family honor. But, the old-school man that he was, he probably relished, as well, a poem that was read aloud at a great banquet for the players on the evening of June 25:

> With you we share
> The love of the Greatest Game
> Played clean and fair With no reward but fame—
> Fame and the Anglo-Saxon pride
> In a goal to get and a horse to ride.

But in 1921, these ideals of "amateurism," of nonchalant competitiveness, were already somewhat wistful. A symptom of their decay could be marked in the fact that with this game, Tommy Hitchcock Jr. had become—in the full modern sense of the word—a celebrity.

On June 18, 1921, in a sidebar in the *New York Times*, alongside a description of the game, the headline read: "Hitchcock, a War Hero, Was Captured by Germans After Airplane Fall But Escaped." The text is worth quoting in full because it was the basis for the publicity that he unwittingly attracted for the rest of his life:

Thomas Hitchcock Jr., one of the American polo team, is a son of Major Thomas Hitchcock, prominent in social circles in this city. Young

Hitchcock has a distinguished war record. He served as a corporal in the Lafayette Escadrille. While he was not the first American to bring down a German machine, he was the youngest (as he was only 17 years old when he sailed for France). He brought down two German planes after he had been at the front for only a few weeks.

He was captured in March 1918, after he had been forced down in a fight with three planes. He was wounded in the thigh and his machine became disabled at an altitude of 1,000 meters. Notwithstanding his wound and the condition of his plane, he brought the machine down in safety. He was immediately captured by several Germans and taken to a dressing station. From there he was sent to a hospital at St. Arnold [sic]. Later he was transferred to Saarbriicken.

It took two months for the wound in his leg to heal but finally he made his escape by evading the guard while on board a train. The guard was taking a nap at the time. Young Hitchcock walked 100 miles and reached Switzerland on August 18, 1918.

Long before he took up flying Hitchcock was noted as a horseman.

His father owned thoroughbred hunters, and his son early learned mastery of the many animals in the Hitchcock stables at Westbury, L.I.

A few days after the last match, there was also a long laudatory article on Hitchcock on the *Times* editorial page. The story of the game also appeared on page 1, right beside another about "the troubles" in Ireland.

The celebrity surrounding Hitchcock would acquire more and more details as time went on. It would be noted that he had graduated from Harvard, attended Oxford, and was in mining. His personal life would be displayed in the press at the time of his marriage in 1928, and then certain adjectives would begin to cluster about his name—"attractive," "soft-spoken," "bold and aggressive," "wealthy," "the greatest polo player in the world." The point is that there was no file like this on Devereux Milburn and never would be; he lived and played too soon. With the International of 1921, polo entered the first phase of what Paul Gallico, one of the great-

---

*This statement, commonly asserted by writers, was untrue: To say that Hitchcock was "a noted horseman" is a little like saying that Gene Tunney was a connoisseur of boxing gloves. Unlike his parents, he did not much like horses, or any "horsey" sports other than polo.

est sportswriters of his time, justly termed the Golden Age of Sport, and riding into that historical moment was Tommy Hitchcock.

After the Internationals, Tommy might have found Cambridge, Massachusetts, a natural letdown. But that was not to be the case. One reason was that he found a new friend during his last year at Harvard, his tutor, the future journalist William Laurence. William Laurence was a free-lance tutor, working his way through school on the fees he collected for his services. His clientele was drawn largely from the Porcellian Club and included Douglas Burden, with whom Hitchcock was again sharing rooms at Claverly Hall. Laurence was quite unlike anyone Hithcock had grown up with. He was Jewish, an orphan, an immigrant, homely, small, and poor. Any one of these adjectives would have served to bar him from the clubs and communities where Hitchcock belonged. Yet there was never anything awkward on either side in the friendship that grew up between them. Snobbishness is a way of making the world small and safe, which was the last thing that Tommy wanted to do. Moreover, he had an aristocratic sense of equality: he was always ready to say to his fellow man, "You're as good as I am." Laurence, for his part, would always reverse the phrase, saying: "I'm as good as you are."

He was so much a self-made man that he had a self-made name. He cheerfully told the story himself. One day he and Hitchcock were sitting around his room after a tutorial session and Tommy said, "Bill, you'll never get anywhere in this country with a name like yours. People can't even pronounce it, much less spell it." Laurence recalled that he was standing by the window at the time, and his glance happened to fall on a street sign. "Okay," he replied, "I'll change it to Lawrence." Everyone agreed that this was a splendid choice, but lest it smack too obviously of Boston (over which a Lawrence presided as Episcopal bishop), or indeed of Lawrence (a textile town named for the family to which the bishop was proud to belong), or perhaps simply because he preferred French to English spelling, "Lawrence" became "Laurence" and Bill was on his way.

He had already come far. Born in Lithuania, the son of a rabbi, he had left there at the age of twelve, wandered around Europe for several years, and then emigrated to the United States, to Brooklyn. Working in a factory and studying at night, he put together enough money and knowledge to enter Harvard. While there he supported himself by working in a drugstore, until toward the end of his undergraduate course he began tutoring. By the time Hitchcock met him, he was on his way to law school.

Like most people who met Hitchcock after he had begun to make his mark in the world, Laurence was intrigued by the contrast in the manner of the man and the reputation of the athlete and war hero. Even forty-five years later Laurence could remember his puzzlement on first meeting Tommy Hitchcock: "He wasn't a client of mine; somebody just brought him around one day. I didn't know who he was. He didn't stand out at all in any way, and when finally somebody told me that he had been a member of the Lafayette Flying Corps, and how he had escaped, and the polo, I looked at him and I thought, my God, he didn't look the part. He didn't look dashing. But, you know, he made himself. A great deal of everything he did was pure character. He needed to excel in everything he did—to do everything as well as it could be done and to be at the top." Tommy Hitchcock was indeed like that. But so, not surprisingly, was Bill Laurence. "He made himself," says Laurence, though not quite in the sense that Laurence did.

A philosophy course was what he and Hitchcock discussed in that school year of 1921–1922. If Laurence's recollections are accurate, their talk ranged from epistemology, to the goodness of God, to the claims of reason and faith, to form and substance, and so on down the list of ancient philosophical problems. They must have discussed other subjects as well. In particular, Laurence remembers Tommy's fascination with the Faust legend. Tommy used to say that he scarcely went to classes in that year except for chemistry.

As the school year wound down, Hitchcock characteristically began to get wound up. "I am very anxious to have a little strife of some kind," he wrote his parents on May 4, 1922, "if it is only on the polo field." Nearly every afternoon he drove the twenty miles or so to the Dedham Country Club for stick and ball or practice games. On weekends he usually went down to Pride's Crossing to play with the Princes. Soon, about the middle of May, an occasion arose for strife of a different and more painful kind.

Hitchcock's "future," that ineffable problem, was settled—at least with respect to his work. He had decided to accept George Gordon Moore's invitation of 1919 to go into business with him, raising money for Moore's mining ventures. Whatever Tommy's parents may have thought of that plan, they were adamantly opposed to another that Tommy was making for the summer. The Princes had asked him to Deauville for the season (June and July) and he wanted to go. A bruising fight went on between Westbury and Cambridge for most of May. At one point Tommy hotly announced that he did not care why his parents did not want him to go. Later he explained that he meant only to say that he had known since "long, long ago" that his parents were opposed not to him but to "French life and customs." His mother had admitted as much on many occasions, he reminded her in a letter, and his father had always been an Anglophile. He, on the other hand, having spent the most "susceptible" years of his life in France, was a Francophile. The conflict, he felt, was unfortunate but serious. "Maybe it is not altogether my fault," he wrote. "Certainly it is not yours . . . But the point is—that it is." He was no longer the seventeen-year-old who had been shocked by "French morals."

In the end Tommy cannily shifted the ground of the dispute from French morals to his own freedom. "I am very different from you," he wrote his parents, "yet I love you very much. Why should these differences . . . be a constant source of friction between us every time we are together? I feel I cannot talk to you as I would like to because you seem always to be hurt by the bluntness and difference of my point of view. You unconsciously think that I should feel and think about everything the way you do. If I did, I should be a much better man, but I don't always." Later, when he had won their approval for the trip, he wrote, "Your opposition meant to me a restriction of the liberty that I have enjoyed ever since I was 17. The trip to Deauville seemed unimportant; the right to decide all-important."

It was the last time that his parents tried to curb his freedom.

At Deauville, society was a public performance, displaying itself brazenly on the broad promenades in the late morning, in the enormous dining rooms in the evening, in the casino all night long. Every conceivable sexual pairing and possibility was on view: age with beauty, nobility with poverty; gigolos, mistresses, *Jeune filles en chaperones*. The dialogues of courtship took place in glances and witty *sous-entendres*, the logistics worked out in murmurs and scrawled messages under the door to one's room. In this ambience the blond young man with the serious face and quick shy smile was bound to stand out.

If he had not known it before, he must have realized in Deauville that he was attractive to women. He was a war hero who had fought for France, and the greatest polo player that le tout Paris had ever seen. Beyond that he emanated a quality of innocence, just the slightest suggestion of naivete, which many women undoubtedly found fascinating.

Toward the end of his stay, Hitchcock, in the proper American fashion, began to worry how he was going to repay the hospitality of everyone who had been kind to him over the past month, his hosts the Princes above all. He had very little money, having been reluctant to ask his parents to support financially a trip they disapproved of morally, and of course he had no house in which to entertain. As it happened, the Grand National Pigeon Shoot was to take place at the resort a few days before his departure. When he discovered that the prize was 20,000 francs ($1,000), he decided to see what he could do. From someone or other he borrowed a shotgun, and when the day came he took his place in the line, in business clothes. (Hitchcock was not above a little gamesmanship.) He stepped up to the line just as he had in Aiken, whipped the gun from hip to shoulder, aiming, and firing, again and again. He won and gave a lavish dinner party with his prize money.

Back in the States, the polo season of 1922 was historically significant in that it marked the first Argentine challenge to U.S. supremacy. Polo came to Argentina via Britain and Ireland. It was imported by the proverbial youngest sons, who came out to Argentina to seek their fortunes and found them on vast estates where nothing was lacking in land, horses, or climate for the best polo. The quality and style of the game changed quite rapidly and in the same way as the American game had done. The English tradition of "not the quarry but the chase" did not long survive in Argentina, nor did the British practice of closing games to the public. In

Argentina, polo became a popular spectator sport, second only to soccer. Finally, because of its wealth (for the most part an agricultural wealth), Argentina could support many more polo players than the United States or England. Thus the country produced real teams that played together often—not, as elsewhere, ad hoc bands drawn up for a game or two.

Argentine poloists also discovered a genetic gold mine in the Argentine cow pony. Within fifteen or twenty years of the introduction of the game, the Argentines were breeding the best polo ponies in the world. Since 1922, Argentine teams playing the tournament circuit in Europe or America invariably sell off the strings of ponies they bring with them, often at enough of a profit to cover most of the expense of the tour. There was a lot of envy behind this accusation: The homemade U.S. polo pony has never matched the Argentine product in price or (with many notable exceptions) in quality.

Argentina's polo players first ventured abroad in 1911, to England, where they enjoyed a string of triumphs against middling teams. Eleven years later they returned, carrying devastation wherever they played and handily winning the British Open. News of this victory probably reached Hitchcock in Deauville, and he must have been pleased to learn that the gauchos planned to come to the United States that fall. If they were half as good as people were saying, they would be good sport.

By the time he returned to New York in midsummer, he knew the names and reputations of the Argentine challengers. Lewis Lacey, a Canadian by birth, was thought to be nearly as formidable a Back as Dev Milburn. John Miles at No. 1 and Jack Nelson at No. 2 were reputed to be amazingly adept hitters, capable of scoring goals from angles (both of body and of position on the field) that seemed impossible. And at No. 3 was David Miles, John's brother, allegedly the most combative player encountered by the English since Hitchcock himself. This was not a team put together catch-as-catch-can; they had been playing together steadily for at least a year. And of course they were supposed to be beautifully mounted.

After dropping in on George Gordon Moore to make sure that when the polo season was over he still had a job, Hitchcock settled down at Broad Hollow Farm to put himself in peak condition. He was soon playing No. 2 for a team called Meadow Brook with Dev Milburn at Back, F. Skiddy von Stade at No. 1, and Elliot C. Bacon at No. 3. Meadow Brook thus accounted for two of the new Big Four. The remaining two, Louis Stoddard and J. Watson Webb, were playing for Shelburne, a team named for the town in Vermont where Webb, a Vanderbilt on his mother's side, had an estate. With them were Raymond Belmont and Robert Strawbridge Jr. Another strong contender was a team called Orange County, composed of Averell Harriman, older than Hitchcock but rapidly improving his game; Charles Rumsey; Malcolm Stevenson, another Internationalist; and Raymond Belmont.

The first tournament of the season was for the Herbert Memorial Trophy, held in late August in Rumson, New Jersey. The Argentines, somewhat to the embarrassment of everyone concerned, lost the first round to Orange County, 13–10, and were eliminated from the tournament. Harriman's team benefited from a five-goal handicap, and the gauchos suffered from the fact that their horses were still weak from their recent voyage across the Atlantic. Still, the Latin American four demonstrated enough skill to whet Hitchcock's appetite to play them.

Meadow Brook won the Herbert Memorial handily, defeating Orange County in the semifinals and Flamingo in the finals. The Open began in early September, also at Rumson, and Hitchcock at last took the measure of the Argentines. Their ponies fully rested, they thrashed Shelburne in the semifinals, 12–6, and Meadow Brook in the finals, 14–7. But it was not the lopsided scores that seemed so astonishing; it was their style. They played a game that could be compared only to Hitchcock's: unrelenting, hard-hitting, and utterly fearless. In the fourth period, for example, the fierce David Miles crashed and badly wrenched his knee. He could not walk, but he could ride, and moments later he reappeared on the field with his injured leg swathed in horse bandages. He managed to play even more ferociously than before, scoring three more goals before the end of the game.

Thus, in the same season, the Argentines had won the U.S. Open and the British Open. With such an important turning point in the game's history, it was decided to field the best team in North America against the visitors from South America. The U.S. Polo Association set a special two-out-of-three tournament for October 4, 7, and 10, which would pit the Big Four against the gauchos.

The Big Four–Argentina match of October 4, 1922, at Meadow Brook also marked the beginning of polo's widespread popularity as a spectator sport. Society was there en masse, naturally, and so was a man who became Hitchcock's great friend and admirer, Lord Louis Mountbatten, a great player and theoretician of the game. But the robin's-egg-blue-and-white stands were also packed with rather more anonymous folk from the city. And if most had never heard the name of any polo player when they arrived, they left knowing at least one—Tommy Hitchcock. The spectators in this series were becoming something hitherto unknown in the polo world; they were becoming fans.

Hitchcock's performance in the first game would have made a screaming fan of anyone. When it was over, he had scored five of the seven American goals (to the Argentines' four), including a hard, high penalty shot, hit with the nonchalant accuracy of a Bill Tilden forehand, just a minute into the first chukker. More impressive even than his scoring, at least to those in the know, was the demonstration that he gave of one quality that came more and more to characterize his play. This was his uncanny sense of anticipation; he seemed to know where an opponent was going to hit the ball even before the man raised his mallet. Thus he was always on the ball seconds before anyone else, intercepting passes, snagging balls out of the air, breaking out of a scrimmage just as the ball skittered free, blocking penalty shots with his horse. Reporters were always writing of Hitchcock that he seemed to be "all over the field," when in fact he was simply where the ball was.

The second game was played in an intermittent deluge, which must have taken the fun out of it for everyone, but especially for the Argentines, whose wildly dashing game depended on hard, fast playing fields. They went into the last chukker behind five goals to two. Nonetheless, they rallied magnificently and scored twice more. Then, with minutes left to play, Hitchcock, in a desperate effort to stave off another Argentine score, fouled Lewis Lacey, giving the other team a free penalty shot from sixty yards out. But, having jeopardized the U.S. lead, Tommy then managed to redeem himself by leaping his horse in the way of the ball, blocking the shot. Seconds later the bell sounded the end of the match.

The Argentines sailed for Buenos Aires on October 21, not without selling their ponies for handsome prices. They had made a great impression on American poloists and had given the game itself an enormous lift in the estimation of the public. They vowed to return, perhaps in 1924.

On the same day in Aiken, Mon Repos burned to the ground, only a few hours before the elder Hitchcocks arrived from Westbury. It was testimony to the growing celebrity of their son that this sad event was conscientiously reported in the *New York Times*.

CHAPTER FIVE

New York, 1922–1927

IN OCTOBER 1922, A SUCCESSFUL POLO SEASON BEHIND HIM, TOMMY Hitchcock left the serenity of Broad Hollow Farm and moved to New York. He had a job, with Moore, and he had a place to live, also with Moore, at 54 East 52nd Street. He would remain in the job and the place for four years, off and on. Whether one thought that was a good thing for Tommy Hitchcock depended largely on what one thought of his patron. And most people had trouble making up their minds about George Gordon Moore.

When Tommy went to work for him in 1922, George Gordon Moore was forty-three. He was also affluent, well-acquainted in America and England, and with a wife and children hovering somewhere in the background. He lived to be ninety-two and died broke in a shabby Hollywood flat off Sunset Boulevard.

More is known about his end than his beginning. Some said that he was born in Canada, others that he was born in Michigan; probably he was born in Ontario and moved to Detroit early in life. He was an Irishman, whether Scots-Irish or Anglo-Irish or Catholic Irish no one knew for sure, but he cultivated his Irishness. He gave money liberally to the Irish Republicans and loved to quote verse after verse of stirring, tearful Irish poetry.

He looked the part. Of average height but strong, he had a ruddy complexion, green eyes, and black hair. His presence, one admirer remembered, crackled with "atomic energy," and the energy was combined with a kind of ferocious charm that many people, almost in spite of themselves, found appealing. He was smart, though perhaps with the sort of smartness that Dickens, to his dismay, found much admired in America: "Is it not a disgraceful circumstance that so-and-so should be acquiring a large property by the most infamous and odious means? He is a public nuisance, is he not?" "Yes, sir." "A convicted liar?" "Yes, sir." "And he is utterly dishonorable, debased, and profligate?" "Yes, sir." "In the name of wonder, then, what is his merit?" "Well, sir, he is a smart man."

George Gordon Moore first surfaced on a big stage in London in 1914. It was said of him that "he moved in a shower of gold," and hinted that the gold was crookedly gained. He was said to be a war profiteer who cornered millions of tons of coal at the first signs of war, then sold it to the desperate British at a profit of a dollar a ton. He had been run out of the States, they said. Of course, people have been saying such things about nouveau riches since the invention of money; but Moore was more than a run-of-the-mill counter-jumper in 1914 London. He was a close adviser of Sir John French, commander of the British Expeditionary Forces in France and Belgium. It was assumed that Sir John was deeply in Moore's debt, probably (but not necessarily) for money. Whatever his power over the general, Moore had the reputation, during the early months of the war, as a man who could pull all the strings. He was, people said, "omnipotent."

Enter, at this point, the intelligent, adventurous, and beautiful daughter of the duke of Rutland, Lady Diana Manners. In the late twenties, playing a nun, Lady Diana scored a spectacular stage triumph in George Cukor's *The Miracle*; later, as the wife of the brilliant diplomat and politician Duff Cooper, she scored a lifelong triumph in international society. Here and there, in three volumes of her autobiography, one may catch a glimpse of George Gordon Moore.

They met in London during the first months of the war. She was nineteen, he was thirty-eight. She was still, she writes, of an age to be under the influence of her mother. He was married, apparently, and had two children. As a suitor he was as delicate as a buffalo. (He reminded her, in fact, of a Red Indian.) The shower of gold nearly drowned her. Each day brought a present: an ankle-length ermine coat, editions de luxe of the French classics, a monkey named Armdie, a poodle named

Fido. And each week without fail there appeared at her door a messenger staggering under the weight of a "box the size of a coffin" filled with lilies.

Her metaphor is just right. Lilies in a coffin expresses the tone of those days and nights at the beginning of the war. The mannered elegance of Edwardian society was intact, but from offstage the sounds of guns and suffering added a certain poignancy to the effect. Young officers, newly commissioned, entrained for the trenches still wearing their evening clothes, changed in the car, and the next morning died in the mud of Belgium. The parties, edged with hysteria, muffled with gallant stoicism, went on and on, and George Moore gave many of them. His inexhaustible gold bought champagne and brandy, the rarest foods, the best dance bands. Lady Diana always sat at his right; but when dawn broke up the party, she would be gone, circling around the Regent's Park with one of her dear friends, holding hands till the time came for him to go to the station, then to the trenches. Some of the guests called Moore's parties Dances of Death; in Lady Diana's memoirs she calls them "orgies."

She used his influence quite shamelessly, and he was delighted to oblige. He arranged for her brother to be attached to General French's general headquarters and to send out to a young friend of hers, wounded at the front, his mother and father and family doctor. With Moore's help she also made plans to set up a hospital in France, where she would serve as a nurse. The project fell through—possibly because Moore wished to keep her in London and didn't pull the strings too hard. Finally, as the war settled down and as the "butcher's bill," in Churchill's phrase, began coming in, the Dances of Death slowed and ceased, and George Gordon Moore left England for America. Lady Diana saw him twice after that, once in 1927 during her tour of the States in *The Miracle*, once again in 1940. He looked that last time, she thought, like "a mammoth toad."

When Tommy Hitchcock moved into the brownstone on East 52nd Street, Moore was again giving parties. They were simple in their lack of formality but complex in the relationships they occasioned. Moore maintained a salon of sorts—for celebrities and for the "nice" young men and women whose admiration lifted the celebrities in and out the door, and whose contacts Moore could use in his business. His business was mining (he was still at it in his late eighties), and his career resembled the progress of a confidence man through the salons of a Mississippi steamboat. He left ruin in his wake. A man who knew him in the thirties recalled one day being in a lawyer's office with Moore while the lawyer explained that a man who had invested in one of Moore's companies wanted his money back. He had a right to it, the lawyer said, because the loan was a short-term one. Moore seemed vastly amused: "Well," he said, "that poor bastard is one permanent investor now!" Ruin, of course, was not all he left behind him; he made several fortunes for himself and presumably for others as well. His trouble was that he had difficulty understanding just where he and his interests ended and where others' began. He was afflicted, one could say, with excessive generosity. He wanted to share everything he had, the bad times and the good.

Mining lay closer to the heart of the American dream than most enterprises. It promised dazzling riches, of course, but more than that, mining was a way of matching one's wits and nerve against Dame Fortune herself, face-to-face. The stuff was there—gold, oil, coal, minerals—waiting to be recovered from a bountiful Nature. When Moore was young, mining was still a frontier gamble, an outdoorsman's risk: the flash of gold in the pan, the dull gleam of ore in dark tunnels, the gusher in the desert.

That surely was one reason why Hitchcock was attracted to it. While at Oxford, he had wanted to go to Morocco to see the oilfields there. Mining was an occupation for adventurers and there was something of the adventurer in Hitchcock. In his milieu, adventuring had the quality of nostalgia. One can see it in the names that they sometimes gave their polo teams: the Meadow Brook Ramblers, the Meadow Brook Freebooters. Wealthy by inheritance, also cosseted by inheritance, for most of them it was easier to risk broken bones on the polo field than risk their money. Hitchcock, being who he was, had to risk everything. Moore would show him the way.

Moore's motives in hiring Hitchcock seem more than a little questionable. It is true that he admired him extravagantly, as a polo player and as a brave and interesting young man. At the same time it cannot have escaped his attention that Hitchcock was uniquely placed to provide George Gordon Moore with access to some of the most socially prominent young men of the Eastern Seaboard and through them to considerable accumulations of wealth, most of it—in the twenties—conservatively invested. That at any rate was what Hitchcock was hired to do: to raise money for Moore's ventures. He was paid twenty cents on the dollar, or so Moore claimed many years later.

How successful Hitchcock was is conjectural. There are rumors that he made a good deal of money. One story has it that with his first $100,000 or so, he bought each of his parents a new car to replace the dilapidated vehicle that they had been driving for years. There are also stories that he lost money, not only his own but his parents' as well. Probably he both made and lost. That was George Moore's pattern, and it was also the pattern of the twenties: easy come, easy go. If Tommy was lucky, he probably came out even in the end.

Many stories were told about East 52nd Street. "We were, you might say, a closely held corporation," said George Gordon Moore years later. Besides Moore, the corporation included Hitchcock, Pyne, Harriman, and John Gaston. All but Harriman lived in the house, and he was a frequent visitor. To hear Moore tell it, life at East 52nd Street was a simple continuation of the "orgies" that he had given in 1914 London. In an interview he dwelt lovingly on the sexual escapades of the various members of the "corporation."* He recalled that a few years after this period, when Gaston was married, his wife accused them all, not entirely in jest, of being "fairies." At that, Moore remembered, "Gaston laughed himself sick. He said, 'If there is any spot in that house, six by four, upstairs or down, where some girl hasn't been laid, I'll eat it.'"

Moore was careful to disassociate Hitchcock from the escapades: "Tommy was a very honest person from his toes to his hair. There wasn't a breath of dishonor in him. Anyone else I ever knew would compromise [to get what he wanted]. Tommy would compromise with nothing." Which is not to say that Hitchcock remained chaste throughout his stay at East 52nd. The well-known journalist Arthur Krock, who came to Moore's parties in those days, said of Hitchcock, "He was fascinating to

---

*In his memoirs, Douglas Burden flatly accuses Moore of being a voyeur.

women and it was difficult for him to fight them off. I don't think he did fight them off too much but it never turned his head and, of course, he never said a word about it. He was never a professional lady-killer; he just took those things as they came."

The best-known story about Hitchcock's amorous life is actually a story about a liaison that never took place. Gaston, it seems, had a special weakness for other men's wives. One of the women who caught his fancy was the beautiful Mona Williams, wife of Harrison Williams, a social figure of the era. Gaston's liaison with Mona, whatever else it may have included, took place on the telephone much of the time. Whenever he got Mr. Williams on the phone instead of the lovely Mona, rather than ringing off without a word, he gallantly left a name, not his name, but Tommy Hitchcock's. Mona, however, had another admirer, Jim Bush, who heard somehow that his beloved had been receiving telephone calls from "Mr. Hitchcock," and it made him angry. One evening the real Hitchcock came early to a party at the Williamses and was walking in the garden with Mona when Jim Bush jumped out of the azaleas so inflamed with jealousy that he flung off his dinner jacket and challenged Hitchcock to a fight on the spot. Tommy was bewildered. Why on earth did this lunatic want to fight him? The problem was complicated by the fact that Bush was a well-known amateur boxer, and Tommy himself was constitutionally incapable of resisting a challenge. He took off his jacket. The two men were just about to fight when Mona, visions of scandal thrilling her heart, interposed her glorious body and pacified them.

Gaston was a man about whom people, both friends and enemies, profoundly disagreed. One group thought he was eccentric; another thought he was crazy. Tommy was much amused by him and forgave him much. According to Arthur Krock, Gaston one day solemnly challenged Hitchcock to go five rounds with him in the boxing ring at the Racquet Club. Hitchcock was incredulous. He had been boxing for several years, while Gaston was in wretched shape and had never put on boxing gloves in his life. Hitchcock knew that once he got into the ring with Gaston, he would beat him, hard. He would have to; that was the way he was. And so he refused.

Gaston kept after him: loudly, publicly, and apparently in dead earnest. Hitchcock reluctantly took up the challenge but set a date sufficiently far in advance so that Gaston could get in shape. In the days that followed, Gaston insisted that he was running and working out in the gym, preparing himself for the great fight.

At the appointed day and hour, all their friends gathered at the Racquet Club gym. Gaston stood in his corner, obviously more than a little the worse for wear; Hitchcock stood in his corner, perfectly in condition. The crowd tossed jibes at the two men, then stilled as the bell rang for the first round. With that sound, as Gaston must have known, the joke was over as far as Tommy Hitchcock was concerned. He moved to the center of the ring intent on getting the thing over as fast as possible. Gaston danced out, shaking all over, flicked his glove at Tommy, and then with a great shriek of mock terror vaulted over the ropes and ran howling to the showers. Hitchcock even forgave him that.

Nineteen twenty-four was an Olympic year, with Hitchcock's beloved France as the host country. In the mysterious, or at least unrecorded, way of American polo, it was decided to send a team to Paris, with Hitchcock as captain. It was his first leadership position and he handled it well, putting together a foursome that was not only the best of the available players but also representative of the new geography of American polo. Rodman Wanamaker, alternating with the No. 3 at Back, was a Philadephian (by origin at any rate); Fred Roe, at No. 3, was a Texan; Hitchcock, at No. 2, was a Long Islander; and Elmer J. Boeseke Jr., all six-foot-four of him, at No. 1, was a Californian. The horses, except for a few belonging to George Moore, were the property of the players, and no fewer than thirty-four of them were on hand at Saint Cloud, just outside Paris, when the Americans arrived at the end of May.

There were three weeks of practice, followed by matches with France, Spain, Britain, and Argentina. Before leaving the States, Hitchcock assessed the competition for a *New York Times* reporter and concluded that the biggest challenge would come from the Argentines. The prediction proved accurate. The French went down to defeat by a score of

13–1, the Spaniards by 15–2, the British by 10–2. In the game against his friend, the marquis of San Miguel, with the stands packed with two Spanish princesses, a clutch of French aristocrats, and a few Rothschilds, Hitchcock managed to score twice in the first two minutes of play. Against Britain, of the ten goals scored by the United States, five were by Hitchcock alone, four others by Boeseke on passes from Hitchcock. Argentina, however, was another matter.

The match was held on the afternoon of July 6. It was a terrible day for polo, hot and muggy with a constant threat of rain. In their handicapping the two teams were almost perfectly matched. For the Americans Hitchcock was rated at ten, Wanamaker at seven, Roe at six, and Boeseke at five; for the Argentines it was Miles, eight, Nelson, seven, Padilla, six, and Kenny, six—totals of twenty-eight to twenty-seven. Never before had a polo match drawn such crowds in continental Europe; six thousand was already a chicken-feed gate in high-goal American polo but a magnificent turnout by European standards.

The first four chukkers again saw Hitchcock dominating the game. In the first thirty seconds, he ran the ball up the field, eluded the Argentine Back, and passed it to Boeseke, who scored. This was the usual American tactic of leaping instantly to a furious attack, and for most of the first chukker it worked: the Argentines were dispirited and confused. By the end of the period, however, they had recovered enough to tie the score, and throughout the second chukker they kept up the attack. Hitchcock rose to the occasion magnificently, "really playing," as the *Times* put it, "two men's games." In one role he continually defeated the well-coordinated rushes of the Argentine forwards, while in the other he snatched the ball from them and sent them madly scrambling on the defensive. Once, in this period he slammed the ball on a beautiful sixty-yard trajectory through the enemy goalposts, a shot that hushed the spectators in amazement.

The third period also belonged to the Americans. Playing in a storm of rain and hail, the Americans and their ponies performed wonderfully, and once again Boeseke, served by Hitchcock, scored a goal to bring the tally to 3–1. The rain stopped in the next chukker, and for the first time the Argentine offensive demonstrated what it was capable of.

In quick succession Nelson and Padilla scored three goals and would have scored more if not for the "superhuman" defensive work of Tommy Hitchcock (again, according to the *Times*), who also managed to score two goals of his own.

This fourth chukker of the U.S.-Argentine match in the 1924 Olympics may well have been Hitchcock's greatest moment in polo to date. Even his opponents were stunned. At the end of the period, one of them, Juan Miles, was overheard saying to Hitchcock, "My God, you should be ranked fifteen instead of ten, Tommy!"

In the fifth period, disaster. From the stands it was impossible to see what happened. There was a scrimmage, no more violent than usual, when suddenly Hitchcock's body convulsed in the saddle and slipped limply to the ground. Evidently he had been hit in the groin. The doctor remonstrated with him to quit the game, his teammates and opponents took the doctor's part. They would finish the match three on three. Hitchcock would have none of it. Slowly he got to his feet, fought against the nausea, found his horse, and grappled himself back into the saddle. The truth was that he had been badly hurt. His play was not the same. In the fifth chukker the Argentines tied the score, and in the sixth, with less than a minute left in the game, Nelson put the ball through the U.S. goalpost to win. For the Americans it was a heartbreaking loss, as the Argentines went on to capture the gold medal with frustrating ease.

Coincidentally, and unknown to Tommy, his future wife was sitting in the stands that July day in Saint Cloud. A few weeks before, she had been Peggy Mellon of Pittsburgh; then she was married to a young man from the same city, a former army captain called Alexander Laughlin, and they were on their honeymoon. They had gone to the polo match on an impulse, for neither one of them was a fan of the game, but it was one of the more thrilling afternoons of her happy honeymoon, and she would never forget it.

In the late summer of 1924, nothing seemed capable of stopping the great liftoff of the United States into what Fitzgerald called its "orgiastic future." The image seems slightly overheated, given the presence of chilly Calvin Coolidge in the White House. But it was Coolidge who said, accurately enough, that "the business of America is business," and the orgy was a fitting image to describe the state of business at mid-decade. Day after day the stock market broke through to higher pitches of excitement, and America's most sensational news lay in the columns of figures printed in the day's stock quotations, for those who could make sense of it. For those who could not, there were reports from Chicago that the parents of poor little Bobby Frank, murdered by those mad metaphysicians Leopold and Loeb, had decided to sell their house. There were stories about the Klu Klux Klan, lynching and cross-burning throughout the South and the Midwest, about the daring U.S. Army pilots who were flying around the world and about daring bandits like Bonnie and Clyde.

There were "social" scandals aplenty, duly reported in the staid *New York Times*. One concerned Mr. Greville Lindall Winthrop, sixty-five, of New York City and Lennox, Massachusetts, a munificent benefactor of the Fogg Art Museum at Harvard. Returning to his Lenox country seat in the early afternoon of September 7, Mr. Winthrop was met at the door by a Miss Holmes, once governess to his children, then his private secretary. She informed him that both his daughters, Emily and Kate, had just eloped, one with the family chauffeur, the other with an electrician who had been working around the place. According to the *Times*, Mr. Winthrop collapsed in deep shock but soon pulled himself together sufficiently to motor over to his mother's estate and tell her the news himself. The *Times* considerately tacked a cautionary headline on the story: "Parent's Frequent Absences in New York Furnished Opportunities for Wooing in Automobile."

But these were the most routine of items. By far the most important story of the first two weeks of September 1924, the story that gripped the imagination of millions, was the arrival in Long Island of the world's favorite royal scion, the heir to the crowns of the United Kingdom, His Royal Highness Edward Albert George Andrew Patrick David, the Prince of Wales. The occasion of his visit was the International polo matches scheduled for September 6 through 14. The occasion was not a formal one: the prince was to be on holiday. No "official" duties would be allowed to spoil, no ceremony allowed to stiffen, the prince's prospects of a lively and liberated vacation among friends.

The public was pleased to see a prince visiting a great democracy in order to enjoy himself. The people with whom he came to play were positively ecstatic. For decades the American aristocracy of wealth had been used, more or less willingly, by the European aristocracy of birth to refill its ancient coffers with dollar bills. The price paid by these Marlboroughs, Churchills, de Castelans, Palfeys, and so forth was fairly modest. In return for countless millions of dollars in refurbished stately homes and castles, restocked game parks, and a firmer hold on such newfangled forms of wealth as stocks and bonds, the European nobleman had merely to marry. Some American heiresses, of course, were no bargain. One thinks of Jay Gould's daughter, Anna, who was called on to *darer le blason* of the Castelan and Tallyrand families. Anna Gould was small, hairy, and vile-tempered. Then, too, there was the lovely but inconsolable Consuelo Vanderbilt, married by the duke of Marlborough for a consideration that was said to have amounted to $250 million, more than enough for a new roof on Blenheim Castle. She wept until she divorced. On the whole, however, the European aristocracy profited not only in wealth but often in good company from their marriages to the common daughters of common American millionaires. The old aristocracy had reason to be grateful; they even had reason to be friendly.

In this sense Prince Edward was the delegate of two or three generations of European aristocracy that had been saved from ruin by American snobbery. He came bearing gratitude. Moreover, the Prince of Wales in 1924 knew already what the Duke of Windsor acted on till the end of his life, that among the American rich he would always find what he wanted—veneration for what he had been, king for a day, and respect for his choice of love over duty, the life of feeling over the life of work. When Edward stayed on Long Island, he stayed among equals, and both he and they knew it.

The visit was a game of fox and hounds, except that while there was only one fox, himself, there were two packs of hounds, the press and the local hostesses. Of the two, Prince Edward may have begun by preferring the hostesses, but he probably ended by preferring the press. The press could be exhausted: he was, after all, only a story. The hostesses, on the other hand, were indefatigable; for them he was the staff of life.

In a sense, though, the hostess hunt was over before it began. Brush, mask, and paws, all went to the James A. Burdens, at whose estate in Syosset, Edward, along with his equerries and aides, was pleased to stay throughout his visit. Yet there were scores, perhaps even hundreds, of invitations tendered the prince—invitations to dinners, to formal dances and informal ones, to luncheons and to lunch, to swimming parties and cruises, not to coffee klatches but certainly to teas; and there were not enough hours in the day, nor days enough in the week, for the prince to accept all of them. Nevertheless, it was clear that he tried.

How he tried! On Wednesday, September 3, for example, he rose early and allowed himself to be whisked over to someone's estate for a cubbing. This must have been exhausting, as he'd been out the night before, first at dinner at the Henry Rogers Winthrops' (distantly related to the unfortunate Winthrop who lost his daughters to his electrician and chauffeur), then at a dance. In any case, after the cubbing, the prince went to ground for a while, surfacing only for an enormous formal dinner given him by the governors and members of the Piping Rock Club, all 175 of them, all male. By royal request the evening was enlivened by the great Will Rogers, who turned up from Broadway around dessert-time, offered Edward a stick of gum, then launched into a twenty-minute monologue on the prince's reputation as a horseman. Everyone remarked on what a good sport the prince was. "He laughed as heartily as all the others" was a typically amazed observation, as if the butt of a public joke can do anything else. After this the prince was observed slipping away from the clubhouse to go to the J. S. Cosden place, where his cousins the Mountbattens were staying, along with the marquis and marchioness of Milford Haven. There he danced until sunup.

One can't be sure how often in the course of his giddy career through the Gold Coast the prince's path intersected with Tommy Hitchcock's. There is a story, related by Bill Laurence, that Hitchcock and Gaston took some obscure revenge on the prince for having tried to seduce a young lady who happened at the time to be Gaston's wife. This sounds right. The prince's visit, with its odd ambience of pomp and silliness, was bound to arouse the mischiefmaker in Hitchcock. At the same time, though, he must have been pleased at what the royal vacationer was doing to promote the sport of polo. To accommodate the crowds at the Internationals, Meadow Brook had built stands for forty thousand people, including bleachers at the north end of the field. The posh seats were still, of course, on the west side: there were the boxes for visiting noblemen, for prominent American families, for their elected and appointed officials in government, for generals and naval officers, for anyone, in short, who could pay the price of a seat that did not, like the ones on the eastern side of the field, face directly into the afternoon sun. Weeks before the opening match, the U.S. Polo Association had received $400,000 for reserved tickets, far and away the largest gate ever collected at a polo match.

More important, in social and monetary value, anyway, was the terrific flurry of commercial activity kicked up by the prince's visit and the Internationals. The button-down shirt, that most durable byproduct of polo, had long been fashionable, since the day four years earlier when an Argentine polo player walked into Brooks Brothers and had one made to order. The polo coat—long, belted, and made of soft camel's hair—was still for the most part used by polo players, thrown over their shoulders for warmth between chukkers, but it would soon drape every prep-school graduate, north and south, from Foxcroft to St. Paul's.

The most determined efforts of advertisers to get a lift from the prince and the polo were not concerned with selling the sort of "apparel" worn by actual polo players. There was no mass market for polo equipment, but there was a mass market (mass sensitivity would be better) for anything associated with "aristocracy." Polo, these advertisers realized, could readily be made into a perfect symbol of aristocracy. For the significance of polo—to Americans such as F. Scott Fitzgerald, for example—was that it summed up all the noblest possibilities of wealth. Polo evoked chivalry, mounted warfare, and a society where privilege was either inherited or, if earned, earned only by good deeds and brave ones. Polo, because of the horse, was also blessed by art. Breeding the animal was considered an art. Painting and sculpting him had been a genre of art since the dawn of civilization, and since the eighteenth century riding him had been considered a delineation of beauty in motion, a performing art. Moreover, the horse was also an ancient symbol of virility, and if the horse meant so much, how much more was communicated by the image of a man who masters the horse, who makes its strength his own, and who, in the war game of polo, struggles for domination over himself, his mount, and his opponents—and wins!

In the image of the players alone, therefore, was a powerful selling device. But there were also spectators: beautiful women and elegant men composed picturesquely in galleries and boxes, arriving and departing in vehicles that whispered of glamour and romance in the night to come. The spectators at a polo match (as an advertiser might see them) combined the glittering tonic of an opening night at the opera with the wholesome fresh-air fun of a Harvard-Yale game. So polo, thanks largely to Edward, Prince of Wales, became firmly fixed in the public mind as of the fall of 1924: a magical image that could endow almost anything—hats, perfumes, a motor oil, a bar and grill—with its own properties of effortless power, violent beauty, and heady romance.

The first match had been scheduled for September 6, a Saturday. All weeklong temperatures had been in the high eighties and low nineties, with reports of hurricanes building in the West Indies. Then the rains came, putting International Field under inches of water. The game was postponed and postponed and postponed. For the press and the hostesses, each additional day was a heaven-sent opportunity to run after the prince. His resistance to the press, petulant at first, was considerably softened when the journalists cannily put forward an attractive female colleague as their point woman. His resistance to the hostesses, never great, stiffened slightly as he talked of continuing on his trip, regardless of the game, to Canada or California or somewhere. In any event, he stayed—and played.

For the other players, the polo players, the postponements tightened the screws of their suspense. Yet in fact there was never much doubt who was going to win the tournament. On Wall Street the odds against the British a week before the match were 2 to 1, and even at that, few people could be found to lay a wager. The British team had been chosen by the authorities at Burlingham only after unseemly disputes involving the selection committee, the backers, and the players themselves. The dissension never ended. When the final choice of a team was made, Lord Wimborne, the principal backer, was so upset that he sailed for home without even seeing the first match. There was no final choice, really; the team that eventually took the field on September 9 was less a team than a desperate guess. It consisted of three army majors (Kirkwood, Hurndall, and Atkinson) and, at Back, the renowned Argentine player Lewis Lacey. The team represented most sections of the British Empire, since the players had learned the game in such varied outposts as India, Cairo, Malta, and Edinburgh. Lacey, though an Argentine, had the good sense from the British point of view to have been born in Canada, which made him a British subject. He was the strongest player of the lot, and the odds against his team lengthened or shortened as reports of his injured arm, and then his case of the shingles, worsened or bettered.

In contrast, the American Defense Committee had been scrupulous and decisive in making up the American team. Never before had they had such an outstanding group of candidates. Still intact was the new Big Four, which had recovered the cup in 1921: Webb, Hitchcock, Stevenson, and Milburn. But Webb was thirty-nine, Stevenson, thirty-seven, and Milburn, forty-three, and while polo is one of the few violent sports in which it is possible for a man to play fairly well into his seventies, International polo is in a class of its own. Besides, among the younger men were players nearly as good as these veterans: Rob Strawbridge, E. W. Hopping, Averell Harriman, and Laddie Sanford. These were Easterners. There was also a new contingent from the West that had been playing with marked success that summer on the East Coast. A team consisting of E. C. Miller, Eric Pedley, Arthur Perkins, and Carleton F. Burke had won the Junior Championship at Rumson, New Jersey. (After the Internationals, most surprisingly, they would win the Open against a team made up of Boeseke, Hitchcock, Lacey, and Stoddard.) So outstanding was Pedley's playing that right after the Rumson series he was invited to try out for the No. 1 position (that is, J. Watson Webb's) on the International team. He nearly made it.

That was in August. By September 10 the cup defenders knew who they were. At No. 1 was J. Watson Webb; at No. 2 was Hitchcock; at No. 3, Stevenson; at Back, Milburn. Malcolm Stevenson was perhaps the weakest link in the chain; he had a tendency to keep the ball to himself, perhaps mistrusting his ability to pass or his teammates' ability to receive a pass. He was a big man, in photographs always scowling as though surrounded by dangerous natives.

Arrayed against them was Lewis Lacey. There were, of course, other men on the British side; there were the three majors. But the three majors were so inept that even the sportswriters ignored them, concentrating instead on the desperate effort of the Anglo-Canadian-Argentine at Back. He was obliged to play four positions, not one, and he did so with remarkable dash and skill. His gallantry, however, offered the principal interest of the game. Its outcome was never in doubt from the first moment of the first chukker, and in the end the spectators were possibly astonished to discover how close was the score, even at 16–5.

For the score only hinted at the extent of the debacle. The majors seemed incapable of teamwork. A basic element of teamwork in polo is trusting obedience to the cry of "Leave it!" Tommy Hitchcock, for example, could cry "Leave it!" and be obeyed, precisely because his teammates knew that Hitchcock had his mount going full tilt and that the horse's momentum would multiply the striking force of the mallet many times over and send the ball flying more than a hundred yards. The unhappy majors, in contrast, were forever checking their mounts as they came up on the ball so that if they missed it the first time, they would have another crack at it.

The consequence of this was that while the Americans took thirty-three shots at the British goal, the British took only eleven. It was the same story the following Tuesday, when the Americans crushed the British 14–5.

Mercifully for everyone—for the press, for the hostesses, and for the prince himself—it was time for Edward to say good-bye. He had learned much during his stay. He had learned, for example, about the abandoned back road into the Burden place with its iron gate that could not be unlocked but could be unhinged. Speculation centered on what uses the prince might have made of the secret drive. Most people supposed that he used it to elude the press as he kept illicit rendezvous with lovely women. The more skeptical supposed that he used it to get back to the Burdens' for a quick nap—while leaving the titillating impression that he had been up all night dancing. On the eve of his departure—by speedboat across the Sound to New London, then to his Alberta ranch—they were saying of him, with admiration, that he could now face a hundred still and movie cameras with the nonchalance of Ruth, Dempsey, or Douglas Fairbanks. The prince had learned, in other words, an indispensable skill in an age of democracy—how to use the press.

There was no International in 1925 to galvanize Hitchcock's physical energies. He played polo, to be sure: mostly with George Gordon Moore on a team that his mother whimsically christened the Meadow Larks. Moore enjoyed a handicap that varied over the years between zero and one, and few of their teammates rated much better. There was thus a certain imbalance of skills on the Meadow Larks, which meant that like Lewis Lacey on the 1924 British team, Hitchcock often found himself playing not one position but four. A vainer man than Hitchcock would have been impatient playing with such duffers. After all, his career spanned roughly twenty years, and for at least fifteen of those years he was indisputably the best polo player in the world: in other words he played among equals perhaps only once or twice a year. By 1931 polo cognoscenti like Peter Visher were writing that Hitchcock was not at his best unless he had teammates of his own class, opponents as well, and an important match to play. This was doubtless true, but the important thing was that none of the mediocre poloists who played with him complained that the great ten-goaler played condescendingly, carelessly, or disdainfully.

The exception was a friend of Hitchcock's by the name of Juan Ligier, a Peruvian who was possibly even wilder a man than John Gaston. Once, in fact, he said something so outrageous that Gaston was rendered speechless. He and Ligier were skimming over the Sound in the Peruvian's chartered motorboat when one of the girls with them fell overboard. Over the side she went, with noble Gaston not far behind. He held her head above water until Ligier brought the boat around and picked them up. "Why did you save her?" Ligier asked Gaston. "We could have gotten another one." This, at any rate, was the man who once told Tommy that his game was deteriorating because Hitchcock had failed to carry Ligier and two other zero-goal players to victory.

One of the qualities that made Hitchcock a legendary figure in the eyes of his contemporaries was his ready willingness to help beginners in the game. It was one of the strongest elements in his character, this eagerness to help, teach, inspire. Peter Grace, A. C. Schwartz, Alan Corey, Jock Whitney, Averell Harriman, all testify to the patience and enthusiasm with which, on the field and off, Tommy inspired them to play better, often better than they knew how.

George Moore was also helped by Tommy. Usually he played No. 1 to Hitchcock's No. 2, which meant that if he were to look good at all on the field it would be because the younger man was setting him up to score. In the early summer of 1925, they lost the Meadow Brook Club Cup tournament to J. Watson Webb's Shelburne and the Hempstead Cup to the Freebooters, a team put together by Harold Talbot. In the latter tournament the Larks were practically an all 52nd Street team, because Percy Pyne was playing with them at No. 1. But even without Moore and the rest, playing with near equals, Hitchcock's 1925 season was not a memorable one.

The following year he was no more successful. He entered the Meadow Brook Cup tournament in June as No. 2 on the Orange County team, along with Moore at No.1, Harriman at No. 3, and J. G. Milburn in his brother's position at Back. They lost in the semifinals by a calamitous 15–4 against the Meadow Brook Ramblers with R. Penn Smith, Sonny Whitney, F. S. von Stade, and Rod Wanamaker, even though they gave up only one goal by handicap. For the Herbert Memorial Trophy, which was played from August 28 to September 4, Orange County changed its lineup. Harriman was No. 1, Hitchcock was still at No. 2, while Louis Stoddard played at No. 3, and J. Cheever Cowdin at Back. They won that one against Laddie Sanford's Hurricanes. But on September 13 they went down to defeat against the same team when the youthful powerhouse Winston Guest replaced Morgan Belmont at Back. Hitchcock seems not to have played in the Open at all that year, but he was again with Orange County toward the end of September in the Waterbury Cup, though his team lost there as well (to Princemere, with Freddie Prince, Harry East, Lord Wodehouse, and Colonel R. M. Wise).

Despite his less than glittering statistics for the two seasons, his performances as an individual were at the usual high level, for there was not the slightest suggestion that his handicap for 1927 be dropped from ten, or that he would not be a certain winner of a place among the International Cup defenders of 1927. The British had challenged, as the rules dictated, the year before. The USPA yearbook announced the event in inimitable style: "Such evidence as is at present before us points to a contest that will be of great interest and, probably, prime importance in the annals of the world's greatest international sporting contest." The gingerly approach reflected the fact that no one really expected the British to give the Americans much of a fight. "The world's greatest sporting contest" it might once have been, though the words would probably have been disputed by the New York Yacht Club, which had been successfully defending the America's Cup off and on since the middle of the nineteenth century. But in the mid-1920s, hardheaded folk in the betting parlors of Wall Street or the drawing rooms of men's clubs were convinced that the British could do no better in the Westchester Cup than they had done in the America's Cup.

The Hurlingham Association, which had managed every challenge and defense of the Westchester Cup since 1886, decided to turn the 1927 endeavor over to the Army in India Association, perhaps in the hope that by going back to their roots the team would gain some magic power lost in the years since they had borrowed the game from the Raj. There were even some Indians participating in the challenge, the maharajahs of Rutlam and of Jodhpur. They, along with Captain the Honorable Frederick E. Guest, supported the expeditions with money and ponies.

And they did it lavishly. In previous International encounters, the British effort had sometimes suffered from lack of organization, which led to bad feelings, bad teamwork, or bad horses—or a bit of all three. In 1927 the organizers resolved to avoid these difficulties by moving a generous pool of both players and ponies to America early in the season. They were put up in Rye, bedded, boarded, and stabled there on a number of estates. After a month of test matches, the association believed that it had found the best combination in Captain C. E. Pert, Major A. H. Williams, Captain C. T. I. Roark, and Major E.G. Atkinson.

On the American side the selection committee enjoyed an embarrassment of riches. The Big Four of three years earlier was still intact, the most formidable foursome ever put together to play the game of polo.

Behind them pressed a group of newer men: Sanford, Hopping, Cowdin, Pedley, Boeseke, Harriman, Strawbridge, and Winston Guest, none handicapped at less than five (though none at more than eight), and all considerably younger than the three elder veterans of past Internationals. Webb and Stevenson were forty-two, and Milburn was a patriarchal forty-seven. In most sports, their ages would have disqualified them. But experience does count in polo, while age, relatively speaking, does not. (It's the horse's knees that must be strong, not the man's.) Nevertheless, in early August it looked as though the Big Four would be broken up, with J. Cheever Cowdin and the young Winston Guest replacing Malcolm Stevenson and Watson Webb. The *Times* greeted this news, saying "youth, not sentiment, must be served." Sentiment, apparently, was all on the side of the Big Four. The Defense Committee—consisting of Louis Stoddard (president of the USPA), the former great Internationalist Harry Payne Whitney, W. Averell Harriman, and Milburn himself—felt from the first that they ought to honor the Big Four; it would be their last chance to play together. Then came the test matches of August 6 and 7, in which Guest and Cowdin far outshone Webb and Stevenson, whereupon the Defense Committee "served youth" and reconstituted the first team, replacing Webb with Guest at No. 1 and Stevenson with Cowdin at No. 3.

The trouble with the youth-versus-age drama was that it did not quite fit the facts. Webb and Stevenson were indeed over forty, and Guest was indeed only twenty-one, having just graduated from Yale. J. Cheever Cowdin, however, was scarcely a youth; he was thirty-nine years old in 1927. Guest, incidentally, was rated that summer at a mere five, but in the enormous power and skill of the man—he was six-four and weighed a hundred eighty pounds—there was every indication that he should have been at least as highly rated as Cowdin.

Hitchcock was not a casual observer of these substitutions. Since early in the season he had been involved in a diplomatic mission that in the end would cause him considerable anguish. The trouble rose over Cowdin. A relative of the two great polo-playing families, the Cheevers and the Cowdins, he had shown promise in his twenties of being one of the all-time stars of the game. Then, in a 1920 match, his horse tripped and fell, crushing Cowdin's hip. But Cowdin was determined to recover his skill and standing, and by the spring of 1927, he had been awarded a handicap of eight. At age thirty-nine this proud and senstive man felt that the 1927 matches with England would be his last shot at International glory. He wanted it badly and in June and early July he played hard and well, so well that the committee tentatively put him at No. 3, replacing Stevenson. The results were not good. One afternoon, after three chukkers with the first-string blue team, Milburn allegedly turned to Cowdin and said, curtly, "Change your shirt." Cowdin angrily rode off the field, vowing to sell his ponies, break his mallets, and quit the game forever.

The vow was mistimed. After a few more test matches, it seemed to the committee that Cowdin was the better player after all. The question then became how to get him back. Milburn was in no position to persuade him: so the mission was given to Hitchcock.

It was a tribute to Hitchcock's gentlemanliness, one of the definitions of a gentleman being that he is a man who never unintentionally gives offense (as Milburn had done). He could also put the most effective pressure on Cowdin, because he was close to the *Times* columnist Arthur Krock, Cowdin's best friend. Krock told what happened then:

> *Hitchcock and Stoddard came to see me and told me I was the only person who could get Cowdin to come back to polo. Would I undertake it, in the interests of an American victory? I said that I would if Tommy Hitchcock would give me his word that Cowdin would not again be replaced, that he would start the International match. Tommy gave me his word. That was good enough for me or anybody else. For Tommy's word was his bond. Cowdin rejoined the squad.*

Webb and Stevenson, however, did not go gently to the showers, as they might have done in a professional sport. In polo few decisions are final; even in choosing an International squad, the ad hoc spirit of the game prevails. The test matches might in theory be over but there would soon be practice matches, which, if they played well enough, they could turn into tests—tests that Guest and Cowdin just might lose.

And so it turned out. Within ten days the Defense Committee had reversed itself again. Guest and Cowdin were relegated to the second team, Webb and Stevenson restored to the first. The reason was that Guest and Cowdin simply did not integrate well with Hitchcock and Milburn. Both were playing positions that were new to them. Guest was a No. 2, Cowdin, a Back, and each found it impossible in the brief time available to adjust to the different tasks demanded of a No. 1 and No. 3. Thus, with much chagrin on all sides they were dropped, and the Big Four was itself again.

For Hitchcock the move was acutely embarrassing. He believed that on a man's word hinged his honor. Honor meant trustworthiness, the willingness to make commitments, and the power to fulfill them. At the same time he could not argue that the committee had been wrong. Between Cowdin and Stevenson, Stevenson was, under the circumstances, the better choice. Thus Hitchcock's loyalty to the sport was in conflict with his faithfulness to his word. He went to Krock and told him what had happened. He offered to resign from the team. Krock released him from his bond. He recalled later, "I never saw a man suffer so much as Hitchcock did."

From the fan's standpoint, and the sportswriter's, the choice of the Big Four was a welcome one. The team had what polo teams usually lack—a history. Even the most occasional followers of the sport knew who Devereux Milburn was, and knew Webb and Stevenson, too. Above all, they knew Tommy Hitchcock. He was "Tommy." Everyone called him that, for everyone is on first-name terms with a celebrity. He was Tommy, the "perfect gentle knight," except on the battlefield of polo, where he was a demonic force, relentless, fierce for victory, "smiting" the ball with tremendous blows that sent it arching 150 yards down the field. And like all the knights of myth, he had a horse—Tobiana, a piebald mare. The crowds knew her name, too, and cheered when she trotted onto the field, always the first.

Thirty-five thousand people packed the Meadow Brook stands for the first match on Saturday, September 10. There was no Prince of Wales this time to magnetize so many (though there were hundreds of replica princes in the fashions that he had helped make famous three years earlier). This time they came for the polo, or, if not for the polo, for "Tommy." He did not let them down.

In the first chukker of the first match, thirty seconds after the throw-in, he scored. No one scored in the second period. In the third, Hitchcock scored twice, and twice again in the fourth chukker. He surpassed even himself in that fourth period, hurtling in and out of the melees unscathed and in total command of the ball, his opponents, and his teammates. "He could do things you simply wouldn't believe," said Pete Bostwick. In those seven and a half minutes, he did them all. The prose of the Polo Yearbook reflected his performance: "It had never theretofore been equaled." In the end the unhappy British were crushed 13–3, with Tommy alone counting six goals to his credit.

In the second game, on Wednesday, twenty-five thousand people came to watch at Meadow Brook, an astonishing turnout for a weekday afternoon at a site more than an hour from New York City. The British had sacked their two Forwards of Saturday's match, replacing them with two other hopefuls, who did in fact give the Americans a better game. One could even call it a tie, 5–5, if one discounted the first period, when the Americans scored no fewer than three goals, all of them slammed in by Tommy Hitchcock and "the immortal piebald Tobiana," as one observer wrote. The day had been cool and partly overcast, perfect polo weather. A reporter handling the "color" part of the story noted that toward the end a single ray of the sun broke through the clouds, illuminating the great Westchester Cup on its midfield table in a splendid column of gold. Fittingly, the presentation of the trophy to the winners was made that afternoon by Mrs. Thomas Hitchcock Sr.

CHAPTER SIX

Courtship and Marriage, 1927–1929

AT SIXTY JAMES W. GERARD HAD AN EYE FOR THE GIRLS. HE WAS AN attractive, distinguished man. A former associate justice of the New York Supreme Court and Woodrow Wilson's wartime ambassador to Germany, he was now a lawyer in private practice in New York, a writer, and a leader of the Democratic Party. One young woman on whom he had his eye was Margaret Mellon Laughlin.

She was the third of four children of Mr. and Mrs. William L. Mellon of Pittsburgh, and the great-niece of Andrew Mellon, then serving his second term as secretary of the treasury under Calvin Coolidge. She had been married, in 1924, to the son of another Pittsburgh family, Alexander Laughlin.

A man of medium height, strong, vital, and with a sense of humor that she adored, Laughlin had graduated from Yale in 1910. He had fought in the trenches during the war, a captain of infantry, and then returned to Pittsburgh to take his place in the family business. He and Peggy had known each other for years; their families were friends. He was thirty-six at the time, much older than she, but apart from that it was the most natural thing in the world that, after a suitable courtship, they should marry in a ceremony witnessed by the pinnacle of Pittsburgh's establishment, a dense crowd of cousins. It was also the most natural thing in the world to suppose that they would live happily ever after. They had eminent social position, an important place in the economic and cultural life of their city; they were intelligent, zestful, and adventuresome.

They also soon had a son, called Alex after his father, born on April 7, 1925. One year and two months later, Laughlin died under anesthesia while having a wisdom tooth removed.

To Peggy Laughlin her husband's death—so terrifyingly sudden, under circumstances of such appalling banality—should have made the whole world meaningless. Yet it did not. In her parents-in-law she had people whose grief was, if possible, greater than her own. He had been their only child. They needed her and needed too the presence of her son, their grandchild. He represented continuity, generational succession. After the funeral she and her child went to the Laughlin summer place in Gloucester, Massachusetts, seeking solace in each other.

The winter of 1926–1927 she spent with her own parents in Nassau. They were on her father's yacht, *Vagabondia*, intending to stay on the boat and take day cruises for bone fishing on the island of Andros. She might have been depressed, but once again an emergency caught her up out of her sorrow. Her mother became ill, and Peggy cared for her. Toward spring Mrs. Mellon was in great pain, which forced a visit to her doctor in New York. While she was convalescing, they stayed at the Plaza, and it was there that Peggy Laughlin fell under the eye of Jimmy Gerard.

He had met her that past winter in Nassau, and he thought it a shame that this attractive young widow should give up her life to her memories, her mother, and her son, as though the only important things in her life had already happened. She was lovely—slender, with wavy, brown hair (bobbed, where a year before it had been long and braided)—and in her company one felt an integrity of spirit that was touching and reassuring. He asked her sometimes if she knew any young men in New York. She always replied that, no, she did not and, no, she did not want to meet any. There was, however, one man whom she saw from time to time, an old beau from Pittsburgh, who had business in New York and who made a point of dropping in on her at the Plaza when he was in town.

One late afternoon in the fall of 1927, Peggy Laughlin and her Pittsburgh beau were having tea in the Palm Court of the Plaza. The beau was a solemn fellow, who probably disapproved of the elderly man-about-town who was taking such an interest in his hometown girl and who just then appeared to be moving toward their table with jovial cries of surprise. Worse, there were two younger men with Gerard. Worse still, the ambassador was telling the waiter to bring up a table so that they could all sit together.

Peggy Laughlin was neither glad nor sorry at the interruption; she would soon have to join her mother upstairs, but she was pleased to see that one of the young men was Jim McVicker: he made her laugh as no one had since the death of her husband. The other man she did not know at all. He was Tommy Hitchcock.

The tea party, she remembered, started badly. Her friend from Pittsburgh sulked, saying not a word. McVicker rose to the occasion, however, and entertained them all with amusing anecdotes of a New York life that she knew only from the sidelines. Sometimes she felt terribly provincial in New York. It was not Pittsburgh, where everyone knew everyone else, what they had done yesterday and what, probably, they would be doing tomorrow. In New York she met people of whom she knew nothing at all. They were just there.

The young man on her right was, for the first few minutes anyway, just there. He was quiet, though she saw that he listened to McVicker's stories and smiled slightly at the funnier ones. He looked sleepy, she thought. She knew who he was. Everyone in the Palm Court knew who he was—by name, anyway. Perhaps she told him that three years earlier she and her late husband had seen him play against Argentina in the Olympics outside Paris, but most likely she did not mention it: His reserve encouraged her own.

Still there was a moment in that first meeting that she treasured afterward. Jimmy Gerard turned to Hitchcock and said, "Tommy, do you realize that this girl just loves riding? Why don't you take her riding in the park?" It was the typical remark of the good host. The content was meaningless; he meant only to stir things up a bit, to get his sleepy friend into the conversation, rope him in, teasingly, just to see what would happen. But what Hitchcock said was, "I don't like riding in parks."

The statement of fact was blunt but also innocent, so that everyone at the table (except the Pittsburgh friend, who was still sulking) smiled. Afterward, she remembered those first words spoken to her by Tommy Hitchcock and remembered thinking, "Here is somebody honest."

The next morning he called her on the telephone. She was astonished; he had hardly even noticed her, she thought. Yet here he was, asking if she would like to go with him to the Huntington Museum—again, the unexpected. The country's most celebrated polo player did not like riding in parks but did like to go to museums—and not the Metropolitan but an out-of-the-way museum that few New Yorkers even knew existed. She went, of course. There was little adventure in her life at that time, and she was already intrigued by this quiet, self-contained man.

Percy Pyne, Hitchcock's St. Paul's friend, went with them to the museum. She suspected that Tommy brought him along to make things easier for her and for himself. He knew that his inability to make small talk was disconcerting to some people until they got used to it, and Pyne was a great talker. At the museum, however, she was surprised at how much Hitchcock knew about the Huntington's collection of Spanish paintings.

Afterward they saw each other practically every day for lunch or dinner. There was nothing elaborate about this courtship, but what they did together was always fun, always touched with the unexpected, so that going out with him was always a bit of an adventure. She learned that his taciturnity was not really shyness, nor arrogance, but something more complicated and interesting, a natural reserve of thought and energy that he had to guard, as one would take care in handling any strong force. It lent an element of excitement to his presence, a quality of something like danger, which she found rare and attractive.

And he was not so taciturn as all that. Especially when she was alone with him, he was wonderfully curious and interesting. Yet here again he surprised her. For one thing he never talked about polo. For another, unlike so many people whom she knew, he had no interest in gossip. He wanted to know what people did in life and how they did it but not why. It was almost as though the private, subjective dimension of life had no existence for him. Certainly he showed no curiosity about it. When he met people for the first time, he questioned them. He asked lawyers to explain a current case, doctors their most hazardous operation, businessmen their most promising deal, journalists their latest story. But their motives or feelings had no interest for him at all. In fact, that bored him. Peggy Laughlin could see that gossip bored Tommy. Let someone start talking about why so-and-so ran off with so-and-so's husband or why a certain man began to drink and went bankrupt, and Hitchcock's eyes would wander and soon he would be asking her to let him take her home.

In the first autumn of their acquaintance, there was not much party-going. Tommy had moved out of George Moore's house almost a year before, taking a small penthouse around the corner from the Racquet Club at 34 East 64th Street and a short walk to his office on Vanderbilt Avenue. (He used the Racquet Club almost every day but only to get some quick, ferocious exercise, usually in the boxing ring with the club's pro.) Tommy was somewhat reluctant to introduce Peggy to George Moore, but inevitably they met, once briefly at the Colony Restaurant, then at dinner at the Harrimans'. She remembered the latter occasion vividly:

One night Averell Harriman and Kitty, his wife, invited us to dinner. Tommy invited Fanny Brice, too, a great big girl, she was, with a gorgeous sense of humor, and the three of us met at Tommy's apartment. I remember that Fanny was all excited about how wonderful it was to be invited to the Harrimans'. She was wearing a lovely new dress and I must have complimented her on it, because she suddenly looked worried and said, "You know, I sweat a lot and I just know I'm going to ruin the dress unless I do something." So right then and there she excused herself, went into the bathroom and stuffed toilet paper under her arms. And as we were leaving she said, "For God's sake, don't let me forget to take it out before we get there."

Well, of course we forgot and she forgot and the next thing I knew there was Fanny going through the receiving line, talking away, just thrilled to be there, and the toilet paper hanging down under her arms. Tommy didn't laugh, of course, or even smile. There was just a way he had: The corner of his mouth would twitch ever so slightly and his eyes would shine.

His eyes were not shining when it came time for everyone to go in to dinner. Harriman had seated Peggy next to George Moore. "Tommy had rather kept me away from George, you see," Peggy recalled. "I think he didn't know what George might tell me at that stage. He needn't have worried though. George did make a few cracks. I remember he said, rather suggestively, 'Why haven't you been around sooner? We could have had such fun at my house on 52nd Street.' But on the whole he was very nice about Tommy. I guess he was really proud of him. In any case, George Moore was practically transparent, he was so easy to see through."

Later she went to a few of Moore's parties, and as she remembered them, they were not so wild as Tommy, by his reluctance to take her there, had led her to believe. She noted that there were a great many servants, that the champagne flowed as if from an everlasting spring, and that the host was wonderfully, perhaps even excessively, concerned that everyone have a good time. She also remembered what his parties were like in later years when things went bad for Moore: "He never paid the servants. He'd hire a batch of them for a party; they'd come, serve, not get paid, and quit. Then, for the next party, he'd go to another agency. I think he must have gone to every agency in New York. He wanted so badly to hold on to the gay, old times. It was rather pathetic. He tried so hard to hold it all together, and finally, later, he lost everything. Once we were having dinner and the lights went out. Nothing was said, but I recall wondering if George had been able to pay the electricity bill that month."

She met many of Hitchcock's friends that fall and winter of their courtship. Bill Laurence was in New York by then. He had graduated from law school, come to New York to find a job in a law office, failed, and then, through John Gaston, he had gone to work for the then great Pulitzer paper, the *World*, under Herbert Bayard Swope. (From there he went on to become the science editor of the *New York Times*, famous for his coverage of the birth of the atom bomb.) Laurence told her stories about Tommy, stories that Tommy would not have told her himself but that helped her to know him better. One of Laurence's favorites was the "Russian spy story."

Laurence's first weeks on the *World* were miserable: The city-desk editors thought that their new Harvard boy was a dud. They could only see him as a longhair, foisted on them by the boss, and they resolved to break him by giving him assignments that would challenge a twenty-year veteran. One involved a Russian spy. The editor got a tip to the effect that somewhere in the city was a Russian spy—nothing else, simply that somewhere in New York was a Russian spy. In despair he called Hitchcock, who said he would call back. Twenty minutes later Hitchcock told him to be at Charles' Restaurant that afternoon at two o'clock. He would see a man sitting with his back to the window who would tell him all about the Russian spy. Incredulous, Laurence did as he was told. The man was there, just where he should have been, and when Laurence introduced himself as a friend of Tommy Hitchcock's, the man said that he was from the Federal Bureau of Investigation and promptly, though not for attribution, gave him the story. It was Laurence's first scoop and it got the editors off his back, for a few days, anyway.

One of the things about Tommy Hitchcock that people always discussed was whether he'd ever been afraid. Peggy Laughlin had not yet, in the winter of 1927–1928, seen him on the polo field except for that time at Saint Cloud. And then she had not known enough about the game to be able to tell whether he was any more fearless than anyone else. It was a side of him that at least initially she had to learn about through listening to others, just as she had later to learn about polo from watching it and talking to others. Tommy never discussed any of this with her—not the game, nor the Lafayette, nor his escape from the train. Still less did he discuss his courage. That involved psychology, and his own psychology concerned him as little as other people's. Still his "fearlessness" was a point of intense curiosity on the part of his friends, and as she listened to them talk, she was struck by the contrast in their fascination over the matter and his indifference to it.

The *New York Times* columnist Arthur Krock, for example, another friend whom she met in this period, was at one time convinced that he had discovered the secret of the riddle after a dinner party that he attended with a group of men renowned for their courage. Admiral Byrd was there and so was Charles Lindbergh, Hitchcock, and others as well. Krock asked them all, one by one, whether they had ever felt fear. Byrd said that the only thing that made him anxious was to get a three-inch penis through five inches of clothing. Lindbergh was not so facetious but confessed that in his great flight he had missed his cat. Hitchcock said, no, he could not remember ever being afraid.

Some months later, however, he and Hitchcock were invited out to Long Island to fly as passengers in a newfangled contraption known then as a gyro, subsequently as the helicopter. The pilot was a friend of theirs who they both realized, too late, was reckless to the point of lunacy. However, neither one of them spoke about it while waiting around the landing pad, or during the terrifying flight itself.

Afterward, driving back to the city, Krock blurted out, "Why the hell did we go up in that thing? I was scared out of my wits."

"So was I," said Hitchcock.

"Well, why didn't you say something, for God's sake?" Krock said.

"Why didn't you?" Hitchcock answered, with the hint of a smile.

The question answered itself. It had been a challenge. Men didn't walk away from a challenge.

By Thanksgiving time Peggy Laughlin knew that even if Tommy Hitchcock were not sure of her, she could be sure of him—if she wanted to be. He came to her with a long face one day and told her that he felt terribly bad about it but that he had to leave her for ten days to go to Aiken. He was extremely apologetic: His mother was counting on him to participate in a drag hunt, an annual affair, and he had promised her he would be there, and so on. A young widow, with a child and an ailing mother, as straightforward in her way as he was in his, Peggy Laughlin made no show of being hurt at his "abandoning" her. She said that of course he must go.

He suspended his courtship again in February when he went to California to play in the Midwick Country Club Tournament with George Moore, Harriman, and Aiden Roark. It was a trip in which pleasure mixed with business and polo in some confusion.

He flew out from Chicago, refueling every two and a half hours and changing planes every five hours. "The seats were not especially comfortable," he noted in a letter to his father, "but the Pratt and Whitney 450 horse-power motors ran like clocks." From the tourist point of view, he thought that flying over the plains was monotonous but that going over the mountains was most pleasant, observing that except for a forty-five-minute stretch over the Sierra Nevadas there was no danger because the plane could have been put down safely anywhere along the route.

His first stop in California was at George Moore's ranch in Carmel. It was an enormous spread, some fifty square miles of the most beautiful landscape in northern California, as wild as on creation day but also somehow like a vast park. The drive from the front gate was twenty-six miles over a mountain road that pitched and turned so badly that visitors often felt seasick. Moore raised cattle on the place, but he also had it well stocked with game. The piece de resistance of a visit to Moore's ranch was a pig-sticking contest in which everyone who had the stomach for it would ride out into the bush, rout the pigs, and try to stab the fast and agile little beasts with twelve-foot spears. Whether Hitchcock went pig-sticking that week he did not say in his letter to his father. He did say that he played polo every day with Moore, Harriman, and others.

The ranch was beautifully sited on a high plateau with a view of the mountains and an awesome stand of redwoods in the distance. As he did in New York, Moore took good care of his guests. Each had his own servant. The wine and champagne were excellent and inexhaustible. The stocky, red-faced host constantly pressed everyone to drink and be merry and not to worry about the consequences. "The climate will look after you," he would say, pouring another glass. He himself, unknown to most of his guests, drank only ginger ale. After a week at the ranch, Hitchcock, Harriman, Moore, and Aiden Roark,* the brother of C. T. I. Roark, went to Hollywood and put up at the famed Garden of Allah for the duration of the Midwick Tournament.

Hollywood in 1927 was, as more than one observer put it, an American Babylon. The era of silent movies was ending and the era of sound was about to begin. Torrents of money fell on the town, on producers, actors, directors, on the talented and the merely lucky, on the decent and the vicious. Few of these people knew what to do with their wealth; they had no roots in the place to steady them, no convenient social models to emulate. Everything had to be built from scratch, like the vast

---

*Aiden Roark later married Moore's wife of the time and later still the great tennis star Helen Wills. His brother, considered by some (including Hitchcock) one of the best polo players in the world, was killed some years later in a polo accident.

papier-mache castles and Egyptian temples and coliseums built for *Robin Hood, The Ten Commandments,* and *Ben Hur.*

The successful in Hollywood were frantic for "class." Mary Pickford and Douglas Fairbanks imported European aristocrats for their parties much as others in the colony imported art for their walls. They prostrated themselves before White Russian generals, viscounts, lords, barons, and dukes—all of whom were charmed to be treated so royally, but who coveted roles on the silver screen as hungrily as any would-be star from Des Moines. When the Princess Beatriz de Ortego y Braganza of Spain turned up, the colony was beside itself with excitement, until it came out that she was a typist from San Francisco, playing a part just like everyone else.

Movie people took to polo much as they took to aristocrats. It was a "class" game, and though most of them played badly, they played enthusiastically. It followed from this that if one could play it well, and especially if he were also a member of what, in Hollywood, was the next best thing to the European aristocracy, the Eastern upper class, he was bound to be lionized in Hollywood. Tommy wrote his father in amused wonderment at the tremendous "fuss" that the papers made over "our polo." They must have played well, however—Moore, Hitchcock, Harriman, and Roark— for they won the tournament against some talented opposition (most of it, like the Marquis de Portago, imported). Moore and Roark, he said, "played better than they knew how," while Harriman, too, was "riding harder and doing more work."

He did mention, half ironically, that his own celebrity had gone so far in Hollywood that he had been approached by one of the companies to make a movie playing himself. Nothing came of this, but he was amused to note that a piebald mare (molded after his own Tobiana) had been cast in a polo picture with William Haines, at a rental price of $500 a week.

Typically he did not describe, in his letter, the bits and pieces of Hollywood social life that he saw during his triumphal tour. But he made some lasting friends there: Hal Roach, the producer of the immensely popular *Our Gang* series, and Will Rogers, the cowboy comedian. Both men were ardent, though not good, poloists. He also met the movie star Bebe Daniels.

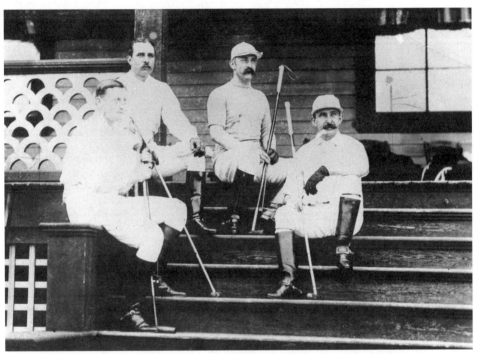

The Meadow Brook, New York, polo team in 1910: O. W. Bird, Thomas Hitchcock Sr. (Tommy's father), R. D. Winthrop, and August Belmont.

BOY AVIATOR HITCHCOCK
ESCAPES FROM CAPTORS

Westbury Youth Leaps From Train and Walks 80 Miles to Swiss Frontier.

By the Associated Press.

BERNE, August 30.—Lieut. Thomas Hitchcock, Jr., of Westbury, L. I., who while a member of the Lafayette Flying Squadron was captured by the Germans last March, has escaped from a German prison camp and has arrived here.

Hitchcock, who is the eighteen-year-old son of Major Thomas Hitchcock, jumped from a train near Ulm, in Württemberg, and walked eighty miles to the Swiss border near Schaffhausen. The aviator is returning to the United States immediately.

Lieut. Thomas Hitchcock, Jr., son of Major Hitchcock, commander of the training department at the Mineola aviation field, was captured on March 6 after a combat with three enemy planes. He fell behind the German lines after he had been wounded in the side. He was first taken to the prison camp at Saarbrucken. Later he was transferred to Giesen and again to a camp in Bavaria.

Before the United States entered the war, Lieut. Hitchock was widely known as a horseman and polo player. A student at St. Paul's School in Concord, N. H., last year, he tried to enlist in the American flying forces, but although he passed the 100 hours endurance test in the air he was rejected because of his youth. He is now 18 years old.

Going to France in June, 1917, he underwent further training in the French air service and was assigned to the famous Lafayette Escadrille with several

Lieut. Thomas Hitchcock, Jr.

other Americans. He had not, however, been transferred to the United States forces when he was captured.

Last February he brought down two German fliers and received the Croix de Guerre with two palms, and the prize money awarded by the Lafayette squadron. After he had been flying for several months he was promoted from corporal to sergeant. Last July while he was still a prisoner he was made a lieutenant by Gen. Petain in recognition of his "gallant work."

Associated Press story on Tommy's escape from the Germans during World War I.

Thomas Hitchcock Sr., Tommy's father, was also a legendary 10-goal polo player and avid sportsman, as well as a World War I aviator.

Tommy Hitchcock at the height of his legendary polo career.

Tommy arrives at a match.

Grooms and polo ponies are at the ready.

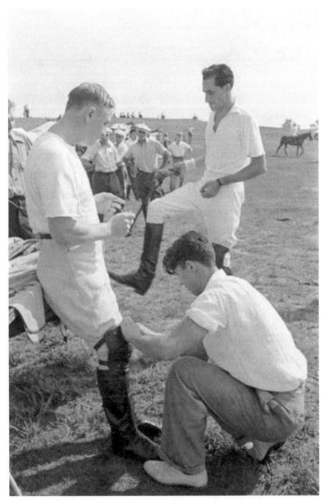
Suiting up to play.

In between chukkers.

Time for another chukker.

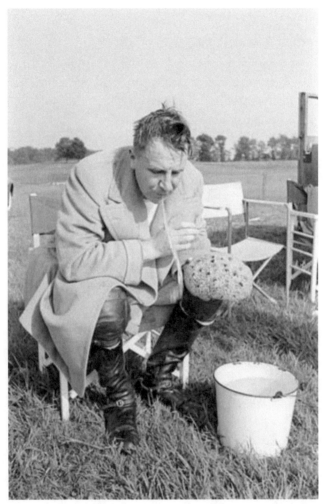

Hydrating.

Tommy playing polo at Meadow Brook.

Louise Hitchcock with her father, Thomas Hitchcock Jr., between polo chukkers, in the early 1930s.

Tommy and his polo equipment at Meadow Brook, the most famous polo field in the country in the 1930s.

Tommy (on left) with his victorious fellow polo team members John Hay Whitney, Mrs. Jack Nelson presenting trophy, Gerald Balding, and George ("Pete") Bostwick in 1926 at Meadow Brook.

Tommy (on left) with his father, Thomas Hitchcock Sr., at a polo match in the 1930s.

The Sands Point, New York, house was built in 1934 for Tommy and Peggy. Designed by
Maurice Fatio, it was one of the first houses on Long Island to have central air-conditioning.

Tommy peering through a telescope in Sands Point with wife, Peggy, reading a magazine on the terrace overlooking the Long Island Sound.

The tennis court at Sands Point. Bayard Swope's house can be seen in the distance.

Tommy had a wooden "horse" made so he could practice polo shots at home in Sands Point.

Tommy at work at home in Sands Point.

Tommy at Sands Point. He was an outstanding all-around athlete who excelled in polo, tennis, and skiing.

Thomas Hitchcock Jr. running on the beach in Sands Point, New York. He ran every day to stay fit.

Tommy at Sands Point with a Labrador retriever and a monkey named Chico.

Tommy salmon fishing in 1933 on the Cascapedia River in Canada with the family of Winston Guest.

Tommy and Peggy with Louise aboard the *Vagabondia* in 1936 shooting clay pigeons in the Bahamas. The yacht was owned by Peggy's father, W. L. Mellon, chairman of Gulf Oil.

Tommy (left) with his friend and lawyer, William Harding Jackson.

Tommy and Peggy Hitchcock with their five children in 1943.

Tommy and Peggy Hitchcock with their newborn twin sons.

Tommy in his World War II uniform.

Hitchcock, Ace in 1918, Joins Air Corps Again

Thomas Hitchcock, Jr., partner in the investment banking house of Lehman Brothers, has received a commission in the Army Air Force, the N. Y. Journal-American learned today.

Mr. Hitchcock was a member of the famous Lafayette Escadrille in World War I, and his exploits included escape from a German prison camp.

For years he has been one of the world's outstanding polo stars and rated at 10 goals.

Mr. Hitchcock first joined Lehman Brothers 9 years ago in the stock department. He was made a partner on Jan. 4, 1937.

Born Feb. 11, 1900, he is a member of a family socially prominent for generations.

Rejected by the U. S. Air Force in 1917 because of his youth, he joined the Lafayette Escadrille. He was in 10 dog fights and brought down 2 planes. On March 6, 1918, he was shot in the thigh in a fight with 3 German planes and landed behind the enemy lines.

After 6 weeks in a hospital he was started for a concentration camp but leaped through the window of a moving train and made his way 100 miles to freedom over the Swiss border.

He has kept up his flying and commutes by seaplane part of the year from his Long Island home.

Tommy joins the World War II war effort.

Central Gunnery School, Sutton Bridge, England, May 15, 1943 to June 15, 1943. Tommy is in the front row third from right.

Tommy's widow, Peggy Mellon Hitchcock (seated in middle) with her five children: Thomas Hitchcock, Alexander M. Laughlin, William M. Hitchcock, Louise H. Stephaich (on left), and Peggy M. Hitchcock, in Palm Beach, 1991, on Peggy's 90th birthday.

Tommy Hitchcock's bootjacks with attached nameplate.

Tommy Hitchcock's riding breeches.

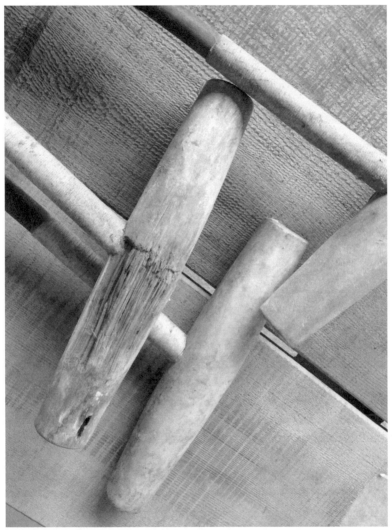

A recent photograph of Tommy Hitchcock's polo mallets.
COURTESY OF GARRICK STEELE. PHOTO BY MISSY JANES, STONE BARN PHOTOGRAPHY.

Eight months later, on Friday, September 10, 1928, a notice appeared in the gossip column of one of the New York tabloids in which Bebe Daniels announced her engagement to Thomas Hitchcock Jr. The accompanying story said that Bebe, the famed film star, then in New York for the opening of her latest box-office sensation, was soon to become the bride of Tommy Hitchcock, the greatest polo player of all time.

At any other moment, under any other circumstances, Tommy Hitchcock would have smiled at this preposterous item: Movie stars were creatures of their agents, and agents, acting under the ruling public relations theory that "halitosis is better than no breath at all," as one of them said, would spread any nonsense about their clients if it would get their picture in the papers. The trouble with this piece of nonsense was that he was by then engaged to be married to Peggy Laughlin. The trouble would not come from her; she had no reason to doubt his faithfulness. But there were her parents to be considered, two people whom he had recently come to like and respect.

The William L. Mellons had been mildly disapproving of their daughter's falling in love with a celebrity. They were of a generation and place that had been touched scarcely at all by the Roaring Twenties, and what they knew of it they did not especially like. Furthermore, despite (or perhaps because of) the controversies that spun around their relative, Secretary of the Treasury Andrew Mellon, they had a feeling that perhaps the old adage was a good one, that a lady's name should appear in the papers only twice, once when she marries, then again when she dies. In Hitchcock their daughter had found a fiance whose name was appearing in the papers every day, though in honorable company and admirable contexts. This time, however, their future son-in-law was in doubtful company and the most dismaying context. What would they think?

Bebe Daniels, in 1928, was no aspiring young starlet. She was at the peak of her fame as a silent-movie actress. A comedienne of considerable talent, she had played opposite the great Harold Lloyd in his *Lonesome Luke* series; she was with Gloria Swanson in *Why Change Your Wife?* and she played opposite Rudolph Valentino in the costume drama *M. Beaucaire*, in the role of the aristocratic lady whose love cannot survive the revelation that M. Beaucaire is only a barber. She was not especially beautiful, but she had a certain sulky charm, and she was funny, intelligent, and independent-minded. Tommy knew her and was amused by her. He might have met her through Hal Roach, for she had worked for him in the Harold Lloyd pictures. Or he might have met her at one of the Malibu parties given by William Randolph Hearst and his consort Marion Davies, for she was part of that circle, too. Bebe may have set her sights for him; there were rumors that at least one movie star had fallen "madly" in love with Hitchcock during his stay in Hollywood. There were also rumors that she was after Averell Harriman. Whatever the truth of the matter, what she was really after, that September, was publicity. And she got it.

Tommy's friends, however, instantly did what they could to see that the gossip went no further. George Moore telephoned her agent and made dire threats. But the man who finally smothered the thing—with laughter—was Will Rogers. Rogers was also a friend of Daniels's, but he had come to idolize Hitchcock as a man and as a polo player; his column, which appeared three days after the compromising photo, was almost indignant.

"Our clever little movie star, Bebe Daniels," he wrote, "doesn't overlook many sporting events. On the eve of the International polo games here she has just decided that she is to marry Tommy Hitchcock. Just before the tennis match she denied an engagement to Tilden, and during the Olympics she publicly denied a betrothal to Charley Paddock. On November 4th, I hope she has the good judgement to refuse both [Al] Smith and [Herbert] Hoover, and when Christmas rolls around, if she's going to marry Santa Claus, why keep it a whispering secret?"

That was the end of that. The February trip to California was not all polo and parties. Hitchcock clearly had business on his mind as well. In writing to his father, about the possibility of doing a movie playing himself, the tone in which he mentioned a fee of $100,000 was not wholly lighthearted; he evidently needed the money. He went on, "However, at the moment I am feeling very optimistic as we have just been offered $1,800,000 for our oil property (under your hat). The United Electric mined 150,000 tons last month. I expect to get our money out of Siosi within 60 days."

Hitchcock may have been in financial difficulties in the years before the crash, that is, before the foundering (temporary, as it developed) of his strip-mining business. Most of the people who knew him in those days remember being vaguely worried about his association with George Moore, that it could come to no good, and might even lead to disaster. There were rumors of gold mines with no gold in them, oil wells with no oil. But there are no facts to go on. Hitchcock was one of those people, as Averell Harriman said, who never talked about his personal affairs unless there was a reason for the other man to know about them.

One evening in Hollywood that winter, he broke away from the usual round of parties and went to dinner with a man whom he had not seen for almost eleven years, since the early morning of March 6, 1918, when he had been shot down behind German lines. Bill Wellman, professionally speaking, had arrived. After the war he had stayed with the Army Air Force and found himself stationed in San Diego. Somehow the young flier met Douglas Fairbanks, who liked his spunk and found him a job in the movies as an actor. Too aggressive and ambitious for that, Wellman switched to directing and, by 1927, had a few minor films to his credit. In that year he got his great chance, and he grabbed it with both hands. This was *Wings*, the story of two American fliers in World War I, the first aviation picture ever made. Written by another ex–fighter pilot, a former Yale Rhodes scholar named John Monk Sanders, *Wings* was staged on what was, even for Hollywood, an extravagant scale. The War Department contributed a whole regiment for battle scenes, in which entire French villages were to be destroyed, and the air force lent dozens of pilots to the project (among them Hap Arnold, who would become a general in World War II). The movie was a hit with the public and the critics. Even today it remains, as one film authority put it, "one of the most excitingly directed war pictures of any period." Wellman would go on to make hundreds of "talkies" as well, including *Public Enemy* and *The Ox-Bow Incident*, but just then, in the winter of 1928, he was basking in glory as the director of *Wings*.

In contrast, or so at least Wellman recalled many years later, Hitchcock seemed terribly depressed. Tommy never went into details—naturally, for Wellman had no "need to know"—but the trouble seemed to be George Moore. As Wellman remembered the scene:

> Tom . . . as a kid was everything I'd love to have my kids be, but when I saw him that night, I realized that things weren't quite what they should be. I won't say he looked badly. He didn't; but he did look like a different person. Still, I remember him as that kid, that remarkable kid, deep thinking and wonderful, who used to say his prayers every night. Now there was something about the guy that was sad, unhappy. Of course, when I knew him in France, he hadn't lived, hadn't been drunk, hadn't had dames, and now he was a lot older.

Wellman too was a lot older. Still, there is no reason to doubt his general feeling about Tommy that night.

> I could tell he was really serious because now and then he had a stuttering way of talking. Not really a stutter, just a momentary thing: "Butabutabut . . ." That sort of thing. And he stuttered then when he said, "Bill, this working with George Moore, what do you think of it?"
>
> Christ, I didn't know what to say. I thought Tom was great. I didn't know Moore personally, but from what I'd heard about him, I was sure I hadn't missed anything. So I told Tom he was terrific and we let it go. But it was bothering him, I could tell, and plenty. You know, a lot of people used to say he was never scared. Hell, he wasn't nuts. Of course he was scared sometimes. He just controlled it, that's all. And it was the same way with his other feelings, like his worries about working with Moore. He hid them, but he had them.

Of all the remarkable men who befriended Hitchcock in the course of his short life, none was more astonishing than Merion C. Cooper. Born in 1894 of a well-to-do Florida family, Cooper was appointed to Annapolis and would have graduated, had he been anyone else, with the class of 1915. Being Merion Cooper, however, he was bilged in his third year. Undismayed by this setback he greeted the outbreak of World War I with joy and relief and hurried over to England to enlist in Britain's fledgling air force. Rebuffed, indeed deported, he cursed his luck and made his way to Minneapolis, where he took a job as a police reporter on the Cowles family paper. He lasted eight months and then went down to Des Moines to work for the other branch of the family, on the *Register*. His first major story was a city-hall expose that won him a byline. His second was an account of the riots that broke out in the black ghetto after a showing of *Birth of a Nation*. He quit after the editors changed his copy. Next he went to Pulitzer's *Post-Dispatch*, where he was saved from firing, rebuff, deportation, pique, or some such inevitable calamity by President Wilson's mobilization of the National Guard against the Mexican bandits.

He never saw any Mexican bandits to fight with, but he made up for this by fighting with members of his own unit. He recalled one fight for the titillation of an interviewer many years later:

> *I got jumped by a big blacksmith, and I put him out of commission with one of the tricks I learned in Minneapolis. The only weapon I had was a blackjack; I carried it with a thong around my wrist, and the rest of it in my sleeve, held by a rubber band, so if I flipped my hand it came right down ready to use. I knew the blacksmith had a knife. When he jumped me I kicked him in the balls, and when he doubled over I hit him on the back of the neck with my blackjack. I only weighed about a hundred and fifty pounds . . . and at Annapolis I'd learned to fight fair. But I had to unlearn all that. I learned the trick of going against a pistol, too. One Mexican in El Paso got five shots at me, but I got him. You just go in very low and hit him around the knees, then whip him with your blackjack.*

When the United States entered the war, Cooper was still inflamed with desire to fly in combat. Several obstacles lay in his path, one of them being Colonel Hap Arnold, but "Coop" overcame them—possibly by going in low and whipping out his blackjack. He learned to fly at the training field in Mineola, where, providentially, he met Major Hitchcock and heard for the first time of his son Tommy, who, of course, was flying in the Lafayette. Coop, then twenty-three, got to war at last, flying DH-14s, bombers jocularly known as Flaming Coffins for the vulnerability of their gas tanks to stray bullets. True to form, Cooper's DH-14 went down in flames behind German lines. True to form, Cooper survived, ending the war in a German prison camp.

The outbreak of peace was a distinct frustration to Cooper, who immediately set out looking for another war. Having discovered one on the Polish-Russian border, he founded (with a man of fitting name, Major Cedric Faunt-le-Roy) a squadron of foreign mercenaries, named for the Polish officer Kosciusko, who had fought with the Americans in their Revolution against the British. He managed to survive this experience, too, despite being once again shot down and once again imprisoned, this time by the Bolsheviks, who kept him imprisoned for ten months in Moscow before he managed to escape. "A woman helped me," he later told an interviewer coyly, "but that's another story. I only had a pocket-knife, but I killed two guards with it, and got away. I finally made it to Poland, too, and that's another story, and a long one."

Back at last in the States, he soon grew restless and shipped out as a navigator-writer on the *Wisdom II*, skippered by the traveloguist Edward Salisbury. Throughout the twenties and thirties, there was a lucrative market in America for movies of exotic places and themes, accompanied by lectures. The voyage of *Wisdom II* was dogged by disaster and disillusion, but Cooper, of course. survived. Teaming up with a brilliant cameraman, Ernest Shoedsack, and an angel by the name of Marguerite Harrison, he next put together a feature-length documentary about a south Persian tribe, the Bahktiari, called *Grass*, which was a commercial and critical success. *Grass* also yielded, for Cooper, a book contract and many profitable months on the lecture circuit. Audiences were thrilled to hear of the awful perils that Coop and his team had survived in the course of the expedition—murderous natives, malaria, treacherous mountain rivers, avalanches, precipices, fatigue, despair, and near death.

That was in 1924–1925. As a famous filmmaker, explorer, and adventurer, he was taken up by an admiring circle of Long Islanders, including

Douglas Burden. He visited Major Hitchcock, too, and through him met Tommy, though only briefly. But comfort and security worked on Cooper with the effect of itching powder. Soon he and Shoedsack were off again, this time for the jungles of Siam, where they made a documentary-with-story called *Chang*. Audiences were ecstatic with terror and delight. *Chang* had elephant stampedes, man-eating tigers, leopards drooling blood, adorable monkeys, and adorable Siamese children who were constantly in danger from the elephants, tigers, and leopards, or else playing with the adorable monkeys. Naturally there were perils aplenty for Coop, too, including a near drowning, near evisceration by a ravenous leopard, near mauling by a tiger, and near crushing by a grief-stricken mother elephant in search of her lost calf. Naturally, however, he survived these near catastrophes and returned to the States, film in hand, to make a million dollars with it.

As a filmmaker, Cooper even survived the coming of sound. (Douglas Burden, for example, did not: his own Cooper-like effort, an Indian epic laid in Quebec and called *The Silent Enemy*, bombed at the box office when it came out in the early days of sound.) Coop did it with a film that was partly intended as a parody of his adventures with Schoedsack and Marguerite Harrison. He set it not in Persia but in Africa and New York, introduced a fantastic ape, and called it *King Kong*. The perils he endured in making *King Kong* were mostly financial, but he survived them as triumphantly as usual, emerging a millionaire many times over.

Coop and Hitchcock were to cross paths many times after their first brief meeting in 1924. For Hitchcock the most significant encounter came in World War II.

Meanwhile, following his trip to the West Coast with Harriman and Moore, Hitchcock returned to New York and Peggy Laughlin. If she were still not quite sure of her feelings for him, he was more certain than ever that he loved her and wanted to marry her. He wanted her to see Aiken, to know the place where he had grown up. He arranged for her to be invited by Sonny and Marie Whitney, who had a house there, and the four of them went down by train along with Averell and Kitty Harriman. It was an overnight trip, and late in the evening Hitchcock asked her if she would like to get off the train at Charlotte, North Carolina, early the next morning to meet an old friend of his, Elliot Springs. The plan was to spend the morning with the Springses, then fly south to Aiken in Elliot Springs's plane. Harriman strongly suggested that she stay on the train: Springs was reputed to be a wild man in an airplane, and she had never been up in one before.

Nothing daunted, she went off with Tommy to the Springses the next morning at six o'clock, and after listening to a torrent of war reminiscences from Springs, who was a splendid storyteller, the three of them—Tommy, herself, and their host—clambered into his plane and took off for Aiken. Peggy Laughlin never forgot her first flight with Tommy Hitchcock:

> *We took off on a bumpy cottonfield and started south. After a while Elliot yelled to Tommy (we were in the front cockpit, which had dual controls), "Hey, where is Aiken?" Tommy yelled back that he should just follow the railroad. A short time later, Elliot was yelling again, "Is this Aiken?" Tommy looked over the side and shouted back, "Yes! There's my father's stables." With that, Elliot made a loop-the-loop, which really startled me, and began to land on the nearest field. "No, no, no! That's the best polo field," Tommy yelled. "You're going to cut it all up!" Elliot just shrugged his shoulders and made motions for Tommy to take over the controls. I don't know whether he'd ever flown that kind of plane before, but he managed to bring it down anyway—in Averell's practice field. It was all such a blur, I don't know what happened then, but the next thing I knew I was all alone in the Hitchcock house—Tommy had changed for the hunt and was gone—and in came his father. That's how I met Major Hitchcock. I had to introduce myself. He was a dear man, very polite, and he gladly drove me over to the Whitneys' where I was staying.*

She and Tommy had a happy week together at Aiken; and soon afterward he asked her to marry him.

She refused him. She still felt bound to her Laughlin in-laws, an obligation compounded of gratitude for their kindness to her and the consciousness of a shared grief. It seemed selfish to marry, all the more so that the man she wanted to marry was the most vital and vivid human being she'd ever met.

It was not, however, a definitive refusal. She had, as a matter of fact, a perfect excuse to gain the time she needed to think it through. Her father was building a new boat in Kiel, Germany, and he had asked her to go over with him to help decorate the cabins. Her mother, still convalescent, needed her company as well, and she was supposed to help persuade her younger brother, who would also be along, to give up an infatuation with what used to be known as "a most unsuitable girl." She told all this to her crestfallen suitor but also promised that she would return in plenty of time to see him play in the International match with Argentina at the end of September.

He was there to greet her at the dock. So, to his dismay, was avuncular Jimmy Gerard. Then he was disappointed again. She had to go straight to Gloucester for the weekend to see her in-laws and collect her son. Tommy, therefore, threw himself into preparations for the upcoming games.

The prize officially was the championship of the Americas, but the most knowing fans of the game realized that a match between Argentina and the United States was a match for the championship of the world. Not only were the stakes high; it was a toss-up as to who was going to win them. On the American side particularly, signs of nervousness and doubt were evident.

There was terrific potential in the Argentine team. With Arturo Kenny at No. 1, Jack Nelson at No. 2, John Miles at No. 3, and Lewis Lacey at Back, they had everything required of a superlative team: great individual players and long experience in playing together. They also had depth. The powerful Manuel Andrada was with them, and a few others as well. Their ponies were probably as fine a collection of mounts as had ever been put into play on an American field. One, Jupiter, would be sold after the tournament to Laddie Sanford for the incredible price of $22,000. The ponies had been struck by influenza in late August, so the opening match had to be postponed from September 3 to September 29, adequate time for them to recover most of their strength.

The Americans, in contrast, found themselves in an unusual state of disarray. The Big Four had ceased to exist. Milburn, Stevenson, and Webb had withdrawn their names from consideration by the selection committee, leaving it and Hitchcock—who was elected captain in place of Milburn—with the difficult task of choosing a team from a list of candidates, all of whom were more or less equal as individuals. Moreover, none of the candidates had ever played regularly either with each other or with Hitchcock. There was room here for trouble. Most of it fell on Hitchcock.

The only fair and effective way to make up a polo team for a match as important as an International is to bring together all the candidates in a series of practice and test games, work them in various combinations and positions, and proceed to a final selection by a process of elimination. The difficulty lies in the number of variables. A might play badly with B, C, and D, for example, but the fault might be in B, C, or D; or it might be in the quality of A's horses; or it might be in the fact that he was playing Back when he should have been at No. 3. Hitchcock had an onerous job that summer. He tried every conceivable combination, every combination, that is, except one: no matter whom he played with, he always played at No. 2.

By the middle of August the contenders for No. 1 were Averell Harriman and Laddie Sanford; Winston Guest and J. Cheever Cowdin were competing for Back; and there was a free-for-all for No. 3. None of the candidates played the position well. Tommy and the committee pleaded with Malcolm Stevenson to try out and he agreed; so for the moment Hitchcock felt secure about that position. Later, it became apparent that despite Guest's young age and his relative unfamiliarity with the position (he was used to playing No. 2), he was clearly Cowdin's superior at Back. So that position was filled. It remained to choose between Sanford and Harriman.

By the end of August, it seemed as though Hitchcock and the selection committee had made up their minds: No. 1 would go to Harriman. And so it would have, if the Argentine horses had not fallen ill, thus postponing the opening match for twenty-six days. Perhaps the wisest course would have been for the American team to fill the interval with a few practice games, hard-paced enough to teach them how to work together but no more. But this was Hitchcock's first major captaincy; he would be personally responsible for American victory or American defeat. Inevitably, then, he worried—about his choices, about forging a team out of them. His response was to do something. And so he put his team through a series of tough test matches, playing them against, among others, the dropped Sanford. At first everything seemed to confirm him in the rightness of his judgment. Then came a game on the Monday before the Saturday of the opening match.

Averell Harriman recalled that what happened in that game arose from a misunderstanding. Believing that it was to be a relatively leisurely practice game—after all, they were coming down to the wire and there was no reason to risk injuries—Harriman left his best ponies at home and played at a pace that was something less than flat out. Sanford, on the other hand, played as if his life depended on it and rode the best of his well-stocked stable. The contrast threw the selection committee into consternation. After the game they went into a huddle with Hitchcock. He wanted Harriman, but he had doubts about Harriman's competitiveness. He did not want Sanford, but he had to admit that the man had been playing well. In the end, he and the committee eventually decided to replace Harriman with Sanford.

Hitchcock of course was personally close to Harriman, not intimate but good friends. Harriman remembers that Tommy was terribly upset when he delivered the news that he was to be cut from the team: "He told me that it was the toughest thing he'd ever had to say, that he was sorry, but that he simply had to do it." He must have been surprised at how cheerfully Harriman responded. "Don't bother yourself about it. We're going to have one more game before this thing is decided, and I think you'll find me back on the team."

Harriman had his dander up. He recalled that he planned his comeback with great care. For this he persuaded the powerful, thick-set Manuel Andrada to play with him at Back. "I told him, 'Now, you keep Sanford off the field.' And Laddie, you know, was not the most courageous man in the world and Andrada was one of the toughest, a real gaucho. The upshot was that he knocked Sanford to hell and gone. I don't know if Laddie was a better player than I was, but he was no good

179

that day, I can tell you. It's an amusing incident, but I was determined to get back. I just could not believe I couldn't beat Laddie. Because, you know, he was soft."

Again there was consternation in the selection committee, but this time, embarrassed at having publicly to change their minds again, they passed the buck to Hitchcock and told him to do as he wished. He did not hesitate. Sanford was out; Harriman, back in. Whether he would regret it remained to be seen.

The opening game of the tournament took place on a cold gray day before a capacity crowd of thirty thousand. Special trains had been put together to take people out from New York, and a special track laid to deposit them near International Field. The *Times* still had a society page writer covering the event. (Peggy Laughlin was not one of them, for she did not like to sit in the clubhouse box, where everyone, she felt, was always talking. She sat elsewhere, accompanied by Merion Cooper, who wore a red tie, which he believed would bring good luck to their friend on the field.) But there was a perfunctory tone to the "social" report that underlined the growing popular appeal of the sport; it might just as well have been a football crowd, one writer observed happily. The game itself, despite an occasional drizzle, offered the most thrilling and beautiful polo that anyone had seen in years. The play, surging back and forth in regular, powerful rhythm, repeatedly brought the crowd to their feet, cheering wildly. Once again, as they always did, the Americans began the game with a blitz attack designed to gain an early lead and demoralize their opponents. Within minutes both Harriman and Hitchcock had scored. The Argentines were anything but demoralized, however, and in the next two periods racked up five goals to take a lead that many people, noting the inexperience of the U.S. team, thought would stick. Yet the Americans in the next three periods held off the Argentines and scored four times, Hitchcock and Harriman getting two each. In the sixth period Jack Nelson put one through for Argentina, so that they went into the last chukker tied 6–6. It was here that Harriman capped his triumph. Midway through the period the Argentines cleared the ball from in front of their goal and began a rush into American territory. Stevenson turned the play midfield, and Harriman, playing on a mare called Miss Mark, wheeled about to get on the ball. Lacey simply was not fast enough, and the tall American got between him and his own goal. With two carefully placed strokes, he sent the ball bounding through the posts for America's winning goal. Minutes later, Hitchcock, smiling radiantly, told reporters that the victory had been "no easy task." (Which put it mildly: just before the whistle the Argentines had had two shots at the American goal, missing by only inches.) The next match, scheduled for that Wednesday, would be even less easy a task.

The United States had gone into the first game as underdogs. They went into the second clear favorites. They lost 10–7. What went wrong?

The Argentine ponies were in better shape, for one thing. In the first game their mounts still showed the effects of the influenza that had laid them low in August; but they were at peak condition for the second match. Secondly, Arturo Kenny, the gauchos' No. 1, had been at a slight disadvantage in the first match: not only had he to pit his diminutive frame against that of Guest, one of the biggest players in all polo, but he had also to cope with his glasses, which occasionally fogged over in the drizzle. In the second game he still had Guest to ride around, but the weather was merciful to his glasses. Finally, most observers believed that Johnny Miles, the Argentine No. 3, played that day the sort of polo that only Hitchcock could rise to, and then only when he was in top form.

The Argentines blunted the American blitz from the outset. The Americans didn't score once in the first two chukkers and gave up three goals to Kenny. They rallied in the third period, however, with Hitchcock scoring twice and Harriman once to tie the score, 3–3. The fourth period ended evenly as well, 4–4, with Harriman scoring for the United States. But from then on the gauchos had the game in hand. Kenny scored once in the fifth and again in the sixth, while wiry Jack Nelson also scored once in the sixth. In the seventh, Miles scored once and Lacey once, the latter despite having been pinned under a horse for nearly two minutes in an earlier period. In the eighth it was Miles again. In the meantime the Harriman-Hitchcock duo had hit the ball home only once each, and Guest once. It was not enough.

Afterward, Robert Kelley of the *Times* found nothing to say about the U.S. team except that they were outclassed. Yet there must have been something wrong, something serious, because the remedy certainly was.

Only once in the history of International matches had the Americans changed their lineup in midseries. Polo is not football. The dynamics of team play are extraordinarily delicate, and even if they are not working well, it is best not to try to create new ones at the last minute. One risks making things worse. Yet Hitchcock took that risk—with consequences that were momentous both for himself and the sport. Just before the deciding game on the following Saturday, it was announced that Malcolm Stevenson had been dropped, that Earle A. S. Hopping would ride in the No. 2 slot, and Hitchcock would play at No. 3.

It was a great gamble. Stevenson was the most experienced man on the field—a grim, resourceful, and unflappable athlete who had been playing international-level polo since before the war. Hitchcock, more-over, knew his game intimately from having played with him so often, and it was he who had persuaded the older man to come out of retirement for this series. But the risk was not simply in removing Stevenson; it was also in the fact that he would take Stevenson's place. Hitchcock had always played at No. 2, the position that seemed best suited to his particular combination of skills—his long-ball hitting, his relentless riding, and his amazing accuracy. The classic No. 3, as defined by Harry Payne Whitney, was as different a position in polo as, say, a quarterback is different from a wide receiver in football. Whitney's No. 3 was a play-maker, a pivot, a feeder of passes to his forwards, a relayer of passes from his Back. His strengths had to be steadiness and accuracy, which, while vital to the team, were scarcely the sum of Hitchcock's strengths. What good would be the terrific pace at which he usually played? What good the stunning 150-yard payloads that he could put on the ball? But that was not all the risk. To take his place at No. 2, he selected a baby-faced, genial young man of twenty-one, a virtual infant in polo who had been playing for only three or four years, Earle Hopping.

Something must have gone wrong. In reading between the lines of Kelley's report, and according to Harriman, what went wrong was Stevenson's game in the second match. "Stevenson," Kelley wrote, "was not the great defensive man he was on Saturday, for the very good reason that the visitors were riding him out of the play." This is more damning than it seems. If a player is consistently ridden out of play, it may well be because of a weakness of nerve, of competitive spirit, of "heart," in the horseman's phrase. Moreover, in the second game Stevenson had more than a fair share of fouls called on him. Perhaps for the loss of nerve he substituted recklessness. So, as he had with Harriman, Hitchcock took another big chance and substituted Hopping for Stevenson.

The night before the match, Hitchcock, as was his habit, dined with his parents at their place in Westbury, went to bed early, and slept late. The pregame regimen was habitual with him: the jog of a mile or so, exercising the ponies, then the concentrated routine of stick and ball, each of the classic shots made over and over, rehearsing them as if he were an actor and his strokes a kind of speech that he had to make perfectly his own. Sometimes, he used a special mallet, made three times heavier than normal by soaking it in brine. Then he bathed and had a light lunch.

The Argentine ponies were led in by a half-dozen mounted gauchos, impassive, decked out in their black porkpie hats, booted baggy trousers, and scarlet sashes. The players arrived in limousines with flags fluttering from their fenders. There was Miles, grinning affably to everyone; the tiny, elegant figure of Lewis Lacey, as familiar a sight in that place as he was in Buenos Aires; Nelson; and the bespectacled Kenny. Hitchcock was mounted, having said what he had to say to his team. From the stands Peggy Laughlin could see him putting his famous pony, Tobiana, through her paces behind the goalpost. She could not see his face; indeed, she scarcely had seen it all week.

It was instantly clear that Hitchcock's great gamble was going to pay off. The U.S. quartet's new lineup was an inspiration. They were inexperienced, unused to each other, and terribly conscious of the stakes they were playing for. Once again Harriman vindicated his captain's faith in him, scoring six goals to Hitchcock's four, Hopping's one, and Guest's two. Asked how he managed to score so often in the first International tournament of his career, Harriman credited his ponies, which, he said, were so much faster than Lacey's that he could often take advantage of the Argentine Back's forward rushes so as to get between him and his own goal. Once he did that, the Argentine could not possibly catch up, provided, of course, Hitchcock or Hopping or Guest passed him the ball. And this they did time and time again. The result was a resounding American triumph, 13–7, which Hitchcock, jubilant, explained as a consequence of everyone's superb teamwork.

The Argentines for their part were bitterly disappointed. One of them, Miles, blamed the ponies, a strange remark for someone who within the week would sell those same animals for the largest sums ever paid up to that time for polo ponies.

It is conventional to speak of a man's marriage as a turning point in his career. Often it is not anything of the sort. Men marry, or they take a job or find a place to live, more or less as chance and instinct prompt them. Not so for Tommy Hitchcock. He married fully conscious of what he was doing. For him marriage was a turning point, and he knew it.

The wedding was on December 15, 1928, at the Plaza Hotel, in a simple ceremony conducted by Dr. Hugh Thomson Kerr, pastor of the Shady Side Presbyterian Church in Pittsburgh. The Plaza might seem a curious place to have a wedding, but it was appropriate for them. Mrs. Mellon, again under the care of her New York doctor, was staying in the hotel: Mrs. Hitchcock Sr. had broken her ankle in a riding accident and was in a wheelchair. Moreover, because Hitchcock was a Catholic, at least nominally, and his mother a Catholic in a far stronger sense, and because the Mellons were devout Presbyterians, a church wedding might have rubbed some sensibilities the wrong way. The Plaza was, to put it mildly, a nondenominational setting.

Peggy had wanted a small wedding—she, after all, had been elaborately married once already—but Tommy discovered, when asked whom he wanted to invite, that there were more and more people he wanted to have. In the end there were some forty guests, most of them his friends, including Roddy Wanamaker, Percy Payne, Averell Harriman, John Gaston, Millicent Hearst, the woman whom Hearst had abandoned for Marion Davies, and Lucretia Bori, the opera singer. There were a good many polo players but also friends from journalism, the business world, and the theater. Frank Hitchcock was best man. Peggy had no attendants and wore a beige-rose dress. She was given away by her father.

The center of attention at the ceremony was Peggy's three-and-a-half-year-old boy, Alex. This was Hitchcock's doing. His tact, his generous sense of how hard it is sometimes to be manly and brave, all worked together to make him, from the first, a splendid father to his stepson. Before the ceremony the twenty-eight-year-old and the three-year-old entered into serious negotiations on the subject of being quiet. The man had a vision, a glorious vision of ice cream—swirls and peaks and valleys of undulant ice cream. And it would all be the little boy's—if only he were quiet. The vision, apparently, was too vivid. In the middle of the ceremony a bright little voice was heard: "Do you think I'm quiet enough? Do you think I'll get any ice cream?"

Husband and father, all at once—the twenties (his twenties, too) had been in many ways a perilous passage. It had begun with an escape, a giddy rush of freedom, a sense of liberation. But into what? For several years he stood seemingly bewildered, unable to make up his mind. He went to Harvard, to Oxford, back to Harvard, and back again to his beloved France. Most young men starting out in their twenties haven't a past to contend with, only a future. But he had been in the war, had what was known as "a good war," was in fact a hero—and he had to make sense of that, too. He was haunted by a feeling of something still undone that ought to be done and by a temptation to rest on the laurels the world had awarded him. Against the temptation, he developed an almost fierce modesty. But against the sense of incompleteness there was no defense— unless it was a plunge into action.

At first he confused action with activity. And George Moore offered plenty of that. In business the activity was a gamble, the atmosphere of quick calculation and decision in which his nature thrived. Socially the activity was even more perilous. George Moore's were not the only parties he went to in the twenties—far from it. Still, unlike many of his contemporaries, Tommy Hitchcock managed to survive these festivals of experience. He did not drink hard liquor. Nor did he lose himself in sexual intrigue. Power, as many have discovered, is a great love potion.

Athletic prowess is a form of power, and prowess at polo—with its ata-vistic symbolism—is a notorious aphrodisiac. It seldom tempted Hitch-cock—perhaps because it was too easy, perhaps because there was so little of the narcissist in him. The narcissist puts the image before the act; he loses himself in a picture of himself in action, not in action itself. Action saved Hitchcock, for that was what he lived for.

And so at the end of the twenties, Tommy married—perhaps just in time. How long could a game hold this basically turbulent man together? Once married—to a young woman of beauty, good sense, and humor—there was no more danger of exploding out of control. Marriage and fatherhood did not tame him, did not take him out of himself (for he was always controlled and never self-absorbed), but it steadied him and made the self-discipline far easier to bear. This was what he turned toward. The twenties were what he turned from.

Their honeymoon began unconventionally. They went to Pittsburgh to spend Christmas with Peggy's parents and little Alex. But then they were off in grand style. She brought her maid, Ruth, and he brought the French valet whom he had employed since moving out of Moore's place two years before. They went by train to Pasadena, where her ex-aunt-in-law, Mrs. Worden, gave them her house, then by boat to Hawaii via San Francisco. Neither of them was prepared for their reception in the islands. They found themselves being tossed around like two babes in a blanket—banner headlines, stares, the handshakes of perfect strangers, obsequious hotel managers, whispers, knowing glances, and invitations to everywhere, for everything, from everybody. Invitations, especially, to play polo. Back in Pittsburgh Peggy had begged him, "Please, no polo in Hawaii." But when they got to Hawaii, it was as though a doctor had come on holiday to a village that had not seen a medical man in years. Walter Dillingham arrived for breakfast one morning at the Royal Hawaiian in Honolulu, where they were staying, and pleaded with Tommy to come out and hit a few balls, ride around a little, show them a few plays. An all-brother team from Australia was also there, and they wanted him to play. A family called Baldwin begged him to come over to Maui, where they had a polo field right in front of their house. Tommy would have preferred to master a new sport (to him), "surfboarding"; nevertheless he took his doctor's bag out of the trunk and went off to help the natives.

They returned to San Francisco after two weeks and went up to George Moore's ranch. Moore laid on some pig-sticking, but most of their stay was taken up with the Pacific Coast Polo Championship, held that year in Del Monte under the auspices of Samuel F. B. Morse. Tommy was on the winning quartet, the San Carlos Cardinals, playing at No. 3 to Lindsey Howard's No. 1, Averell Harriman's No. 2, and Billy Tevis's Back. They won even though in the finals Moore, handicapped at one, replaced Howard, a far better player, and despite the fact that against them were Eric Pedley and Elmer Boeseke, each handicapped at eight—the two finest players in California—as well as Hal Roach and E. G. Miller. Hitchcock had discovered that with anyone playing a Back less able than Devereux Milburn—which is to say, anyone at all—he could serve the team best by playing at No. 3. Earlier in October, after the Internationals, he had begun the Open (playing with Sand's Point) at his old position at No. 2. The team had done poorly until he went back to No. 3, when they surged ahead. The new niche represented some self-sacrifice on his part, for the No. 2 position was the most glamorous on the field in many ways, while the No. 3 was (at least before he took it over) one of the most obscure.

There was some debate among the house party at Moore's over where they should go after the championships. Tommy told Peggy that she could go wherever she wanted, because practically anywhere in California were people who would be glad to put them up. She had heard that Santa Barbara was a lovely town and suggested they go there. Some of the guests, all bachelors or summer bachelors, groaned at the thought: Santa Barbara was to the West Coast what Boston was to the East. But they went anyway for a few days and then to Hollywood. It was Peggy's first visit to the Babylon of America; she remembered a slight culture shock on entering a society where everyone seemed to behave as if he were acting a part, in full makeup and costume, before a small audience of sharp-eyed men and with no one agreed on the script. Hollywood social forces in those days were manipulated by the Pickford-Fairbanks couple and the Hearst-Davies ménage. An invitation from the former, however, was like being summoned to the palace, while Hearst and Davies gathered a more informal and amusing crowd. The Hitchcocks were invited to both places but turned down a Hearst ball on the grounds that if they went, Tommy would be showing disloyalty to his friend Millicent Hearst.

After a brief stay at Pasadena, where Hitchcock played polo at the Midwick Club, attracting crowds that nearly rivaled those at Meadow Brook, they returned to New York in early March. They had planned to settle down in their apartment, a penthouse at 53 East 66th Street, but it was not yet ready for them. They stayed at the Lombardy Hotel until it was.

The couple found waiting for them in New York an extraordinary accolade on the editorial page of the *Times*. Hitchcock was now definitely in the pantheon of heroes of the Golden Age of American sports:

> *By a widely approved decision of the national polo authorities, Thomas Hitchcock, Jr., has attained that eminence in his particular sport which is shared in others by such men as Tunney, Babe Ruth and Tilden. He is the only 10-goal man accredited by the United States rules. . . . Mr. Hitchcock's youth and his showing at the last series with the South Americans entitles him to be held the highest-goaled player in the world. . . .*
>
> *The young captain's official certification as the world's greatest polo player means that no other nation is likely to gain international honors for some years. A rapidly growing public for polo now has Mr. Hitchcock as one of those athletes whom the American people particularly delight to honor.*

If this sort of thing affected Tommy at all, it turned his concerns more toward his new family and his business interests than toward polo. As the spring of 1929 moved into summer, he, Peggy, and Alex moved out to Sands Point, where they lived in a sort of compound not far from the house of Mary Rumsey, Averell Harriman's sister. Other nearby neighbors were the A. C. Schwartzes, Cissy Patterson, the Julius Fleischmans, the Swopeses, and Robert Lehman. They were also only a short drive from the Hitchcock place in Westbury.

The Hitchcocks lived quite modestly, buying from Harriman, Payne, and Moore the little group of bungalows where Tommy and his friends had been summering for the past couple of years. The conditions were primitive at first. The bedrooms had no closets, the roofs leaked in storms, the plumbing was rudimentary, and there always seemed to be sand on the floor. No matter—they loved it, and even afterward, when their own children came and the place was fixed up, they looked back to the bungalow compound at Sand's Point with a special nostalgia.

It was here that Hitchcock began his long, sometimes desperate love affair with tennis. On the tennis court, he was not the incarnation of power and grace that he was on the polo field. The blacksmith's arm and tremendous strength of his back were outsized in this game. His hand-to-eye coordination was astounding; his reflexes were instant and true; but the sum was often less than the parts. He kept at it, sometimes playing as many as six sets in an afternoon, determined to beat not only his opponents, which he did often enough after a while, but also the devilish imp in him that held him back from the perfect prowess he sought.

Quite often, as Alex grew older, Tommy would play tennis with him. "Daddy was a very patient man," Alex recalled, "and a good teacher. He would always include me in a game when I got older, if he could, and I became quite good at it—much of which I attribute to him." With Alex he also discovered that he had a happy talent for fantasy and storytelling. He could talk to the boy about what he never talked about among men, the war—perhaps because with a child he could make child's play out of it. But he also told long rambling stories about animals and men, making them up as he went along.

His business affairs also absorbed him. The strip-mining operation was in full swing, but he was also involved in a new venture called Prestcoke. Prestcoke was the trade name for a high-grade smokeless fuel that could be sold for three dollars a ton less than mined anthracite. It was, in effect, an artificial form of anthracite, a forced transformation of bituminous (i.e., soft, smoky, and relatively inefficient) coal into a hard and efficient coal, a transformation that in nature takes millions of years. The process was the invention of Clarence S. Lomax, a chemical engineer who invented the coke oven in 1914, and Hitchcock's partner in the business was C. E. Poyer, the grandnephew of Thomas Edison. They had been working on it for eight years. Environmentalists would say that Prestcoke in a sense redeemed Hitchcock's sins as a strip miner, for the little pillow-shaped briquettes promised, when they came on line, to thin out the clouds of smoke that hung over industrial cities. But there were not many environmentalists in those days, and their voices, such as they were, would soon be silenced by a more immediate crisis.

In September 1929 the Hitchcocks moved to Chicago, where the Prestcoke plant was being built. Peggy was pregnant, expecting the child in January, and she thought it appropriate that a new life should begin in a new city. They took rooms in the Drake Hotel until they could find a permanent home, and during the day she explored that corner of the city on foot, much as she would in New York. She learned her mistake from a friend. It was the era of the great gangland wars for control over Chicago's immensely profitable underworld. It was a dangerous place. For Hitchcock it was also a filthy one. He spent many days in the plant in south Chicago, coming home in the evening covered with soot from head to toe, to the consternation of the doormen at the Drake.

In October came the crash, or "the drop," as Peggy called it. It is impossible to know exactly how much money Hitchcock lost in the early months of the Depression. Much of it was on paper, and for a time his principal investment, United Electric, continued to make money. But as more and more businesses and industries failed, as one-third of all workers were thrown out of their jobs, people began not to have enough money even for coal. United Electric went into a kind of bankruptcy then, and it seemed for a time as though Hitchcock and the others (Moore, particularly) were going to lose everything. Yet Hitchcock had a talent for pulling his chestnuts out of the fire just in time. In the past few years, he had occasionally run into a brilliant young engineer named Robert Koenig, who had graduated from Harvard a few years after Hitchcock. He found Koenig and put him in charge of United Electric; within a few years the business was on its feet again.

On the whole, however, Hitchcock's modest fortune was badly mauled in the Great Crash. Peggy remembered that when they moved back to New York just before the New Year, they had to do some fairly drastic economizing. "It was good for Tommy," she said. "He took a beating and we pulled in our horses. I began looking at the bills and decided he was wasting too much money. He told me not to worry about it, just keep on sending the bills to his office as usual. But when the Depression really began to hit bottom, I told him I wanted to handle the accounts. He said, 'Oh, no, you won't.' But I did. I cut everything in half. We had a small apartment then, but we had a butler and he was always going out to buy expensive things for the house. He must have been selling them, for I never saw anything but the bills. We got rid of him. Then there was the chauffeur, Leary. Tommy was crazy about him; he knew all the policemen and he could go tearing along to the theater or out to Long Island, right through red lights, park anywhere, and Tommy loved that. But the man was buying new tires every month. I asked Tommy what on earth he was doing with all those tires. He hadn't even looked at the bills and Leary was just squandering money. We got rid of him, too."

On New Year's Day, 1930, at the Harbor Hospital, Peggy gave birth to a girl, whom they called Louise after Tommy's mother. He was delighted to be a father in his own right, though he must have wondered what sort of world the girl was to grow up in. On Wall Street the night before, the Stock Exchange had given a party, a ritual to propitiate the angry gods of the market. The gods, it was hoped, would bring a nice new year for American enterprise.

CHAPTER SEVEN

The Thirties

THE YEAR 1930 WAS NOT NICE AT ALL, AS IT TURNED OUT, BUT THE POLO world carried on as if there had been no trouble at all in the economy. During the first five years of the Depression, the United States Polo Association (USPA) showed a steady growth both in the number of players and in the number of member clubs. This would seem to demonstrate, first, that the top echelons of the well-to-do in America were only marginally affected by the Depression and, second, that polo can be played, certainly on the club level, for rather less money than is usually thought possible. Polo is, and always will be, a rich man's game, but rich men are more common in America than they like to think, and polo is no more expensive than, say, yacht racing, which virtually became a popular sport in the thirties.

At the Meadow Brook Club, on any given Saturday in the thirties, five polo matches would be playing simultaneously on all but the International Field (which was saved for the most important tournaments). Within twenty minutes' drive of Meadow Brook there would be at least eight other matches, with high-goal polo at Sand's Point Club and Bostwick Field and various low-goal matches being played at the Whitney's field or the Phipps'. And around all these fields, there would be a thin ribbon of onlookers. This was American polo's original and still most powerful constituency, its principal university, its library, its news center, and its command post led by Louis Stoddard.

It was a fairly homogeneous constituency—but there were discernible rifts in it. Meadow Brook itself, for example, like virtually every so-called country club in America, discriminated against Jews. The Sand's Point Club began partly in response to this policy. Founded by Julius Fleischmann, the yeast manufacturer (and, after the end of Prohibition, a major liquor producer as well), the Sand's Point facilities were modest indeed compared to Meadow Brook's. The membership was small, but most unusually it was not exclusively Jewish. Hitchcock was a member, and so was Averell Harriman. The most prominent Jewish players were A. C. Schwartz and Robert Lehman. An innovation at Sand's Point was Sunday polo, which Meadow Brook did not permit.

Another source of conflict in the polo world was the issue of "professionalism." It was a question agitating all sports in the thirties, endlessly debated in the press, in gentlemen's club rooms, and in colleges. For example, did a college baseball player forfeit his amateur status if he played on a semiprofessional team in the summer? (Yes.) Was a tennis bum (who played for bed and board) a professional? (Sometimes.) What about the enormous yachts, some of them carrying more sail relative to hull size than any boat in history, that raced for the America's Cup and other trophies? They all had paid hands. Did this jeopardize the "amateur" status of the blazered and white-flanneled man who owned the boats and sometimes skippered them? (No.)

The professionalism issue did not arise in boxing or baseball: those sports had long since been abandoned to professionals, and people—even purists of the "amateur" spirit—were generally pleased that the country offered a ladder to financial success for such "brutes" (the word is Paul Gallico's) as Babe Ruth and Jack Dempsey, or even to such "self-made men" as Gene Tunney (who made a million dollars in one night in the famous "long count" fight with Dempsey). The trouble arose in sports that had once been considered an exclusive preserve of the privileged class, football and tennis in particular, and track. What was at stake here, it seemed to defenders of amateurism, was the "infection" of sports with the "disease" of money.

This was true enough: Gallico wrote of college football in this period that it had grown to be the greatest "money industry" of all sports. "I watched the game degenerate," he said, "into the biggest and dirtiest sports racket the country has ever known." Moreover, there was an ugly hypocrisy in the conduct of colleges, and sports promoters generally, that nauseated sports lovers. As tennis, for example, became an increasingly popular sport, tennis clubs such as Forest Hills began charging admission to tournaments. At the same time, however, and by no coincidence at all, the U.S. Lawn Tennis Association began enforcing the "amateurs only" rule with ever greater strictness. The tennis clubs were thus left with a monopoly of the gate receipts, while the players (unless they were independently wealthy) were left with the option of either vanishing into the limbo of professionalism or the ignominy of being "tennis bums."

Track, in the years of Paavo Nurmi and Jesse Owens, also attracted big money—and clothed it in hypocrisy. Many people wondered, for example, why track stars didn't exercise their right as amateurs to refuse to compete. Why didn't they just call up the promoter of a track meet at Madison Square Garden, say, and beg off on the grounds that they didn't feel like running that night? Jesse Owens did just that in a Swedish track meet where he had been booked to appear, after winning four gold medals in the Olympics. The American Athletic Union suspended him.

In polo the problem was both more complex and simpler. In 1933 the famed English supporter (and player) of polo, Lord Wodehouse, the earl of Kimberley, rose before a luncheon meeting of the British Sportmen's Club and blamed professionalism for the decline of the sport in England: "The canker of professionalism has crept into our game. Our polo today in some cases—I only say in some cases—is almost on a par with professional association football. Certain patrons, rich patrons, bid for these players and the highest bidder gets them. The state of affairs has discouraged many young and promising players from taking up the game seriously, because they felt they had no chance in present-day polo without a 'hired assassin'* on their side."

The heart of this argument is not quite where it seems to be. After all, these "young and promising players" who were inhibited from getting into the game because they could not afford a "hired assassin" could always, if they were truly serious about the game, become "hired assassins" themselves. Evidently, what really bothered the earl was the

---

*The term "hired assassin" is still being used by men who deplore professionalism of any kind in polo.

"bidding," not so much the canker of professionalism as such but the growing importance of a market. If the demand for good players rose, the players would naturally start raising the price of their services. Traditionally, the relationship between patrons and their less-rich players had been a purely personal one. The patron supported his players much as a feudal baron supported his tenants, providing them with the wherewithal to feed and shelter themselves and taking in return some portion of their time or the fruits of their labor. Into this happy hierarchical arrangement intruded a deplorable new factor—cash payment. The old order giveth way to the new, wrote Tennyson at the end of his version of the Camelot myth. But the old polo order of England refused to give way. The Burlingham Association passed a flat rule: "No player shall pay or receive payment for playing polo."

In American polo circles many doubtless applauded Lord Wodehouse's sentiments. For them, however, the threat posed by professionalism was not money, not cash payment, not a seller's market in polo-playing services. Having no feudal tradition in their version of aristocracy, having, in fact, risen to aristocracy by the same market that so appalled the noble earl, and having, as a class, rather more cash than their English counterparts, the notion of buying and selling held no terrors for the American polo world. What did dismay some of them was that the game would be taken over by people who were not "gentlemen."

In the early twenties some people expressed this fear quite openly. Once, at least, this target was none other than Tommy Hitchcock. Douglas Burden remembered that his father, after seeing Hitchcock play one afternoon, grumbled that the young man's aggressive style was not gentlemanly, that he played polo as though it were a form of football, that if this caught on, the game would go to the dogs. In the thirties, social anxiety found another target, the West Coast players, who were not gentlemen almost by definition. Perhaps it was to blunt this sort of talk that Will Rogers got off his celebrated remark that people called polo a gentleman's sport for the same reason that they called a tall man Shorty.

In polo, there had always been a few players whose personal histories lacked many of the features by which gentlemen recognized one another. They may not have gone to the familiar private schools or colleges; they may have been born to families of modest social standing. Malcolm Stevenson was one such player. There were others, more and more of them in the thirties, who made their living—often a good one—in and around polo, as trainers, breeders, or dealers. The most prominent were the Preece family, the Hoppings, and the three Balding brothers, Englishmen who worked for various polo families on Long Island and elsewhere. To what extent were these men professionals? In any strict sense of the word they were. It was rare, to be sure, that a specific cash payment was made by a patron in return for which the player agreed to serve on the patron's team for a game or tournament or season. On the other hand, it often happened that they were employed by the patron as his personal dealer, trainer, or breeder, and it was understood that they would play for him, or his friends, as well. Yet the fact is that few people took alarm at this sort of professionalism, and the USPA never felt obliged to issue any rule similar to that supported by Lord Wodehouse. Why was that?

In the last analysis the answer was money. There was plenty of money in the American polo world, but there was not in the English. Well-known British polo commentator Harry Cottingham singled out one aspect of the money question when he wrote in 1931 that "it must not be overlooked that the public . . . especially in the U.S. has been educated to exceedingly high-class [he means high in skill, not social standing] polo and that this play is the only type which will attract the twenty to forty-thousand 'gates' without which modern polo could scarcely exist." And money, Lord Wodehouse notwithstanding, improves the quality of a sport, up to a point.

But the interesting thing is the way in which the Americans circumvented the professionalism issue. They did it simply by endowing the word "gentleman" with a generous elasticity. The attitude of the USPA was succinctly expressed in an article in *Polo* magazine for January 1930: "If he's an all right person, he's an all right person." Robert F. Kelley, the *Times* polo writer, turned to the dictionary: "Let us have one sport," he wrote, "without the bickerings and red tape and nastiness of eligibility rules and arguments, a game played for the fun of it, all comers welcome so long as they have a 'sense of honor, regard for obligations and considerations for the rights and feelings of others.'"

Cottingham fell back not on Webster but on knighthood, and added a note of relief: "When all is said and done, however, the gods be thanked that the highest class polo is still more essentially amateur than almost any other leading sport. It has also retained the chivalry of sport to a much greater extent than any other game."

The polo world accepted Webster, and certainly Tommy Hitchcock did. He valued gentlemanliness, and if it came in the person of a horse dealer or a movie-producer or an army officer or a Jewish financier, it was all the same to him.

The death in 1930 of Harry Payne Whitney, the great captain of prewar American polo, seemed to remind the USPA that it had a player as qualified as Whitney to do what no one had done since Whitney: assume full responsibility for the defense of the Westchester Cup against the English challenge. That year Hitchcock was made captain—which was nearly inevitable—but he was also made chairman of the Defense Committee, with full power of appointment. The men whom he chose reflected not only his own unsnobbish views but the broadening constituency of the sport. They were Carleton F. Burke, a Californian; Stewart Iglehart, father of two of the most youthful high-goal players in the game; George H. Mead of Dayton, Ohio; A. Charles Schwartz; and an upcoming player and patron, John H. Whitney. He added a sixth member, making the announcement in May with particular pleasure. This was Tommy's father, whom he put in charge of the ponies collected by the USPA and stabled at Mitchell Field. The appointment was greeted warmly by the fans of this family sport, especially because the elder man was the last of the original quartet to play for the cup in 1886 and was recognized as one of the greatest horsemen and trainers of his time.

As if to underline the polo world's pleasure in this father-son team, the *Times* carried two stories on it—one with five-column headlines on the sports page, the second on the editorial page. It was already becoming a rare thing, the opportunity to celebrate family solidarity, and the *Times* made the most of it, bringing in Tommy's mother as well.

No one had done more for the sport than the Hitchcock family, but Mrs. Hitchcock had in many ways done most of all. At Aiken and in

Westbury, she had—over the years—trained and encouraged many of the high-goal players in the East, her son being by no means the first. In the 1929 season, for example, a new team called Old Aiken had won the Junior Championship, the third Westbury Challenge Cup, and the Herbert Memorial Cup. The boys—Stewart and Phillip Iglehart, Robert Gerry, and J. C. Rathborne—were in their late teens and early twenties; all had been Mrs. Hitchcock's proteges; two, Stewart Iglehart and Rathborne, were among the candidates to play in the 1930 International.

Hitchcock went about the selection of his defense team more systematically than had been done before. In the winter he alerted seventeen players that they were being considered and expressed the hope that they would be able to participate in the various tournaments—the Meadow Brook Cups, and so forth—of June and July. The candidates were (in no specific order) Laddie Sanford, rated at seven; Elmer Boeseke, eight; Eric Pedley, nine; E. A. S. Hopping, eight; H. E. Talbot, seven; Stewart Iglehart, seven; Winston Guest, nine; Earle W. Hopping, six; Robert Strawbridge, seven; J. Watson Webb, seven; Cecil Smith, seven; Rube Williams, seven; J. C. Rathborne, seven; J. P. Mills, six; Pete Bostwick, six; and Lieutenant M. McD. Jones, five.

Again, like the defense committee he appointed, the list is significant for the care he took to make sure that the various facets of American polo be given a fair shot at a team position. Youth was served, and so was age. It was also the first time that any army man was asked to be a candidate. The big difference, however, was the number of Westerners. There were four: Boeseke, Pedley, Cecil Smith, and Rube Williams. Williams and Smith were professionals by almost any definition of the word, and Smith went on to claim a place in the pantheon of this amateur sport almost as honored as Hitchcock's.

Cecil Smith was born in Texas. He was a cowboy, the genuine thing—a laborer on horseback. However, he grew up in polo country and was encouraged to play by his employer. His aptitude for the game caught the attention of a visiting veterinarian from the Chicago area, a Dr. Macmillan, who encouraged him to find a patron in one of the better polo centers of the nation. Smith did just that, making his debut into the handicap rankings of the USPA in 1925 at zero. His rise was steady, advancing one goal a year until he reached ten in 1934. A big, round-faced man with a short lock of blond hair always down over his forehead in the Will Rogers manner, he rode like a cowboy, well back in the saddle, heels flailing as if a cattle stampede were gaining on him. He had a remarkable way with horses. The great Indian poloist, Rajah Rao Singh, said of him, "I have never seen a man spend more time taking care of his ponies than Cecil . . . [it] was one thing which made him a great player."

He also made his living by breaking and training ponies not only for himself but to sell. The Argentines did the same, of course, but Cecil Smith also gave exhibitions of his skill as a polo player and charged admission. Happily, however, he was easily rescued from the taint of professionalism by Webster's definition of a gentleman. Everyone liked Cecil Smith, including Tommy Hitchcock. He was one of Nature's noblemen, even if not one of Lord Wodehouse's sort, and in America that made all the difference.

In the end Smith was not able to compete for a position on the 1930 defense team—he couldn't get East—so Hitchcock's task was simplified. Throughout the summer he put the candidates through practice games and test matches, shifting positions and combinations. For several weeks he himself was out of action with an injury. Ultimately he decided that the team he had put together for the final game of the 1928 series against Argentina offered the best combination of individual skill and teamwork. Winston Guest would be at Back, Hitchcock at No. 3, and Hopping at No. 2. The No. 1 slot was open, for Harriman had decided to rest on his laurels. Hitchcock named Eric Pedley.

If the American team for the first time reflected the growing nationalization of polo, both teams taken together reflected its internationalization. On the British side, again, there was the small, wiry figure of Lewis Lacey, the Canadian-born Argentine who was playing in his third International series, his second for the British. Gerald Balding was playing for his native country, but he had been employed by Americans for some years and made his home in the States. Captain C. T. I. Roark was also an Englishman, actually an Anglo-Irishman, but in recent years he had been playing polo almost entirely on U.S. soil, primarily for Laddie Sanford's Hurricanes. To make the salad complete, on the American side was Winston Guest; born in England of an Anglo-Irish father and an American mother, he had learned his polo in American indoor arenas and at Yale. Pedley, too, was the son of a British army officer.

For the first time in a number of years the Westchester Cup series opened on schedule, on September 6. And for the first time the press concentrated on the game and gave relatively short shrift to the "society" aspect of the day. The turnout was the largest ever seen in the history of polo; forty-five thousand people packed the stands on either side of the field and stood five deep behind the goalposts. The standees needn't have felt sorry for themselves; from beginning to end everyone was on his feet.

The Americans won handily, 10–5. Nevertheless, at the postgame press conference, Hitchcock, exhausted and sweating, told reporters, "It was the hardest and fastest game I ever played in . . ." He was elated and his customary reserve broke down when he saw his father standing nearby and rushed into the older man's arms.

The victor's postgame remarks were not mere polite hyperbole designed to take the sting out of the British defeat. It probably was the "hardest and fastest" game of his career. He had come onto the field just before the throw-in, one of the handful of supreme athletes given to each generation. The crowd knew it and roared. And, of course, his opponents knew it, too. As a result he found himself harried and harassed and checked and covered as never before. The more ferocious the struggle, the more he was exhilarated. But he had scored only two goals (a modest sum for him), while Pedley had four and Hopping, three.

Pedley was the star of the first match. An able No. 1 is expected to score more than his teammates, but Pedley that day seemed to do things with wild passes from his Nos. 2 and 3 that most players could not have done with good passes. In the second game, on September 10, he did better, scoring no fewer than nine of the fourteen American goals, as many as the total British score. Yet, in this second game it was Hitchcock who was recognized as the true genius of the team. The crucial period was the sixth. At the throw-in, the Americans were behind by one point, 7–6. The *Times* called on the forces of nature to describe what then happened to the British: "The thunderstorm struck." First Hopping tallied, then Pedley; then Hopping again, then Pedley again. Each time they had been set up by their No. 3, Hitchcock. "Captain Hitchcock was everywhere," the *Times*'s Kelley wrote. "The Britons could not send the ball away from him. Lieutenant Humphrey Guiness drove in a perfect 80-yard hit from behind his goal, only to have Hitchcock come streaking through to set it up again. The British launched an attack, only to have Hitchcock cut across to turn the tables. His mallet whipped the ball from every angle. . . . Hitchcock earned the chief laurels."

Another sign that polo came into its own in the thirties was the growing literature on the sport. "Literature" does not mean that novelists and playwrights, or even autobiographers, suddenly began to write about the game, still less that it was taken up by epic poets, like those of Persia fifteen hundred years ago. Literary writers have not concerned themselves with polo or polo players. Kipling, Edith Wharton, Churchill in his autobiography, have written about the game but no one has ever brought to it the fineness of feeling or perception that Turgenev brought to shooting, for instance, or that Trollope brought to riding to hounds. The polo literature of the thirties was of another genre—journalistic, technical, and theoretical. By 1930 the polo audience had grown large enough so that such magazines as *Spur* and *Horse and Horseman* devoted more and more articles to the game and its players, and one magazine, *Polo*, was completely specialized. Much of the attention was strictly reportorial—detailed accounts of particular games, personality profiles of the players, and photographs. Many articles discussed questions of tactics and strategy, the breeding and care of polo ponies, in hair-splitting debates on proposed changes in the rules, and inevitably the governance of the sport.

"Gone were the days," wrote Cottingham wistfully in 1931, "when polo was a private matter, publicity abhorred, everything thrown in the way of reporters to discourage them, and everything done to veil the personality of the player on the field."

Modern times were bitterly received in some quarters. Indeed, at every stage in the evolution of the sport there had been people—mostly players, but also some fans—who bemoaned the fact that, in the words of one observer, polo was being "ruined by faster mounts, by the virus of winning, by high speed and other things." It is unlikely that Tommy

Hitchcock took part in this sort of debate. If someone had said to him that the desire to win was a "virus," he would have shaken his head in disbelief and tried to change the subject. He did make other contributions to the polo literature, however. In the winter of 1930, he directed a film for Jock Whitney that was in part a documentary of that year's International and in part a how-to demonstration. This film unfortunately seems to have been lost. Also in 1930, before the Internationals, he issued a set of instructions to all candidates for the team, which set down his views on how the various positions should be played. They are as valid today as they were then.

Dispute did arise, however, over his general introductory remarks concerning individual play. He reminded people that polo was not hockey or soccer and that the field was enormous. Thus he advised, "Do not dribble the ball. Take a full swing at it every chance you get. There are few exceptions to this rule." This dismayed conservative players who lacked confidence in their capacity to hit the ball in regular thirty-yard trajectories, as he could do. On the other hand, he displeased the hotshots with his suggestion that players "not take the ball by hitting under the pony's neck; for a backshot, no matter how feeble, is safer than a shot under the pony's neck, which is very difficult to make."

But the point that caused recurrent argument was a leitmotif that ran through the entire set of guidelines. This was: "Play the man rather than the ball. The ball won't travel by itself if you eliminate the man. This is especially important when a man is trying to dribble the ball behind you. All you need do is to check and bump into him hard, and that will spoil his play." The slogan, "Play the man, not the ball," echoed down the ranks of American polo players until, in 1936, Grove Cullum felt the time had come to squelch it.

Cullum felt that the American tactics, having been learned originally from the English, still carried a lingering resonance of the offside rule, which limited the task of the No. 1 to riding out the opposing Back so that his No. 2 could come smashing through to score. If he tried to get between the Back and the goal to receive a pass, he risked being ruled offside. It was time, he said, that the No. 1 spot be considered analogous to a forward-pass receiver in football, as should the No. 2.

Cullum also castigated the presence of so many "ball hogs" on the American polo field. There was too much individual aggressiveness, he said, and argued that it stemmed from the practice of building teams around one or two superlative players. The "ball hog" is more often made than born, he said. Or rather, his natural aggressiveness is exploited by his teammates, who early in his career give him the "none too pleasant task" of riding out or otherwise lambasting the one or two high-goal players on the opposing team. He is the spoiler, the hatchet man, and "once having tasted blood, his appetite becomes insatiable."

Against this rather lurid picture of wild young polo players swooping around the field like rabid bats in search of blood, Cullum paints another picture—of technical mastery over stick, ball, and horse and of disciplined cooperation. At times he sounds—the era, after all, is that of the New Deal—like FDR preaching against the gospel of uninhibited free enterprise:

> *We owe many of our polo victories to the individual aggressiveness of our players. But individual aggressiveness is not an unadulterated virtue, for a too rugged individualism is simply lethal to teamwork. I would never try to suppress the aggressive spirit in a young player . . . but it should be kept under control to the extent that a player is willing to combine his efforts with those of his teammates for the good of the whole.*

Tommy Hitchcock always thought of "the good of the whole." That had been an integral part of his training. On the other hand, he believed that the good of the whole lay in winning; teamwork in other words could never be for him an end in itself. Polo was not ballet. Rugged individualism had its place—perhaps not in the relatively ideal circumstances of International play, where the players were capable of carrying their proportionate share of the weight, but certainly in ordinary tournaments, where inevitably there was a good deal less than equal distribution of skill and resources among the players.

But if on issues of field tactics Hitchcock took a line that might be called "elitist," on issues of polo politics he took a more "democratic" position. In 1936 the United States Polo Association was embroiled in what its then-president Robert Strawbridge termed a "grave constitutional question." Briefly put, the question was whether the governing body of the association—basically consisting of three officers: the chairman, secretary, and treasurer—was sufficiently representative of the various interests and areas in American polo. Founded in 1890, with 8 member clubs and 142 registered players, the USPA had burgeoned into a nationwide institution that, in 1935, counted 65 member clubs and listed 1,200 civilian and 1,300 army players.* Moreover, in those forty-five years the geographical balance point had shifted dramatically from somewhere on a line running down the East Coast to a line running from Chicago to Houston.

Neither of these developments, the numerical growth or the geographical shift, had been reflected in the USPA's constitution. After nearly half a century, it was still producing officers and special committeemen who were predominantly of Eastern old-family background, several of them (like Strawbridge) the sons of men who had held these offices. This state of affairs had begun to stir a mild discontent. The officers were responsive, and a meeting was called in January 1936 at which all but ten of the sixty-five member clubs were represented. The agenda was a revision of the constitution.

Debate polarized between two proposals, each championed by men who were old friends and teammates, Devereux Milburn and Tommy Hitchcock. Milburn's plan had the support of the incumbent officers, who, under it, would remain in office until the end of their terms. The plan further called for a complicated system of representation, involving the governors of the six circuits, an army representative, and seven representatives elected by the club delegates at their annual meeting. These fourteen men would form the executive committee, and at their head would be the currently constituted administration.

Hitchcock's plan was simpler. He envisaged a "federal" system whereby the six circuits would convene separately and elect their gov-

*In 1980 there were 1,407 members, none of them military.

ernors, who would appoint their officers. Moreover, he urged that the plan be voted in at the current meeting, so that it could take effect immediately. This was too much for the officers and those delegates who supported the Milburn plan. They succeeded in putting off a vote until the following annual meeting.

Hitchcock was at the zenith of his fame in the early thirties. Happily for him celebrity was not the perilous place it is today, when his habits, his companions, his diversions, his relations with his children and colleagues would have been raked, probed, analyzed, and exposed by paid investigators of the people seeking the magic key to his success or the fatal flaw by which to hook and rip him from his pedestal.

Still, even in the thirties he had to bear the importunings of the crowd. He was recognized wherever he went, and if most people were respectful of his privacy, many were not. He was beseeched by autograph hounds; strangers offered congratulations and advice; old men grew deferential in his presence; young men were abashed; people turned and stared in the street. In print he found his name regularly listed in the sportswriters' lists of all-time greats. It was a time of statistics and hyperbole, the adjectives animating the numbers. Deprived of -est (as in greatest, fastest, toughest, hardest), sportswriters and commentators would have been made mute. But they had the numbers to prove it: most home runs, most knockouts, most mph, most powerful serve.

It was better, of course, when the adulation came from one's peers and colleagues. Then it was based on knowledge. John Hay Whitney, with whose Greentree team Tommy won two Open championships in the thirties, recalled that people said Hitchcock was cruel to his mounts. "It wasn't true," Whitney said many years later. "In polo it used to be good form to ride with long stirrups and a long bridle, to be gentle with the pony, ride with light hands. Tommy changed all that. He had to have the advantage that comes with a sharp 180-degree turn, and for that you had to pull the pony around hard.* It used to be said that people wouldn't

---

*To make this easier, though not on the horse, he invented a special device called the Hitchcock gag.

lend him their ponies because he was so rough on them. But he wasn't. I supplied many of the ponies he used, and I never found one with a cut mouth after he'd used it."

One quality for which his peers particularly admired him was the extraordinary mixture of courtesy and ferocity in his conduct on the field. Eric Pedley recalled an incident in the brutal East-West matches of 1933 when an enraged opponent hit the ball with a tremendous offside forehand, clearly intending it not for the goal but for Hitchcock. It struck his knee, and for a few minutes the game was stopped while he limped around his horse in agony. His teammates called foul, but Hitchcock stopped their cries immediately. "Of course he didn't do it on purpose," he said, "Don't be silly!" When the game resumed, he rode out his opponent with the same flair and relentlessness as before, but no harder.

There are, as well, countless stories of his quick compassion on the field and off. It seemed that he could anticipate an injury or a fall as quickly as he could anticipate the ball. He pulled Bill Jackson back into his saddle and knew before anyone else when Jock Whitney had broken his glasses. He made a point of chatting easily with his opponents before a match. Once, suspecting that Cecil Smith had suffered a concussion in a game three days previously, he went over to the gigantic cowboy and asked, "How's your head?" Smith took his time answering: "I figger that any man fool enough to play this game does better with his brains knocked out."

On the field he never swore, and never yelled, with one exception. When he cried "Leave it!" the sound shredded the air like a trumpet. Seymour Knox of Buffalo, a seven-goal player and the animating force behind the famed Aurora team that won the 1936 International in England, remembered playing with Hitchcock when Knox was just a beginner: "I thought I had a shot at the ball and was galloping after it when suddenly right behind me I heard 'Leave it!' as only he could yell it. It scared me so, I fell off my horse."

His battle cry was not the only thing that scared people. He was, to use an overworked word, tough. Yet, as Seymour Knox insisted, "He was a very clean player, a very careful player. That may sound funny, but it is true. He was a hard player, very difficult to ride off the ball. But he did not smash headlong into opponents at a dangerous angle. When you ride a man off, it must be a small angle, one that makes you just drift into him. Then you use your horse's weight and your shoulders to push him away from the ball. Tommy was hard but clean. He was bold but heady: he used his mind. His force helped to make him a great player, but more important was his finesse. He had great anticipation, always in the right place to hit the ball to the right place, and he very seldom missed it."

The East-West games of 1933 were a milestone in the history of American polo and in Tommy Hitchcock's athletic career. Before this series the basic unit of the game remained what it always had been, the ad hoc quartet put together, often at the last minute, by one or two entrepreneurs who usually had only a local pool of talent from which to draw. In polo there was no such thing as an all-star game. In polo, all-stars were assembled for international play, not national.

For several years the USPA had been under pressure to organize a tournament that would pit the highest ranked players against each other. In the West there had always been a good deal of conscious rivalry with the East. People had been playing polo there for forty years, after all, and though they lacked the depth of talent available in the East, by the thirties they were confident that their best players were more than a match for anyone the East could field. This sentiment grew insistent following the extraordinary performance of Eric Pedley in the 1930 International, and it became clamorous with the rise of the two cowboy stars, Cecil Smith and Rube Williams.

The principal cheerleader, strategist, and promoter of Western polo chauvinism was Carleton Burke, a Pasadena businessman and connoisseur of horseflesh who in 1933 and again the following year acted as the nonplaying captain of the Western forces. But the East-dominated USPA was also eager for an East-West showdown as a way of bringing polo to the attention of a wider public. So, too, was the man on whom the hopes and organizational problems of the East would ultimately rest, Tommy Hitchcock. The tournament was scheduled to begin on Saturday, August 13, at Chicago's Owentsia Club. Chicago, of course, was neutral ground between East and West, but the promoters also had an eye on the huge crowds attending the nearby Century of Progress Exposition. In this they were not disappointed: an average of twenty thousand people turned out for the three matches, a startling audience for polo in the Midwest.

The team that Hitchcock selected to go to Chicago was built on the great promise of Mike Phipps and Raymond Guest and on the known strength of Winston Guest. To accommodate the new, the old had to be shuffled. Thus, with Mike Phipps at No. 1, the best position for him to play, Hitchcock would have to go back to his old slot at No. 2, and because Winston Guest was a player somewhat in his own mold, he reasoned that the powerful, younger man would do well at No. 3. This left Raymond Guest to play at Back. Their combined handicap, with Hitchcock at ten, Winston Guest at eight, and the two others at seven each, was thirty-two, the highest aggregate that he could have put together in the East at that time and probably the principal reason that the East was favored to win (at least in the Eastern press). As substitutes he brought along Billie Post, a slim young Back, and Earle Hopping.

The West, under Carleton Burke's guidance, fielded Aiden Roark, an assistant to producer Darryl Zanuck, at No. 1; Elmer Boeseke at No. 2; Cecil Smith at No. 3; and Rube Williams at Back. Though their combined handicap was similar to the East's, this was deceptive. They had significantly more experience in high-goal polo, Boeseke, for example, having played in that league for as long as Hitchcock, and on the whole they were bigger and stronger men than their opponents. In sheer size, only Winston Guest could compare with Boeseke, Smith, or Williams. The big question was whether the West had the horses to carry these behemoths, and the guessing in the East was that they did not.

The guessing was wrong. The East lost the first game, 15–11, won the second, 12–8, and lost the third, 12–6. In all three the players rode as if they heard the hounds of hell behind them and saw the Holy Grail ahead.

In the first game the East was outplayed and outridden from the opening period. Neither offensively nor defensively could they work together as a team. In part this was because they had had little chance to practice together. But in part it was because Hitchcock had underestimated what he had brought to the No. 3 position. Realizing his error, he switched with Guest in the third period, and from then on the East's performance improved, he himself scoring five goals. By that time, however, it was too late to overcome the West's early lead. The game was played recklessly. Cecil Smith received a concussion when he fell, his horse on top of him. He lay for a full thirty minutes beside a waiting ambulance. Then he got up and continued the game. Rube Williams was also badly hurt when a swinging mallet hit him in the ribs. After fifteen minutes he too continued to play. These would not be the only wounds suffered on that battleground. The next matches would see worse.

For three days Hitchcock held himself incommunicado. Rumors escaped the security of the Eastern camp nonetheless, and by Tuesday afternoon it seemed certain that Earle Hopping would be playing the following day. Whom he would replace was Hitchcock's secret, and he kept it right up to game time.

It was Michael Phipps. Winston Guest was at No. 1, Hopping at No. 2, Hitchcock at No. 3, and Raymond Guest at Back. Improvised though it was, the combination worked. The violence of the previous game drew a crowd of twenty thousand (five thousand more than the opening day), many of them Easterners who had come on a special train to cheer for their side of the continent. They were given something to cheer for.

The bare-bones account in the *Times* the next day is worth quoting in full:

Lake Forest, Ill. Aug. 16

First Period

The East scored quickly on a foul by Williams. Hitchcock took the ball from the throw-in and as Raymond Guest was about to shoot, Williams rode across him. Hitchcock converted from the 40-yard line. Winston Guest and Hitchcock staged a drive from the next throw-in and outrode Smith and Williams, with Guest scoring. Another play of the same kind gave the East its third goal. Hitchcock's mount stumbled and he was thrown, but was able to resume after a five-minute delay. A No. 1 penalty on Hopping, who rode Boeseke down, causing the latter's mount to fall, gave the West its first goal. Score—East 3, West 1.

Second Period

   The Westerners rallied in this period, but wild hitting kept them from setting up a lead. They scored twice to once for the East, on pretty plays by Smith and Williams, the latter following his own long drive from the end zone and outriding Hitchcock and Raymond Guest to tally. Hitchcock scored for the East on a quick solo. Score—East 4, West 3.

Third Period

   Hitchcock took the ball from the throw-in, dribbled to the side and centered it for Hopping, who needed only two swings to score. Hopping missed a pass from Hitchcock in midfield with no one near and Roark picked it up. Score—East 5, West 4.

Fourth Period

   The Westerners tied it up at the start of the fourth on a foul shot by Smith, the foul being on Hitchcock, who crossed Smith. Williams, trying to get away alone, missed, and Raymond Guest dribbled in to score. Hitchcock gave the East another, converting on a foul by Roark, but the West got one when Boeseke intercepted Hitchcock's pass to Hopping and rode in alone to score. Score—East 7, West 6.

Fifth Period

   Each team scored in the fifth period, with Hopping executing the longest successful shot of the series. He picked up the ball from scrimmage at midfield, dribbled for position and his booming drive rolled through. The West pulled up again when Smith, taking the ball from the throw-in, passed to Roark, who tallied. Score—East 8, West 7.

Sixth Period

   Putting on more pressure, the East stretched its lead to three goals. Hitchcock beat Williams to the ball and outrode him to score. Roark got loose, but missed an easy shot, and the Guest brothers staged a drive. Raymond went up and when Smith rode him out, Winston galloped in to take charge, scoring easily. Score—East 10, West 7.

Seventh Period

The West lost Williams in this period and dropped another goal further back. A few seconds after play started Hopping followed Hitchcock up the field. The Eastern leader left the ball to ride out Williams and Hopping scored. As play resumed, Williams was thrown and was taken from the field with a fractured right leg. Score—East 11, West 7.

Eighth Period

The Westerners rallied again in a final drive, but the best they could do was break even. Winston Guest followed Hitchcock in and scored, and a moment later Boeseke with Roark and Smith helping him, rode through for the final goal of the match. Final score—East 12, West 8.

There was more to it than this, of course. Williams, accident-prone to begin with (besides the battered ribs he had sustained in the first game, he had also collided with a goalpost and badly twisted his neck), was out of the series and never again achieved the eminence of national or international polo. Boeseke's fall in the first period was also serious: X-rays later showed that his foot was broken. Nevertheless, he played the next Saturday, his foot so swollen that he had to play in a tennis shoe.

But it was the sentence about Hitchcock's being thrown that left out almost everything. True, the horse stumbled, but only after she had been smashed into by Elmer Boeseke's horse. Moreover, she stumbled and fell on Hitchcock's right leg, twisting it painfully. Finally, the delay lasted not five minutes but twenty, while the Eastern captain was totally unconscious.*

That evening both teams were the guests of honor at a party given by Freddie McLoughlin, a Chicago polo player, and his wife, the dancer Irene Castle. Winston Guest remembered that Hitchcock, most uncharacteristically, talked on and on about himself and the Lafayette.

---

*As a result of this accident, the Polo Association made a new ruling that a player knocked out for more than a minute may not continue to play in that game.

The next day he was persuaded to see a doctor, who suspected a concussion and advised him to go back to New York. Far from going home, he refused even to go to bed. He seemed oddly elated. With his teammates he went that afternoon to see the nearby Exposition. He had a grand time. The following morning he couldn't remember having been there. His teammates pleaded with him to go to bed. He wouldn't listen and called for a little light practice that afternoon. The next day, however, he slept long and late. Waking, he reported that his headache was better. His teammates were pleased to hear it but remained skeptical.

The day of the third and deciding match, his mood seemed to have swung again, from elation to depression. Always quiet and soft-spoken and relaxed before a game, he seemed completely withdrawn. His long face was hollow-cheeked, his eyes lusterless, the lines between his eyebrows deep, as if scored by a knife.

He did more than go through the motions that afternoon. He played, as polo players say, "up to his handicap." He was as aggressive as ever, riding out the opposition, pressing the battle without letup; but his game was off. The anticipation was not there. He missed the ball too often. His passes sometimes went wild—or right to the opposition. He failed to score. In the end he was gray with fatigue, barely able to rise to the ceremonies required of the defeated.

The series was hailed by polo officialdom as having "done more to advance polo than any single factor since the introduction of the game in the U.S."

Mrs. Hitchcock, who had been in the stands to watch her son, had more ambivalent feelings, which she expressed in some light verse she wrote on the train back to New York.

> Though defeated they return
> Our boys were not disgraced,
> For valiantly they battled on
> Though in the end outpaced
>
> Never match was harder played,
> More sternly, grimly fought.

> And through it all a spirit fair,
> Though gentleness was lacking;
> The frequent accidents and fouls
> Were almost too nerve-wracking.

Hitchcock could remember nothing of the East-West game after the first period of the second game. Back in New York he was still plagued with nausea, dizziness, and blurred vison. At length he was persuaded to see Dr. Foster Kennedy and a brain specialist at the Presbyterian Hospital, Dr. Stokey. They were blunt. He must go to bed until further notice, and he must not play polo, certainly not for the rest of the year.

In 1931, with the Electric Shovel Coal Corporation verging on receivership and his briquette factory stillborn, Hitchcock had joined the Bankers Trust.* His pride had compelled him to go to work, but his spirit made that particular work tedious. His father-in-law more than once tried to persuade him to come to the Gulf Oil Company. Hitchcock resisted, partly because the notion of working for his wife's family went against the grain and partly from sound self-knowledge. He knew that he would feel suffocated in a large corporate bureaucracy, even as a top executive. He might be a "team player," but he bore no resemblance to an "organization man."

In the meantime he resolved to learn all that he could about banking, boring though it was, especially in the bond department, where he started. "It's a whole new language they speak down there," he said once to his wife, not happily, when he came home in the evening. They had moved to a larger apartment at 120 East End Avenue. His life was almost a routine. Every morning before going down to the office he would run his mandatory mile. He lunched with friends and associates, and two or three times a week after work he would get a little violent exercise at the Racquet Club. Twice a week he would box with Joe Phitten, the trainer of the International teams.

---

*In 1936, Tommy Hitchcock was a leading force in the rejuvenation of this same company, which strip-mined coal in Illinois and Indiana. Thirty-six years later that company, known as Ayrshire Collieries, was sold to Amax, a large mining and metals company, to become its coal-producing subsidiary.

On the evening of December 26, 1933, a telegram arrived from Aiken that sent him there posthaste. That morning his mother had been in a drag hunt. At a jump her horse had tripped and she had fallen under it. And this time she did not get up, as she had many times before. When her son arrived at Mon Repos, rebuilt after the fire of 1922, the house was hushed; indeed, the whole town was quiet, waiting. The doctor's verdict could not have been worse. The sixty-eight-year-old woman had broken her neck; she was partially paralyzed, and she was not likely to recover.

Somehow her spirit and humor redeemed the months that followed. "Lift up your hearts!" says the Gospel message. Her heart was always indomitable, and she lifted her family's hearts as well. In a letter dictated a few days before her death, she wrote: "I may not send many more letters in this world, so will make this one short and to the point. When next we meet, may it be in the Happy Hunting Grounds. We have had many good hunts together and I hope may have many more."

She had been struck down the day after Christmas; she died on Easter Sunday, surrounded by all her children and her husband.

Years before, seven-year-old Tommy had written his mother from Aiken. It was spring and she was ill in New York, far away. "The garden," Tommy wrote with his Franco-American spelling, "is very pretty, it is full of jonquilles and narcises and violettes. You will find the garden beautiful. I wish I could make you a nice bouquet." The garden was beautiful again.

She was buried beside her aunt Celestine Eustis, the woman who had brought her to Aiken sixty-two years before. On the day of the funeral, by order of the mayor, all stores were closed, to mourn the woman whose force and imagination and compassion had animated the town for more than half a century. Her reputation, of course, went far beyond Aiken. Obituaries appeared in papers from Washington to Boston; Damon Runyon paid his respects in a San Francisco paper. In England a writer recalled the famous story about her first ride to hounds in the Queen's hunt. It was right after her marriage and she stood out in that field, the only woman to sit astride. A spectator asked the MFH who she was, and he replied, "I don't know; she looks like an apparition but she rides like hell."

Perhaps the most fitting tribute—fitting, that is, to her most characteristic moments—came from Will Rogers, who had been some years before one of her less satisfactory pupils in the game of polo. "She won't go to Heaven in a chariot," he wrote in his nationally syndicated column, "she will go on horseback, and she won't holler for St. Peter to open the gate. I don't care how high the gate is, she will give that horse his head and kick him, and she will sail right over that gate, and old Peter will phone up to the Lord's Main House and say, 'Look out, Lord, there's two thoroughbreds coming.'"

In 1932 Hitchcock was rescued from the bond department of the Bankers Trust Company by his friend and Sand's Point neighbor Robert Lehman. As head of the family investment bank Robert Lehman was discerning in his choice of partners and prided himself on the fact that many of the most successful of his associates had no previous banking experience when he hired them. They came from government or the arts, academic life or the law: they might even come from the polo field. The story is that he approached Hitchcock one day with a statement and an invitation. The statement was that he was wasting his time in the bond department. The invitation was to come to Lehman Brothers. Hitchcock accepted. Neither had cause to regret it.

Facetiously people on Wall Street say that in order to be a successful investment banker one must "look British and think Yiddish." What that seems to mean on the "Yiddish" side is that one must have a bit of the hustler in one's makeup—an ability, that is, to sell, promote, and persuade, and the capacity, if need be, to cajole. One must be able to "smell a deal." Even more important, one must know when a proposition is not a deal and how to walk away from it.

On the "British" side the qualifications are more nebulous. In investment banking, more so then than now, contacts—social and political—are extremely important. It helps to know, or be known by, a wide range of influential people in the business world. Whole sectors of the American economy in the thirties were controlled by provincial men, men who loathed "Wall Street" on principle and Jews from superstition. This was especially true in the oil industry, in commercial banking, and in many areas of manufacturing (the Ford Motor Company being a notorious example). Lehman Brothers was perceived by these people as the essence of "the Wall Street Jewish conspiracy." Against this sort of prejudice Robert Lehman had to fight constantly. The Gentiles in his house helped in that fight—not by "looking British" (in Texas and the Midwest that would have been as counterproductive as speaking Yiddish) but merely by being Gentile.

In any event, at Lehman Brothers Tommy Hitchcock found a profession that made full use of his powers. He also found himself among friends. One of those was Joe Thomas, who worked closely with Hitchcock for the next ten years.

"In business," Thomas told an interviewer many years later, "Tommy was a very, very able man. He had a deceptive way of looking uninterested. He'd sit there, draped in his chair, his hair over one eye as though it were half-time in a polo match. But if you fell for that, before you knew it your watch was gone. He was keen, unusually productive and he had tremendous imagination. When opportunities came—as they usually do come, accidentally—he always saw and recognized them for what they were."

He was involved in many transactions in the course of those ten years at Lehman, but none perhaps was more important, or more significant for what he accomplished later, during the war, than the American Export Lines "deal."

Until 1933 American Export was one of the country's leading shipping companies, with lines to South Africa, the Mediterranean, and northern Europe. Like most American shipping companies, it was, even before the Depression, subsidized by the federal government. (Without subsidies this country's shippers could not stand up against foreign competition, partly because American seamen were paid a living wage, whereas foreign seamen were not.) However, with the coming of the New Deal, this subsidy fell under congressional scrutiny and the company found itself in two kinds of deep trouble. One, of course, involved the decline in business and financial troubles as well. The Depression was a worldwide phenomenon, and each country frantically adopted protectionist policies that stifled foreign trade. Second, a Senate investigation revealed that an unconscionable amount of public subsidy money was going into high salaries and fees for the officers and directors of the line and into plushy expense accounts.

Hitchcock sensed a deal here. The company, he felt, was basically sound or could be made so with a change in management. He was optimistic about a revival of foreign trade in the not-too-distant future, and he felt that the government, determined to keep a U.S. merchant fleet in being, would not cut off the subsidy. In 1934, the line fell into the hands of its creditors, the American Shipbuilding Company and several banks. Hitchcock wanted to buy it from them. "He was all for it," Joe Thomas recalled, "and so was I, but really it was Tommy who battled against the negative idea of the Lehmans about buying it."

Such battles are the essence of business life. In prestigious investment houses, decisions are rarely made by fiat of top management. They are nudged into being through an indescribable process of argument, negotiation, discussion, special pleading, lobbying, plotting, reasoning, arm-twisting, and so on—all within the organization. Success requires the persuasiveness of a courtroom lawyer, the guile of a clubhouse politician, and the infectious spirit of a high school football coach. Superficially it might seem that Hitchcock would be completely ill-suited for such activities—generally referred to as "office politics." His father could not have done it. The side of him that Fitzgerald saw as Tommy Barban could not have done it. His first mentor in business, George Moore, could not have done it. Hitchcock turned out to be very good at it indeed.

Together with Thomas he won the reluctant blessings of the Lehmans and put together a syndicate to buy American Export. They paid $1.5 million and assumed debts of $8 million. They appointed a new board of directors, consisting of themselves and two outsiders, and installed new management. That was in 1935. Less than five years later, the line cleared $8 million, of which one-fifth was subsidy.

The following year the line brought in profits of $13.7 million with a subsidy of only $974,000. As Thomas put it, "We all made a tremendous amount of money out of the American Export deal, including the unwilling Lehmans."

As with anything that engaged his imagination and competitive spirit, Hitchcock threw himself into his work at Lehman Brothers.

Banking was his vocation, as polo had never been. Polo was something else—a talent, a great gift, and, in the heat of the game, a tremendous catharsis, a kind of blessing. He did not give it up—far from it—but as the decade wore on, it seemed as though he had more and more to make time for it.

Following the defeat in the East-West series, there were the inevitable rumors in the polo world that Hitchcock was slipping. Polo fans had a new hero in Cecil Smith. The cowboy lent himself easily to popular mythology: a Will Rogers who could really play. There was talk, that winter of 1934, of dropping Hitchcock's handicap to nine. This did not happen (the authorities could tell the difference between "slipping" and a concussion), but he was no longer alone up there in the stratosphere: Smith and Boeseke were also given handicaps of ten.

The 1934 season was focused on the new spectacle of East-West rivalry. Hitchcock was once again to captain the Easterners, with an assist from a special selection committee composed of Dev Milburn, F. S. von Stade, and James C. Cooley. On August 8, at the Piping Rock Club, a test game was held, one of the last before the committee made its choice. On the field the contenders were Michael Phipps, Earle Hopping, Pete Bostwick, and Seymour Knox, the bantamweight leader of Buffalo's increasingly successful Aurora quartet. Peggy was on the sidelines.

Accidents in polo occur in fractions of a second, yet later the mind rehearses the action in slow motion: Phipps attacking, the ball rolling lazily over the green grass toward Hitchcock's goal, Hitchcock closing in on him, galloping at his near side, checking ever so slightly to cut behind him, to hook the mallet raised to strike. Just then the accident begins: the forelegs of his pony catch in the rear legs of the other, the pony stumbles, head and forequarters sink sickeningly down, and Hitchcock's body arcs out from the saddle and falls slowly to the ground.

He landed, amazingly, on his feet. He stood there for a long moment as if studying the gait of Phipps's horse from the rear. Then he fell full-length, backward, on the grass.

This time he was not unconscious for long. Peggy helped him off the field and into a waiting car. They went to his father's house, where they had been keeping the old man company in the first summer of his bereavement. Hitchcock went docilely to bed, and the doctor came and said that he had another concussion—not a bad one this time but a concussion nevertheless. Three weeks later, three weeks of trying in light practice to fend off the inescapable, Hitchcock announced that he would not be able to play in the East-West game.

Very likely there were knowing people in the polo world who said that Tommy Hitchcock was through as a player in 1934. The USPA knocked him down to nine goals.

But when the 1935 season was over, the sportswriters were delirious. Only one thing moves them more than a new hero: an old hero who makes a spectacular comeback. Hitchcock did that in 1935. He played with Jock Whitney's Greentree—Whitney at No. 1, Pete Bostwick at No. 2, himself at No. 3, and Gerald Balding at Back—and they won the Meadow Brook Cups and the National Open. In the Open, it was said, he played the two finest games of his career. The first came in the semi-finals when Greentree beat Templeton (Mike Phipps, Winston Guest, Stewart Iglehart, and Raymond Guest) in overtime, 10–9. That game, said an observer, he won "practically single-handed. His speed in thinking, riding, hitting and anticipating every play was uncanny, and the pace he set was terrific." Once, he stopped the ball in midair and hit it ninety yards for a goal.

In the finals Greentree came up against Aurora, a young team with Knox at No. 1, Jimmie Mills at No. 2, Ebby Gerry at No. 3, and Billie Post at Back. Knox was a thorough man and a lively competitor. Before the tournament he solicited advice on a vital question: how does one beat Hitchcock? From Carleton Burke, the coach of the West team that had won in 1933, he got a long and detailed reply:

> *There is no excuse for [Hitchcock's] being allowed to take command of the field, as he did last Sunday—when he is playing against players of five-goal handicap or better. You fellows are all better mounted than he is, if you make him hurry and make him gallop, and block him whenever possible. Last Sunday he was allowed to slow the pace of the game down to his pace, and he could have played all day at that rate, and so could his old crippled ponies.*

If one of you ride over the ball or block his shot, crank your pony around, just as he does, and block him again and stay with him, for he is always in a position to do some damage. His great trick is to "slip" an opponent—to stop short when he is at a disadvantage and let the opponent slide off his flank. Then he is free to turn and get the ball. So, sit your pony down, and pull up with him. I don't mean that you should follow him around like a puppy dog, but one of you should always be against him.

Burke's counsel is interesting in that it emphasizes an aspect of Hitchcock's game that others do not, his horsemanship. But at the same time he made much of the fact that Knox had no excuse for not bottling up the Long Islander. Not even Hitchcock could always be in a position to do damage if his ponies were as bad as Burke contended. But even if one discounts the remark as somewhat exaggerated, a morale-booster, the question of the quality of Hitchcock's ponies is an intriguing one. "Old and crippled" they never were, but it is probably safe to say that except in the International tournaments (when he could draw on the best mounts available in the country, lent by the best-endowed players), Hitchcock's string lacked the depth of quality that a Laddie Sanford could draw on, for example, or an Averell Harriman, or even a Seymour Knox. He always had two or three superb animals—Tobiana, Katrina—but not a dozen of them.

In the great final game of the 1935 Open, when Hitchcock's Greentree beat Knox's Aurora 7–6 in sudden-death overtime, Hitchcock was said by Arthur Little of *Spur* magazine to have been "better mounted than he [had] been in years." But regardless of his ponies, it was in this terrific match that Tommy Hitchcock once and for all removed the last remaining doubt that he was the most outstanding athlete in his sport. One observer wrote, "He ranks two goals above every other player in the world." Another said, "He has been tearing pages out of fiction and putting in one of the most amazing exhibitions of a great comeback the sport world has ever seen." And Devereux Milburn said, "I have never seen anyone play like that—anywhere!" When the rankings were published in the winter of 1935–1936, Hitchcock was rated back at ten.

And with Boeseke and Smith dropped to nine, he was once again alone at the top of his sport.

By 1936, five years had gone by without a British challenge to retrieve the Westchester Cup. The Depression had struck much harder in Britain than it had in America. The Britons could not afford the voyage. But some Americans could, and the rules of the series were bent slightly so that an American team could defend the cup on British soil. Hitchcock, citing the press of business, took himself out of the running, and a team of Phipps, Pedley, Iglehart, and Winston Guest went over and trounced the English yet again. By now everyone was ruefully saying, in British sporting circles, that polo was an Indian invention, a British sport, and an American profession.

This conveniently left out the Argentines, who had been giving the English a bad time for years. In 1936 it was their turn to give the Americans a bad time. For the second year in a row, Greentree (with Bostwick, Balding, Hitchcock, and Whitney) won the Open, beating Winston Guest's Templeton in an overtime game that was tied three times, once by Hitchcock in the eighth chukker. The victory earned Greentree the honor of defending the Cup of the Americas against an Argentine quartet composed of Duggan, Cavanaugh, Gozzotti, and Andrada. They lost, 21–9 and 8–4, margins of defeat that marked the beginning of the end of U.S. hegemony in world-class polo.

In 1932 Hitchcock had been asked—on a charity radio broadcast that brought him together with most of his peers in the Golden Age of Sport—to name his all-time-great polo team. He left himself off, of course, citing Eric Pedley as the greatest No. 1, Leslie Cheape of England (killed in the desert in World War I) as the No. 2, Pat Roark of England as No. 3, and Dev Milburn as the Back. In 1934 Louis Stoddard was asked to name an all-time-great American team. He chose J. Watson Webb, Monty Waterbury, Hitchcock, and Milburn. In 1937 *Horse and Horseman* magazine was moved to list the "Ten Greatest Players Today" —Thomas Hitchcock Jr., Cecil Smith, Stewart Iglehart, Jose Reynal, Roberto Cavanaugh, Eric Pedley, Manuel Andrada, Andreas Gozzotti,

Rao Rajah Hanut Singh, and Dev Milburn. This list is noteworthy for the equal number of Argentines and Americans on it—and the lack of an Englishman. About this time sportswriter Arthur Little voiced the age-old complaint that in polo the best never got a chance to play against or with their peers. If they ever did, Little imagined that the best, the top team in the universe, would have Eric Pedley at No. 1, Hitchcock at No. 2, Iglehart at No. 3, and Cecil Smith at Back.

Hitchcock had little taste for this sort of celebrity-hyping. His daughter Louise, however, tells an amusing story that suggests that her father was not above pulling rank on occasion: "It was during the [1938] World's Fair in New York," she recalled. "I wanted to go and see the king and queen of England, who were coming to open the British exhibit. Mummy told him he had to take me. She couldn't because she was pregnant. . . . I knew he didn't want to do it, but he did, and he was very cute about it. We had reserved places at the British pavillion but we were late and a great crowd had formed around it and we couldn't get through. We were in one of those little electric carts, with a man driving it from behind, and the horns playing 'The Sidewalks of New York.' We couldn't get through but an enormous lane had been kept open for the king and queen, all lined with police, like a parade ground. "Daddy told the man to drive us down the open lane. 'Just go right down,' he said. He did it, and down the alley we went.

"Everyone started to wave and scream and throw confetti at us. But when we got to the end a big police chief stopped us and asked for our pass. 'Where do you think you're going?' he said. "Well, Daddy just showed him our tickets and we went and sat down and I saw the king and queen. To get somewhere, or get something done, Daddy would do anything. He wasn't shy about that sort of thing. I was terribly embarrassed, yet in a way I liked it." Hitchcock would have gotten his daughter to see the king and queen one way or the other—the royal way just happened to be the handiest route. He took it.

Hitchcock, especially after he joined Lehman Brothers, was a busy man. He worked a full day and more. He and Peggy traveled a good deal—to California in 1936, to Mexico, to Florida occasionally, and elsewhere.

He played polo right up to the war, and he played tennis every chance he could get. In 1937, with Joe Thomas, he discovered skiing and threw himself into *that*.

Nevertheless, his children saw more of him than many of their friends saw of their fathers. Louise recalled, "Every night when he came home from the office he'd always take a bath and always rest in bed. That's when we saw him. He'd tell us stories of the war, and his escape. We just loved that. Or he read aloud to us, chapter by chapter, from the Jungle Books. I used to drive him crazy about my arithmetic. He'd say, 'Now, Louise, if I give you four apples and you eat two of them . . .' trying to make it all as concrete as possible."

Little Peggy remembered, "Daddy and I had a game we played; it was about a family of dolls. I had the whole family, and little dinner plates and furniture and everything, and we made up stories about them. He had a wonderful imagination. When I was three I had many colds and allergies and was sent down to visit in Aiken with my grandfather. He was a darling man, very shy actually but he really didn't know how to keep a three-year-old company. Daddy would write me a postcard almost every day. On the back would be a typed paragraph of an on-going story which he must have dictated to his secretary, ending always in suspense with 'to be continued, Love Daddy.' It was a wonderfully imaginative story in which I was the central character of course and did things like climbing into a tree hole, then flying off with Cock Robin (one of our favorite story characters) to Cookooland where the cookoos all came out of their cookoo-clocks to show me the way (flying of course) down to Florida where Mummy and Daddy were vacationing."

A new element in his life in this period was flying. He bought his first plane in 1934, a Fairchild seaplane. He swapped this for a Bellanca in 1935, and in 1937 he bought a second model and hired a professional pilot, Joey Gaeta, to service it.

He used the plane mostly in the summer and fall, flying it in from Sand's Point to the East River in the morning and back out again in the evening. Alex, his stepson, often would go along with them for the ride. His father would explain to him how to fly the plane and then allow him to handle the controls—great fun for a twelve-year-old boy. All his children (his second daughter, Peggy, was born in June 1933) remember with great delight begging their father and Joey to please "do stalls" over the Long Island Sound. They would first unfasten their seatbelts, the pilot would cut the engine, the plane would suddenly drop, and they'd rise straight up to the roof until the engine started up again. What a thrill that was—better than any roller-coaster ride! Joe Thomas, who flew with him on many occasions, remembers this incident. The wind was from the west, so that in order to take off they had to cross the East River at 23rd Street, where the plane was docked, and angle upwind toward the fifties. "I was sitting there beside him," Thomas said, "and the damned thing just wasn't getting aloft fast enough. I said to him, 'Look, if you don't get up and out of here I'm going to have to order my lunch, because already I can read every word on the River Club menu.' Tommy said, 'Well, yes, I guess I am a little low' and just yanked it up and around as if it was a horse."

On another occasion he and Peggy and Bill Jackson decided to go to Princeton for the graduation of his nephew Julian (Pete) Peabody.* It was a lovely day when they flew down and left the plane moored on Lake Carnegie. But after the ceremonies the cloud ceiling dropped to about four hundred feet and they had to fly very low. It was a bumpy ride, and in the course of it there was a lively discussion about where they were going to drop off Jackson—at the ferryboat landing on 90th Street, near his apartment, or at Sand's Point? Hitchcock wanted to be polite. Jackson believed that politeness was not called for under the circumstances.

"There are dangerous tides around that landing," Jackson said.

"Don't be ridiculous," said Hitchcock. "You don't want to take the train all the way back from Sand's Point. And besides, the tides are the same as down around Wall Street."

"The hell they are," said Jackson, looking at the lowering clouds. "I've seen those currents turn the ferryboat completely around."

---

*Julian's parents had been killed a few years before, frozen to death after their steamship, *The Mohawk*, sank off the coast of New Jersey. Hitchcock had identified their bodies. This was the second tragedy to befall the Hitchcock children of his generation. In 1925, Tommy's younger brother, Frank, had been in a coma for three weeks following a polo accident. He recovered eventually, but it took him a long time to do so.

Hitchcock was the pilot, Jackson, the guest, and so the conversation ended in favor of politeness. Then, as Jackson recalled the scene, "The ceiling now came down to about a hundred feet and the turbulence was so great that I thought the plane might break up. I saw Tommy reach around for his briefcase. I thought he was looking for a map. Not at all; he handed me a sheaf of papers relating to the American Export Air Lines and suggested I look them over from a legal point of view. 'I'll be damned,' I said to myself."

Joey Gaeta, who became his pilot in 1937, believed that Hitchcock flew just the way he did in World War 1—"by the seat of his pants." "He knew no navigation at all, and radio was just out of the picture for him. When they opened LaGuardia they still let us fly by, but we had to have two-way radios and fly close to the water. "We used to fly in real thick weather when LaGuardia was closed down. We would fly right on the water, you know, three or four feet up, so we could see. I'd report to the control tower, and it would come back, 'Bellanca 15300, yes, you're cleared through. How is it out there?' And I'd have to say, 'Well, I just passed buoy number 13.' We'd stay right down and fly under Hell Gate and Triborough and the 59th Street Bridge. He had absolute control of that plane, though. He loved to sideslip. In good weather sometimes he'd fly over the Brooklyn Bridge and put that thing in a sideslip and slip right down and touch the water. It was beautiful."

Peggy, fortunately for their marriage, had complete confidence in him. They flew together everywhere. Reminiscing many years later, she recalled that she got sick only once. "I said, 'I'm going to be sick,' and Tommy handed me his hat. Just like that; no hesitation at all. And I didn't hesitate either. I threw up in the hat and threw the hat out the window. Neatest thing you ever saw. It looked like we had practiced it."

In 1937 he had a different sort of flying venture under way. He wanted to start an airline company, as a subsidiary of American Export. The project, his last major business effort, occupied him right up to the outbreak of World War II, and it caught him up in more than office politics. There was plenty of that, to be sure. Robert Lehman was so opposed to the plan that, according to Thomas, he scarcely spoke to Hitchcock or Thomas for nearly a year. (To no detriment, incidentally, to Thomas's career, which carried him to the presidency of the bank in 1962.) But what was novel in his experience with the American Export Airline Company was that it involved him for the first time in a government bureaucracy, in delay, obstructionism, in-fighting, influence-peddling, and the rest of it. As it happened, the struggle to set up an airline was the best possible training for his mission in the coming war.

He was fortunate in that, while bureaucracy was the name of the game, he had an individual opponent, someone he knew well, Juan Trippe, the president of Pan American. He was a worthy competitor. By 1937, Pan American, largely through Trippe's skills as a lobbyist and salesman, was widely believed to be a national airline. Within the continental United States there was competition among various carriers, but in Central and South America, which in those days offered the only markets for international air travel, Pan Am had a virtual monopoly. Pan Am, Juan Trippe used to say, carried the flag.

Hitchcock's idea was to take advantage of developing aircraft technology and the facilities of his shipping company to set up an air passenger and freight service from the East Coast to Lisbon and thence to the Mediterranean. Transatlantic travel in the thirties meant flying-boats. Even the experts were saying that land-to-land long-distance flying would not be commercially feasible until the 1950s. Thus Lisbon offered the best access to Europe and the Mediterranean, for the Azores lay between as a fueling stop. Trippe, of course, was alert to the possibilities of a European connection for Pan Am; it promised to be far more lucrative than the Latin American routes.

The key to Trippe's ambitions (and Hitchcock's) lay in the hands of what became the Civil Aeronautics Board (CAB). This agency, under the theoretical oversight of Congress, awarded to American carriers the limited number of landing permits made available by the countries of Europe. Not long after he got wind of Hitchcock's plans, Trippe applied to the CAB for all the landing permits in Europe. His argument was simple. No other airline had the over-the-water experience of Pan Am; no other airline had even the equipment to think of such an undertaking.

This was largely true. At that moment American Export Airlines was just a name, a corporate shell. It had no planes, no crews, and no facilities.

But Hitchcock quickly borrowed enough money from the now-profitable parent company to buy one aircraft, and he sent it off, like a wild goose laying down its territorial rights, to Lisbon.

At the same time he filed a protest with the CAB seeking to block Pan Am's grab play. Trippe countered with every political weapon that he had. Nor did he neglect the personal approach. He spent hours with Hitchcock, the two of them alone at Sand's Point or in one of their apartments in town, trying to talk Hitchcock out of his scheme. In the process Hitchcock learned a good deal about the airline business—how expensive it was to maintain and overhaul engines, how terribly slow the manufacturers were in making deliveries, how difficult it was to hire competent personnel, and so on—but he was quite unpersuaded to give up.

He won that first round, though he put most of the year 1938 into the effort. The CAB refused Pan Am a monopoly of the landing permits and authorized American Export Airlines to begin operations. This took time. The original plane that it had bought to stake out its claim had completed the voyage, but the two-engine craft was clearly unsuitable both in point of speed and stability. The firm replaced it first with a Consolidated 28, making nonscheduled flights between New York and Rome, with stops at the Azores, Lisbon, and Barcelona. Then in the summer of 1940, it bought three Vought-Sikorsky four-engine S-44s, which made the New York–Lisbon hop without the island stopover.

Trippe had one more card to play. So low was the demand for transatlantic freight and passenger service at the time that no airline could long stay solvent without a government mail contract. Such contracts were awarded not by the CAB but by Congress, and Trippe had many friends in Congress. In October 1940 a Senate subcommittee turned down American Export's request for an airmail appropriation of $500,000. Pan Am, said *Time*, "stood by as silent and happy as a cat full of canaries."

Undaunted by this turn of events, Hitchcock launched a counterattack that he had been planning for some time, one that struck at Pan Am where it lived. He bought TACA, a profitable rough-and-tumble carrier that was Pan Am's only serious competitor in Central America.

How this battle would have ended cannot be known. In November 1941, the Senate subcommittee again stood firm behind Trippe and again turned down American Export's request for a mail contract. Hitchcock's next stop would have been toward the courts. But the war, which had already darkened most of Europe while the two airlines were struggling over landing permits, made the whole question academic. After December 7, 1941, American Export Airlines had plenty of government contracts, as did Pan Am. By that time, however, Hitchcock had gone on to another sort of battle.

CHAPTER EIGHT

Washington and London, 1940–1944

SUNDAY, DECEMBER 7, 1941, WAS COLD AND RAINING, A BAD DAY TO GO to a football game. Tommy went anyway, with Peggy and Jock Whitney and the actress Joan Bennett. Early in the afternoon history broke up the game. Time stopped, and when it resumed, everyone remembered precisely where he had been.

One of Whitney's trainers brought the first news. He had gone for a beer and heard it on someone's radio. "They're saying the Japanese have just attacked Pearl Harbor," he told his boss. Whitney said nothing, removed his glasses, rubbed his eyes, and looked at Hitchcock. Her husband, Peggy noticed, looked sad and withdrawn. "In a moment," she recalled, "we heard the public-address system calling some general to the phone. Then another one. Everything was dead quiet. Then the news began coming over the speakers, and you heard the noise getting louder and louder. It was almost a panic. Joan Bennett was crying. Her children were in Hollywood, and she was worried that the Japanese might poison the reservoirs. There were all sorts of rumors. She came home with us and telephoned their housekeeper to be sure to boil all the water. Tommy called Washington. After that everything was different. That was the end of a wonderful era."

Until that moment Tommy Hitchcock had been an isolationist of sorts. This was not a popular position in his milieu. A number of his friends had long since acquired commissions in one or another of the armed services.

Merion Cooper was back in the Army Air Corps, in Air Intelligence, "the oldest captain in captivity," as he put it. Hitchcock, he said, thought that he was crazy. Joe Thomas and John Fell, his Lehman Brothers partners, had been commissioned in the naval reserve in January 1941. When they returned to New York, Hitchcock, according to Thomas, told them that they were damned fools, that the United States would stay out of this one. Thomas replied that he did not like the idea of war any more than Hitchcock did, but he knew that the country would get into it, one way or another, and when it happened, he wanted to be able to call the shots on what became of him. "I just want to choose my own misery," he said. Tommy grinned and said, "Well, I can't blame you for that."

Closer to home, his nephew, Helen's twenty-one-year-old-son Avy Clark, acted out almost to the letter the great adventure of Tommy's own youth in the previous war. Clark joined the Clayton-Knight program, which trained American volunteers for the RAF. On December 7 he was already on his way to England to learn how to fly Spitfires. By early spring of 1942, he would be in one of three Eagle Squadrons, British analogues of the Lafayette Flying Corps, flying over occupied France. His other nephew and namesake, Thomas Hitchcock Clark, was preparing to leave Harvard and join his older brother.

Tommy knew what was going on in Europe. Two years before, in the summer of 1939, somewhat against his inclination, he had agreed to play in the June International tournament against the British. The Americans won handily. The talk was not of polo, however, but of war. Two months later, on August 23, 1939, Hitler and Stalin signed their nonaggression pact. One week later Hitler invaded Poland; England and France declared war; and Europe was again a battlefield. History moved in stop-time as events succeeded one another in frozen frames of horror: the fall of France, Belgium, Holland, Dunkirk; the Battle of Britain.

Hitchcock often sat late into the night listening to the news on the radio. Yet he was convinced that this was not America's fight. Hitchcock dreaded what was happening in England and France, where he had so many friends. He had no sneaking fondness for fascism either. But from his own experience in World War I, he abhorred war.

Why, then, was he isolationist? One factor was the timing. His career at Lehman Brothers was just beginning to take off in the late thirties. The investment banking game continued to enthrall him even after he was in the war. In a letter he wrote home from England in 1943, he said he longed for the war to be over, so that he could compete with Juan Trippe again. Then, too, in 1939—actually right in the middle of the final game of the 20-goal International tournament—he became the father of twin boys, Thomas Hitchcock III and William M. Hitchcock. Then his beloved father died on September 21, 1941, leaving him the head of the family. His life, in other words, was coming firmly together—career, marriage, and children.

But these circumstances, happy and fulfilling though they were, could not remove the warrior in him completely. He was an isolationist not from feeling but from conviction. Hitchcock had come away from the first war impressed by the devotion and bravery of ordinary officers and men but also by the cynicism and stupidity of the governments that threw them into battle. He remembered the inefficiency of the training camp at Avord, the faulty machines that caused the needless death of so many young pilots, the bungling when his squadron tried to get Spads to replace the obsolete Nieuports. [This mindless apparatus of bureaucrats, war profiteers, and bloodthirsty politicians seemed to be back in place—and he wanted no part of it.] He would have agreed with Churchill's words on the significance of the First World War: that it had been fought "in helpless violence, slaughtering and squandering in ever increasing numbers, till injuries were wrought to the structure of human society which a century will not efface." And it was happening again, not after a hundred years but twenty-five.

There was also the fact that France, which Hitchcock had once regarded as his adoptive country, had collapsed in the face of German power like an old lady of leisure under the advances of a husky butcher boy. France, by allowing herself to be overcome, had proved her decadence. One might be charmed by a decadent society, but not to the point of fighting for it.

England was a harder case. The gallantry of the pilots in the Battle of Britain was impressive but, again, not enough to shed American blood for their cause. Like many Americans he was also under the illusion that Great Britain was a mighty empire and could take care of itself. He was not aware that the Empire had already become a liability, that the British economy was antique in equipment and lackluster in performance, and that its social structure was doddering toward collapse. With a little help—and he supported Lend-Lease, then under the leadership of his friend Averell Harriman—he fully expected that Britain would be able to stave off a German attack. Germany, or so went the argument, would then negotiate a peace with Britain and turn her aggression on the Soviet Union, with only two possible results, one better than the other, but both good. Free of enemies in the West, Germany would destroy the Communist state. Better yet, Communism and Nazism would destroy each other.

From the moment America entered the war, there was only one thing that Tommy Hitchcock wanted to do. In the end he did many fine things and one magnificent thing. But there was only one thing he wanted to do. That was to fly fighter planes in action.

The day after Pearl Harbor, he was on the phone again. One of the people he called was Bill Jackson. Jackson recalled the ensuing conversation:

"Well, what are you going to get into?" Hitchcock asked.

"I haven't had much time to think about it," Jackson replied.

"Flying fighters will be the big game, Bill, like playing on the number-one field."

"For men in their forties?" Jackson asked.

"Sure," said Hitchcock. "Let's go to Washington tomorrow and look around."

They went to Washington.

Someone once said of Hitchcock that he knew more people than God. Contacts, knowing people in the right places, were the basic currency of the world in which he had been brought up. Moreover, he was a famous man, which meant that although he knew many people, many more knew him. Jackson remembered that in Washington they went right to the top, to the chief of the Army Air Force, General "Hap" Arnold, and to most of his high-ranking subordinates as well. They saw the top brass in their offices at Langley Field; they even entertained the top brass at their hotel. On Hitchcock's side there was no beating about the bush; he came to the point immediately. How could he get to war in a fighter plane?

In reply they asked questions: How old are you? How much flying have you done since 1918? What sort of planes have you flown? How long? Under what conditions? How much navigation have you had? Why do you want to fly fighters? You can be much more useful to us on the ground, don't you know?

He didn't know, or didn't much care. All sorts of commissions were offered him, in intelligence, in administration, in research and development, in production. He didn't want any of it. But for what he did want he got no encouragement whatever.

He couldn't have been surprised. On paper he was, as they say, "technologically unemployable." The American air force had not done much to prepare for war. As far as aircraft production was concerned, it was almost as badly off as it had been at the beginning of World War I, but it had kept up with technological developments, and such planes as it had were as good as any in Britain or Japan (though not as good as Germany's). Hitchcock had no experience flying P-47s or anything comparable in terms of weight, instrumentation, range, or maneuverability—not to mention gunnery. He was, they kept saying, too old, but what they meant was that he was too inexperienced. He had not kept up. And he was probably too old to catch up.

Finally, it was true that he could contribute more to the war effort on the ground than in the air. He was the president of an airline, a partner in one of the most powerful private banks in the country, a man who could get things done, and, of course, he knew "more people than God." Such men were harder to find than people who could learn to fly modern fighter planes. Fighter pilots, in World War II thinking, were no longer mythical creatures, knights of the air. They were troops, and, as such, expendable.

The dominant faction in the air force did not consider pilots to be important troops. This group believed that the war would be won by strategic bombing carried out by airborne battleships, by flying fortresses. Since

Napoleon, at least, wars had been won by artillery, in the final analysis by machines, not men. Strategic bombing was just artillery. Given a sufficient number of bombers, these air generals believed, they could defeat Germany almost alone, without army, navy, or fighters. By the pattern bombing of cities they could demoralize the German civilians; by the precision bombing of factories and transportation facilities they could devastate the German industrial capacity. All that would be left, after the bombers had done their work, was for the army to come in and mop up the mess. It was the beginning of a new myth, not the romantic myth of a chivalry of the air but a technological myth, and it proved far more misleading.

In the early weeks of 1942, however, these issues were scarcely perceptible. Hitchcock had only to find something to do, something that would not permanently close the door on the possibility of his joining a fighter squadron. He found it within a week.

Merion Cooper was a braggart. Yet he was also an able man, and when Hitchcock needed him, he was well placed to help. He took him on at Air Intelligence, recommending (which he had the authority to do) that Hitchcock be commissioned a major.

In the two weeks needed for the commission to come through, the Hitchcocks went up to Stowe, Vermont, for some skiing. The instructors were half-awed, half-amused by Hitchcock's approach to the sport. "I know this isn't your first time out, Mr. Hitchcock," they would say, "but perhaps we should try this slope over here, the Intermediate." And he would reply, "No, let's try the Nosedive. It's always best to jump right into these things, isn't it? Besides I haven't much time." And up they'd go to the top of the trickiest, steepest slope on the mountain. "People thought he was reckless," his wife remembered, "but he wasn't. When he came to the rocks, or a narrow twisty part, he'd take off his skis, sit, and slide down on them. He wasn't in the least embarrassed, as most people would have been. Then after three or four days he'd go down anything. He took a terrific beating, of course, but he stuck to it and stuck to it and by the time our two weeks were up he was doing wonderfully well."

When he returned to Washington, an air force major, he expected to stay there, for a time at least, and he wanted his family to be with him.

He rented the journalist Joseph Alsop's house on Dumbarton Street in Georgetown. Alsop was covering the war in China at the time.

Cooper, by his own account, had a project that he was trying to sell to the top brass just at the time Hitchcock joined his task force in Air Intelligence. It involved a demonstration to the world, not least the American electorate, that the United States had the capacity to carry the war to the Japanese home islands, by bomber. Politically the plan was a symbolic morale booster, revenge for Pearl Harbor. Militarily the strike was supposed to demonstrate the viability of bomber doctrine. One leg of the attack was already in the works, Jimmy Doolittle's raid on Tokyo from the decks of the U.S. carrier *Hornet*. The other leg was Cooper's idea, a B-17 strike from Chennault's Flying Tiger airfields in China. This was still in the planning stages, and Cooper wanted Hitchcock to be part of it. The catch to the plan was that B-17s did not have the range to fly to Japan from China and back; the men on the return flight would have to crash-land in Japanese-occupied Manchuria and somehow make their way out on foot.

In the week or so that it took his family to leave New York (the two girls were at school), Hitchcock saw a good deal of Cooper and his wife at their home in Alexandria. Dorothy Cooper remembered those evenings vividly, doubtless because of the strong contrast between her husband and his friend.

"I knew, of course, about his tremendous reputation as a polo player and how aggressive he was in polo and business," she recalled, "and Coop had spoken a lot about his war record and how brave he was." What impressed her most about Hitchcock was "the gentleness in his voice and manner, his simplicity and straightforwardness, his consideration and his joy of life. I had expected a harsh, aggressive person, and he was such a contrast to the picture I'd had of him. Of course he was a very powerful man, physically: he had wide, thick shoulders and big arms. Yet one knew that here was a man who had complete control of himself and of his life. He had such an air of completely relaxed, easy self-confidence."

Socially, wartime Washington was like a Harvard-Yale football game, except bigger, more jovial. Everyone was either literally or figuratively in uniform, and in uniform, liberal Harvard lawyers could sit down with conservative Yale coupon-clippers and rejoice in their solidarity, their common memories and common purpose. Washington in uniform was a pleasant place to be, charged with the special poignancy of parting and loss.

Peggy Hitchcock remembered that the one time in her life when she really enjoyed entertaining was when they first moved into Joe Alsop's house. Everyone they knew, it seemed, was in Washington then. Bill Jackson stayed with them for a while and later moved over to Helen Clark's house on M Street. Tommy's sister was with the Office of Strategic Services (OSS)—as Jackson would be before long—and her husband was in England with the Red Cross. Part of the pleasure of having people to dinner was that they had an excellent cook; part of it was that everyone went home at 10:00 p.m.

Cooper's plan was authorized in February 1942. But preparatory to leaving for China, Hitchcock received the usual battery of shots and inoculations—and immediately fell ill. He ran a high fever and was bedridden for several weeks. Cooper went to China without him, and Hitchcock, though still with Air Intelligence, was without a specific mission. He was also further away than ever from a fighter squadron.

This, however, he could do something about. As soon as he was well enough, he determined to get his wings, a relatively simple matter of being tested by an instructor at Anacostia Field, just outside Washington.

One Saturday in early March, he drove out with Bill Jackson and Joey Gaeta (soon to be a test pilot for Grumman Aircraft Company)* and climbed into an AT-6. It had the same horsepower as the Bellanca, but in one crucial respect it was a completely different plane: landing or taking off, one could not see directly in front; the nose of the thing stuck up too far in the air. For Hitchcock, though, his check-out flight was the ski slopes all over again, only this time the instructor was not in the least amused. Jackson remembers that when it was all over, the man staggered out of the plane, white and shaking.

---

*Though he had left Italy at the age of four, Gaeta was not allowed, in those first months of the war, to serve in the armed forces. The Grumman job was Hitchcock's idea, and he used his contacts to get it for his friend.

Later, Hitchcock explained to Gaeta what had happened: "As soon as we got settled, the tower told me to taxi out to the runway, which I did, zigzagging all the way because I couldn't see in front of me. Well, the instructor finally got me in position and the next thing I heard was the tower saying 'You're cleared for takeoff. Take off! Take off!' So I opened up the throttle and we started moving. But I still couldn't see where I was going, so I zigged a little, and at that speed, the plane almost went off the runway. By this time the instructor was screaming, and the tower was screaming, and by the time the tail came up so I could look over the cowling, there was a big bomber parked right in front of me.

"Well, I pulled on the stick and got it up in the air. Once I was up there I threw her around all right, but I realized what a bad start I'd made. So I said to myself that I just had to make a decent landing. After a while I turned to the guy in back and asked if he'd seen enough. 'Hell, yes!' he said, and I headed back to the field. In making the descent, I held the nose down so as to be able to see, but in that plane if you hold the nose down, it just goes faster. So I leveled off and hoped for the best. Well, we just bounced all over the field."

Hitchcock could always laugh at himself, but he was also somewhat chagrined. His wife recalls that he came home that evening "like a dog with his tail between his legs." He knew he'd flunked. But first thing the next morning, he went out to try again. Jackson drove him. He noticed that Hitchcock could hardly walk and asked what was the matter. Hitchcock laughed and said, "My knees were shaking so badly up there yesterday, my thighs are stiff."

He got his wings that afternoon. When he wanted to, he could be the most persuasive man on earth. He asked the airfield commander to let him have all day to work up from the slowest plane they had to the official trainer and if he checked out in that, to let him have his wings. The colonel not only agreed; he would teach him himself. All day long they worked at it, right through lunch, and at the end of the afternoon he went up alone in the trainer and passed. Later Hitchcock used to say that he had heard the colonel whisper to the checkout pilot, "You'd better pass him. If you don't he'll be back every day and crack up so many airplanes that we'll have to ask for a new budget."

For a short time in late March, it seemed as though the air force had succeeded in putting Hitchcock where it believed he was best suited to serve. Unlike the army, which made a point at that time of taking engineers and putting them to work as pastry cooks, the air force tried to find occupationally appropriate jobs for its people. Hitchcock had been the head of an airline, the director of a steamship company. What better place for him, then, than the Air Ferry Command under General Olds. For a week or two, he was in Rio de Janeiro, shipping materiel to the British in North Africa, then hard-pressed by Rommel. Whether he liked the work or not, he had no time to discover. Olds was transferred to the Pacific theater, and in April Hitchcock was back in Washington. Then occurred one of those chance meetings that novelists can invent but biographers seldom discover.

Lunching with his wife at the Shoreham Hotel one day, he encountered Gil Winant, his old teacher at St. Paul's, now U.S. ambassador in London, who was in Washington briefly for consultations. Winant knew that his friend's knowledge and feeling for pilots and fighter aircraft held the key to the problem of where he could best serve. At that juncture of the war, bomber doctrine might be riding high among the generals of the American air force, and within the RAF. But for a few officers and officials in both countries—not to mention the public—the most celebrated and interesting of all the Allied arms of war was the RAF Fighter Command. These were the men and planes that had fought and won the Battle of Britain. Their prestige was immense. Winant knew this, knew, too, that Hitchcock was well connected in England. He asked him to write him a letter giving a job description of an assistant air attaché to the U.S. Embassy that Hitchcock could fill.

Hitchcock wrote the letter. He asserted (which was true) that RAF fighter-training procedures were far better than the American, that its experience with aerial gunnery was unsurpassed, that its progress in design and engineering was impressive, and that its knowledge of fighter deployment and tactics was far greater than our own. The Americans could learn from the British, he wrote; indeed they had to learn. The job description, in short, was that of a liaison between the American air force and British Fighter Command, via the American Embassy in London.

In late April he was on his way to Britain. As he expected to be back and forth, Peggy decided to keep the house in Washington for the time being.

It was paradoxical, but Tommy Hitchcock felt that the war appeared to be somehow farther away in London than it had been in Washington. The blitz was over, of course, but the rubble seemed only to emphasize the quiet and pedestrian orderliness of the people. The ruins might almost have been intentional, like bits of the old Roman wall left standing for the edification of tourists. Everyone, to be sure, was in uniform, dark brown or navy blue; but people went about their business with the usual English air of vacuous hauteur, distracted by purpose. Washington had been all bustle and confusion, soldiers and bureaucrats scurrying around with an urgent sense of their own importance but no very clear idea of what to do. The English had been at war for so long, that by the spring of 1942, they had managed to domesticate it, like some large and fierce-looking dog that had unaccountably wandered into the drawing room and been allowed to stay.

There was also the sense, in Hitchcock's case a poignant one, of being suspended between two strong desires, neither of which seemed likely to be fulfilled. One desire pulled him back toward home. Many men rush to war as a merciful vacation from the drudgery of work, from the tedium of stale marriages, from debts and dissolution. Hitchcock felt no relief at all going to war. His letters to Peggy are filled with love and an almost wistful loneliness; he wanted to be kept informed of every detail, how the children were doing at school, whether the twins were learning to swim so that they could go out on the water. "I miss fighting Trippe," he wrote at one point. "The Germans seem much less accessible than Juan." But that, of course, was the other desire pulling at him. He wanted to fight Germans, he wanted to fly in combat again. Avy, his nephew, was doing it. Yet here he was, engaged in a job that everyone said was more import-ant, that was more important, and it made him restless and sad. Action was reality, and in London it seemed terribly far away.

He never complained. On the contrary, he threw himself into his liaison work with all his usual energy. From May to November, his first overseas tour, he wrote some two hundred technical reports for Washington on many subjects involving performance of American and British fighter aircraft. At that stage of the war, before our armies and navies were ready for action, the United States served the Allies primarily as an arsenal. The most powerful industrial plant in the world, crippled by the Depression for almost a decade, revived and went to work furnishing guns, tanks, ships, planes, and all the other materiel of modern warfare. It was the most stupendous demonstration of productivity in the history of the world. Since 1940 the British, who with the Russians were sole survivors in Europe of the Nazi onslaught, had been working closely with American producers of arms and armaments. Nowhere was this more true than in the production of aircraft, and of no aircraft was this more true than the P-51 fighter, its nom de guerre: the Mustang.

The Mustang had been built by the North American Aviation Company, and by the time Hitchcock took up his job in London, the plane was undergoing performance testing to determine its strengths and limitations. The testing was being performed at the RAF Air Fighting Development Unit in Duxford. Duxford had high priority on Hitchcock's list of must-see installations.

A great many hopes were pinned on the Mustang. The Spitfire was the most famous plane in the annals of warfare, and, two years after its heroic service in the Battle of Britain, it was in its ninth generation of development and still the mainstay of Britain's air defense. Avy Clark was flying Spitfires even then with the Eagle Squadron. The plane was characterized by an acrobatic maneuverability in combat, a terrifically fast rate of climb, and high speed at high altitudes (above twenty-five thousand feet). Though by 1942 it was being used for probes and sweeps over the Channel into France, the Spitfire's principal function was defensive. Radar had been one key to success in the Battle of Britain, but the other had been the Spitfire's ability to rise to radar warning of incoming high-altitude bombers. For the coming phase of the war, however, which the Allies planned to take into Germany, the Spitfire was inadequate. Its range was limited, which ruled out bomber escort, and its relatively slow speed and poor diving capacity made it inefficient as an attack plane against troops, airfields, or other ground targets.

The Mustang was designed as an attack plane: faster than the Spitfire at medium to low altitudes, faster in diving, longer-ranged; it was just as handy in combat. It was sturdier and heavier than the Spitfire and embodied some new principles of aerodynamics, in particular the laminar flow wing. It was powered by an Allison 1720 engine, which was a specifically American contribution to its design and one of which officials at Wright Field were proud.

At Duxford, Hitchcock spent long hours poring over reams of charts, graphs, and statistics that set out the comparative performances of the Mustang and the Spitfire IX. What he discovered he put into a report of May 29, 1942. The important point was that the Allison engine, the pride of Wright Field, was not turning out to be the best engine for the plane:

> *Not only is the Mustang considered an excellent low and medium altitude. The Spitfire is drawing 290 more H.P. to get slightly less speed. The conclusion is inescapable that the drag of the Mustang is less than that of the Spitfire. This in spite of the fact that the Mustang weighs 8,000 lbs., and the Spitfire 5 B weighs 6,475 lbs. Though the poor climb of the Mustang is a disadvantage, it is more than made up for by the greater speed and diving ability. . . .*
>
> *Mustang is 30 mph faster than the Spitfire at 5,000 feet, 35 mph faster at 15,000 feet, and 1 or 2 mph faster at 25,000 feet. It is interesting to note that the Merlin engine of the Spitfire 5 B delivers 950 horsepower at 25,000, and the Allison engine delivers only 660 horsepower at that altitude.*
>
> *It is recommended that the Mustang be speedily equipped with the Merlin 61 engine now being used in the Spitfire IX. It is estimated by the Rolls Royce people that the Mustang equipped with the 61 engine will have a top speed of 440 miles per hour, and will have a speed curve of somewhat more than 20 miles per hour faster than the Spitfire IX.*

The summary contained four points: "1. The Mustang is the best American fighter plane to reach England. 2. The Mustang is faster than the Spitfire 5 B up to 25,000 feet. 3. At 25,000 feet the Mustang has the same speed as the Spitfire 5 B but uses less H.P. in attaining this speed than the Spitfire 5 B. 4. A cross-breeding of the Mustang with the Merlin 61 engine would produce the best fighter plane on the Western Front."

The "best fighter plane on the Western Front" was precisely what the Mustang, equipped with the Rolls-Royce Merlin engine, eventually became. The significance of this cannot be exaggerated: without the refurbished Mustang the Allies would not have been able to gain dominion over the skies of Europe, and without that dominion they would not have won the war against Hitler. The most important part of Hitchcock's contribution to the making of this plane was still to come, in Washington, where he helped batter down powerful opposition to the project. But already one can detect a characteristic Hitchcockian flair in the matter. The "best" was an ideal in which he believed. Ideals are not attainable, he knew, but they are approachable. And because they are approachable, it is the obligation of individuals, organizations, societies, to try to realize them, whether in matters of personal conduct or cooperative endeavor, or the production of a machine.

All that summer and into the fall, Hitchcock traveled in the Embassy's Beechcraft from station to station, gathering data and drumming up support. He was often at the Rolls-Royce Experimental Installation Plant near Nottingham, where the transplant operation was about to be performed on four Mustangs. He reported to Washington that Mr. Hives, the Rolls-Royce works manager, was highly optimistic and hoped that the U.S. authorities would "make every effort to capitalize on the Mustang airframe with the high-altitude engine." He found an ally in Sir John Slessor, chief of the RAF's Coastal Command, and in Brigadier General Frank O. D. Hunter, head of the Eighth Air Force Fighter Command. He enthusiastically endorsed a report by Dr. Edward Warner, an American aeronautical engineer, who wrote: "The RollsRoyce Merlin is still, as it has been for several years past, well in advance of the Allison in actually demonstrated power output and ability to deliver its power at high altitude. The installation of the Merlin is a clearly indicated step. . . . If the handicap under which the American machines labor . . . is removed . . . by replacing their present engine with that which the Spitfire carries [the Merlin] . . . both the Mustang and the P-39 would have within their grasp a top speed far superior to anything that has yet been employed in combat by either the British or the German Air Force . . . [and] the Mustang would be the better airplane of the two. . . ." He also had the support of perhaps the most significant officer in Britain, for his purposes, Brigadier General Alfred J. Lyon, chief of the Air Technical Station in Europe. Lyon was a dying man, but he put his prestige behind the campaign for the Merlin-equipped Mustang.

By October 1942 the transplant operations on the initial four Mustang airframes were well on their way to completion. This, of course, would be the crucial moment, when the plane was actually flying. All the campaign so far had been based on estimated performance; the estimations had been scientifically arrived at, but they were still only on paper.

The Mustang, Hitchcock knew, was by far the most significant aspect of his mission in London. On June 18 he wrote his wife, "When I wake up here I wonder what the hell I am doing in a strange city miles away from everyone I love and care about. This war, as all wars, seems so senseless. Life in London . . . is much too easy to make one think that one is actually engaged in waging a war." War, for him, was combat, and though he didn't want to say so to his family, he still yearned for it. Compared to combat, he could only say of this effort, "In a small way I am doing a little good."

He found some solace in what was also part of his job: learning everything he could about the fighter planes that were already operational. This meant flying them himself. On June 26 he wrote,

I have been getting in quite a bit of flying. I have had a little more time on a Spitfire, a Link trainer, and a couple of days ago I had a nice ride in a Mustang (albeit still equipped with the Allison). . . . I went up to 15,000 feet to try some acrobatics. It is about 21 years since I have done this and my technique was a little rusty. The first two barrel rolls that I tried ended in abrupt pull-outs from dives at around 300 mph; all the blood immediately drained away from my head, with the result that I completely blacked out. My last barrel roll was much better. With a few more rides I would feel quite at home in a Mustang. My knees have ceased knocking together when I ride in the hot stuff.

Moreover, while life in London was "much too easy," it was not without interest. He stayed at Claridge's for the first few days of his tourand then took a furnished flat near the embassy with Captain Manning Jacobs. His cousin-in-law David Bruce, then with the OSS, passed through, as did Averell Harriman. Jock Whitney was with Air Intelligence, and he too was trying to get into action. The Hitchcock-Jacobs apartment, Whitney recalled, sometimes seemed like a club room of the combined general staffs: "Tommy invited me to stay with him . . . and the first thing I knew he'd invited General Spaatz and all the other brass he could lay hands on to meet me. Imagine, a new almost-civilian captain arriving to join the air force, meeting the commanding generals, American and British, socially. This was the kind of thing Tommy would do, very typically; he didn't really care about customs or regulations. If I'd said, Please, for God's sake, don't do anything like that, he'd laugh like the Devil and say, that's what you're going to do. And I would do it very happily. More often than not, whatever he had you do was exactly the right thing to do."

His nephew Avy Clark often came to stay for a couple of days between his ten-day tours of duty. Clark was always on his best behavior with his uncle. Hitchcock, for his part, was fond of Avy and learned much from him about the realities of fighter warfare; but he did not encourage intimacy, not from his nephew or anyone else. Once, at a party, an extremely self-important and very rich American made the error of condescending to a small red-haired British officer, a major in the Commandos. The dispute was over a girl, and something in the American's manner finally enraged the major. He chopped him neatly behind the ear, and the American sank to the floor like a wounded buffalo. Hitchcock instantly dispatched Avy, a big man himself, to remove the stricken guest as quickly as possible and return him to his hotel.

By the end of October, the first Mustangs had been converted to the Merlin engines, and Hitchcock was understandably eager to try one out. Avy Clark, who was on leave at the time, went with him to the Rolls-Royce plant at Hacknall. "We took off in the Beechcraft," Clark remembered. "It was a four-place plane and we had two bomber pilots in the back seat who were hooking a ride. It was one of those days in England where you couldn't see anything through the haze except straight down. We got lost, but soon found a field and went down to ask where we were. The bomber pilots took a train from there on, but we got to the Rolls-Royce factory in time and went out to the field where the new Mustang was.

I was a little worried. I said, "Look, Uncle Tommy, you'd better not fly that thing. The test pilot is the only guy who's been up in it and besides, you're going to get lost." He said, "Oh, the hell with that," and began looking around for the Rolls man in charge. He told Uncle Tommy to go ahead and take it. He had a right to fly it, after all; it was mainly his idea. After he'd taken off, I said to the Rolls man, half-jokingly, "Well that's the last time you'll see that airplane," and the guy panicked. He called all the airfields in the area to watch out for a wandering P-51. Sure enough, we soon got word that a P-51 had just landed at a field twenty miles away. I flew over and picked him up. He'd gotten lost, but he was pleased as punch with the plane. That was the important thing.*

In November Hitchcock returned to Washington to carry the campaign for the Mustang to the last remaining stronghold of opposition, Wright Field. The word "channels," like the word "no," was an utterance he sometimes could not hear well. Channels meant lobbying the research and development people at Wright Field, the same people who had made a large investment in the Allison engine. That meant time, and time was what he did not have, and so he planned on going straight to the top, to General Hap Arnold.

He arrived on Helen Clark's Georgetown doorstep unannounced early one morning, hardly a resplendent military figure. His long raincoat looked as though he had slept in it, which he doubtless had, and he carried no insignia of rank anywhere. Peggy had let the Alsop house go earlier that fall and returned to New York and 10 Gracie Square with the

---

*Apparently, Hitchcock often got lost. In addition to weather problems, all the airfields in England were heavily camouflaged. Only later, when he got his own command, did he learn to fly on instruments instead of by the seat of his pants.

children. She was flying down that afternoon to stay with him at his sister's. Waiting for her, he sat down to prepare the presentation that he had to make to Arnold that afternoon. He had with him an impressive dossier of backup material: letters from General Eaker and General Spaatz, from Air Marshall Portal, and from Arthur "Bomber" Harris. Sir John Slessor of the RAF Coastal Command would soon be in Washington and the indispensable Alfred J. Lyon was already there, having left his sickbed in London to make the trip and plead for the new Mustang. (He died a few weeks later.) What he did not have were the actual performance figures, only estimates, but these were expected to come through any day.

He was unusually tense. He showed his sister the notes he planned to use as the basis of his presentation. They were blunt, even aggressive, and she cautioned him to be more diplomatic with Arnold, who, she felt, did not like him much in the first place.

Lyon and Slessor went with him to the meeting, and they plastered the general's office with charts and sheets of figures. Arnold was impressed but unmoved. To Hitchcock it was maddening that the general seemed not to realize the urgency of the matter. Arnold had other things on his mind. The people at Wright Field were happy with the Allison engine; it was good enough for the job; it was an American engine; why hurry with this Merlin thing? He had priorities, and, frankly, the Merlin-Mustang coupling was not one of them. In any case he could not do anything without the actual performance figures.

Hitchcock, with his experience of bureaucracy, felt more disheartened than he should have been. His wife, when she rejoined him that evening, thought she had never seen him so depressed. He hardly slept all that night. Nevertheless, in the next few days, while they waited for the performance figures to be sent over, he continued his lobbying efforts.

The performance figures arrived early in December. They went through "channels." The process was surprisingly fast, however, and it was not many days before the matter arrived on the desk of the undersecretary of war for air, Robert Lovett. Lovett, an investment banker in civilian life, had known Hitchcock since World War I, when Tommy was with the French and Lovett was a naval airman flying under British command. Moreover, he had flown planes equipped with Rolls-Royce engines and remembered them as absolutely reliable. The Wright Field people exerted a good deal of pressure, Lovett recalled. "The Allison had been in part designed and ordered by them, and to have their baby thrown out with the bathwater was a very serious blow. It finally came up to Hap Arnold and me. I remember insisting that we could not fool around with an inferior product when a superior one was available, and once we had the performance figures, Hap agreed with me. There was no question of what to do, really. We decided to start producing Merlin 61 engines at Packard, and to produce the P-51 B, as the hybrid was called, with the highest priority."

A few days later, when President Roosevelt sent a note to Arnold, casually mentioning that "a friend just back from England" had apprised him of the merits of the P-51 B, the general was pleased to report back to his commander in chief that twenty-two hundred of the planes had just been placed on order.

Years later another president, Harry Truman, used to say that the hardest lesson that he had to learn in the White House was that nobody ever did what one told him to do. Giving orders was easy; seeing that they were carried out was something else. From November 1942 to February 1943, Tommy Hitchcock, now a lieutenant colonel, had the task of seeing that the production order for the P-51 B was carried out. The job sent him back and forth across the country, mostly between Wright Field and the Packard plant in Indianapolis. Everywhere he went, as he wrote Peggy in New York, he spent "all day talking airplanes." On at least two occasions he talked airplanes to the press, and the interviews that he gave are remarkable for his sensitivity to what might be called the public relations problem of the P-51 B. The original Allison-powered Mustang had been extensively publicized in the press, somewhat misleadingly, as an American plane, a brilliant contribution of American technological genius to the war effort. The problem was to explain to the public that the Mustang was indeed a splendid aircraft, but that it could be made just a little better with a Rolls-Royce engine. Hitchcock handled himself in this delicate business with admirable skill.

In an interview released by the War Department, he was quoted as saying of the Merlin-Mustang,

It's best described as a pilot's airplane . . . Fliers feel that they have always known how to fly the plane after they've been in it only a few moments . . . Our fliers are good and are giving all they have to keep control of the air for us. This is not easy, nor is it easy to equip them with a plane better than the best the Germans can make. We are drawing freely and indiscriminately on the engineering skill and productive power of both England and the United States to beat the Germans in the race for air superiority . . . A well-developed instinct of self-preservation in the British people, plus the Rolls-Royce engine, will assure the English a plane in the front rank of fighter planes, while the resources of the U.S. and the engineering skill which has developed the laminar flow wing used on the P-51 will assure American fliers of fighter planes worthy of their skill.

In the conference rooms of the War Department, where he had to confront the Wright Field people, he was even more diplomatic. A transcript of his comments on one occasion has survived, in which he begins by downplaying the whole question of U.S. jealousy of England. "This fighter plane business in Europe is a little bit like the women's dress business," he said.

The question of styles and fashions keep changing. When I went to England . . . the English fighter command wouldn't look at anything that wouldn't fly 28,000 to 30,000 feet and have plenty of speed. Since then the Focke Wulf has come into active participation on the Western Front; and now all the talk you hear is about greater climb and additional acceleration. That is because the Focke Wulf has these capabilities to a very high degree.

The Focke Wulf will climb away from the Spitfire 5 B, dive away from it, make 30 miles more per hour, and do everything but turn inside it. . . . The only evasive maneuver that the Spitfire has is to

wait until the Focke Wulf gets within firing distance and then make a sudden turn—and the FW goes by.

When you talk about engines, you get practically down to the Rolls engine—that is, the Rolls Merlin engine. . . . Now when I first was sent over there, I was rather surprised to run into a report that the Mustang, which is our P-51, was 35 miles an hour faster than the Spitfire 9 at around 15,000 feet. At 25,000 feet it went a few miles an hour faster and was pulling 290 less horsepower. That indicated there must be something aerodynamically good about the Mustang. Dr. E. P. Warner, prominent aeronautical engineer in this country, came over to England. . . . He reduced it to coefficient of drag. . . . The Mustang has a very low coefficient of drag. . . . It has the lowest coefficient of drag of any plane in that theater.

They said, "Now, if we can put a high altitude engine in this plane we will have the answer to a maiden's prayer." So they put a Merlin 61 engine in it; and they got us to put one into it in this country. This is the plane that goes about 426 miles per hour at 21,000 feet. The Spitfire carried about 85 Imperial gallons and the Mustang carries about 140 Imperial gallons. This new version of the Mustang carries four 50s and four 303s on it, and carries quite a lot of ammunition. The rate of climb is somewhat less than the Spitfire's.

The white hope of the English, in order to combat the FW-190, and particularly the Focke Wulf with the fully rated engine, is by putting the Merlin 61 into the Mustang. They believe that it will be the best fighter plane for the next year or two; and their preliminary tests indicate that they are right.

About those fighter sweeps over the French coast—it is really remarkable that they have gone as well as they have. The Spitfires have been not only fighting over enemy territory—but largely with equipment inferior to the Focke Wulf. The Germans really didn't care if they came over or stayed home. There was no military damage they could do over there. They couldn't get the German to fight unless they gave him the advantage. The German would wait around—and if there was a straggler, he'd jump on him. On the whole, those English boys did pretty well, and, until the Fortresses came along, there was no reason for the Germans to join in combat. . . . I think that phase is over now; because we have enough bombing planes there to make it worthwhile for the Germans to fight. The bombing planes have gotten to their objectives and bombing has been accurate and they have been hitting very well.

Between trips to Washington and the Midwest, Hitchcock returned to his home at 10 Gracie Square in New York City. The twins, whom he scarcely knew, were four. Every morning he would signal that it was time for them to come into his bedroom by putting a record on the phonograph. It was always the same record, "Chattanooga Choo-Choo." They would come tumbling in like puppies and for a while all three of them would wrestle on the big bed. Then it was time for him to shave, brushing the boys, too, with soap mustaches, and put on his uniform, explaining what the bars meant and the eagles on the buttons, the heraldry of the modern soldier. His girls Louise, thirteen, and Peggy, about ten, remember that their father appeared different. Ruth, the maid, also noticed a difference: he no longer left his clothes lying all over the floor.

They had Christmas of 1942 together, but the interludes at 10 Gracie Square amounted to little, and when he returned to London in February 1943, he missed his family more than ever. On arrival he wrote Peggy, "I am afraid that as far as I personally am concerned my trip back home was a bad idea. It was so wonderful seeing you and the children again that it makes the separation all the harder." And, again, a week or so later, "I have taken deep roots with you and the children. . . . No war, no flying, no Mustangs—no matter how good or how plentiful—can replace you." Years later Robert Lovett would say of the Merlin-powered Mustangs, "Tommy Hitchcock was largely responsible for the P-51 B, for keeping pushing on that project until it got through. . . . The only person who could have done [this] was someone who was both knowledgeable as a pilot and who had the qualities of leadership to take a grasp of disparate people and get them moving in a common direction." Hitchcock must have known what he accomplished, but he was not the sort of man who ever looked back with pride.

At the War Department briefing in February 1943, he had said that the air war in Europe had entered a new phase. The Flying Fortresses, put into operation in 1942, had begun to give the Germans some cause for alarm, so much so that the Luftwaffe had begun to gear up its fighter defenses to attack the incoming bombers. The consequences of this development had taken time to become clear to the bomber doctrinaires.

The first American heavy-bomber raid took place on August 17, 1942. Twelve B-17s, escorted by Spitfires, attacked Rouen, easily within range of the fighters' eighty-five-gallon fuel capacity. The raid was hailed as a success: enemy fighter opposition was negligible. Four days later a similar raid was not so lucky. Twenty-five Focke Wulfs and Messerschmitts rose to defend the target. Even so, all planes returned safely, with the loss of only one life. On September 6, however, during a raid over an aircraft factory in Meulte, two bombers were lost, many damaged, and there were fairly serious casualties. If that seemed ominous, subsequent missions, to Meulte again and to Lille, took losses from heavy fighter interference that were considered quite bearable. Indeed, until well into 1943, American bombing experience seemed to preserve one prized assumption, that with a minimum of fighter escort, the big planes could take care of themselves.

Hitchcock stated this belief himself in a letter to his father-in-law, written after the 108-bomber assault on Lille in mid-October 1942. "The outstanding thing of interest in the air war in this theater," he said, "is the success of the Flying Fortress in daylight bombing. While . . . their objectives have all been within the range of fighter aircraft cover, on three occasions, for various reasons, the Fortresses found themselves unescorted, and had to engage in battle for fairly protracted periods with German fighter planes. As near as I can find out, as a result of these engagements about thirty German fighter planes were destroyed and others damaged, with the loss of only two Flying Fortresses."

A two-to-thirty kill ratio is distinctly bearable, even if one supposes a Fortress to be the equivalent of four fighters or even six. The trouble was that the whole thing was an illusion, or rather one big illusion made up of many little ones. Nothing like thirty enemy planes had been destroyed that day over Lille, in fact, probably only two were. The Nazis kept meticulous statistics, and after the war the Allies found that in this period American reports of the damage inflicted on German fighter defenses could be routinely discounted by as much as 90 percent.

How this pathetic misunderstanding could have happened is one of the wonders of the war. It was actually simple, however. To find out the destruction inflicted on German fighters during any given raid, the military statisticians asked the gunners on their return how many enemy planes they had shot down or crippled. Then they simply added the total, subtracting a certain statistically arrived-at number to compensate for wishful thinking. What they did not reckon into their calculations, incredibly enough, was the fact that in the middle of an air battle, any number of gunners in the same plane could claim in perfect sincerity to have shot down the same plane. Thus one aircraft would have been destroyed, but six or eight or ten might be recorded as having been destroyed. This was the illusion, but it fit to perfection the grand illusion of the bomber generals that the big planes could go it almost alone.

Hitchcock, of course, knew none of this. No one did, until after the war. By August 1943, however (two months after the original target date for the Eighth Air Force's domination of the skies of Europe), bomber doctrine was in a shambles. So long as the Eighth kept pounding away at France and Holland, the Germans had offered little resistance. But when they extended their attack into Germany itself, all hell broke loose. An omen of what was to happen came on June 13 when 102 B-17s bombed the port city of Bremen. One-fourth failed to return. But it was the Schweinfurt-Regensberg raid of August 17 that once and for all destroyed the myth that the bombers "could do it on their own." The target was a ball-bearing plant and distribution center. The available fighter escort with the longest range was at that time the Thunderbolt; it could fly 340 miles, fight, and return. This meant, of course, that in the crucial minutes around the release point, the bombers would be wide open to fighter attack from the ground. The result was catastrophic: 315 planes reached the target; of these, 60 were lost; but of those that returned, half were almost completely destroyed. The human losses were even worse. Hardly a plane came home without a cargo of dead and mutilated men.

Schweinfurt was the Eighth Air Force's Verdun; the men were on the verge of mutiny, refusing to fly into Germany without the sort of escort that could protect them, not just as they "coasted in" and "coasted out," when there wasn't much opposition anyway, but over the target. Hitchcock (and many others) had foreseen that the bombers, once they struck at the Fatherland itself, would need all the help that they could get. Even at his most optimistic, in the letter to his father-in-law, he had made the success of bomber doctrine contingent on their being "strongly enough defended." In fact, he had always stressed that one of the best selling points of the Mustang Merlin, equipped with a supplementary fuel tank, was that it was a "fighter with legs."

The first big shipment of P-51 B's would not arrive in England until the middle of September 1943. It was February when Hitchcock returned to London for his second tour. The assistant military attaché for air still had to work on a number of bottlenecks on the English side of the ocean; but by and large, from February till December, Hitchcock had no firmly focused mission of the scope and importance that he had had on his first tour. He was a troubleshooter, an authorized enemy of bureaucracy, his principal targets inertia and the SNAFU. Bill Jackson, who was in London in that period, assigned to the problem of clearing the Channel of U-boats by dive-bombing them when they came up for air, wrote Peggy Hitchcock that no one was better suited for his job than her husband. "I hear him calling up Ira Eaker, Jack Slessor, Geoffrey Blake, Gil Winant, Lord Portal, and many others whose rank or exalted station give me the cold shivers. Not Tommy; he talks to them just as he talks to me, and they love it . . . I simply could not do my job without him. I get fussing around with a ball of red tape and Tommy comes roaring up behind me and knocks it the length of the field. I gallop away as proud as if I had hit it myself."

He was also an investigator, gathering information from all over England on the myriad of technical, tactical, and training developments taking place in the fighter arms of the RAF and the USAF. In his absence the embassy had overhauled his Beechcraft and he used it constantly, glad to get away from his desk.

On his previous London tour, this sort of work had provided a measure of excitement. "Now," he wrote Peggy toward the end of March, "for some strange reason it has worn off. I am getting very restless over here." A rather comfortable domesticity had enveloped him, and he felt vaguely threatened by it. David Bruce, in charge of OSS activities in the European theater, and Hitchcock had taken a house at 3 Lees Place, near Grosvenor Square. There was a bedroom and bath for each of them, and a large living room and dining room. There was also a guestroom, which was for Avy Clark, Tommy Clark (who arrived in England for RAF training on March 21), or any others who might be passing through.

Hitchcock did a modest amount of entertaining and took pleasure in it. Every once in a while, Peggy would get in the mail a little package of place cards that he had made for a dinner party and then retrieved for her as a souvenir. When Robert Lovett came through London in May, Tommy gave a dinner for him to meet the top English RAF people. The place cards read: Air Marshall Sir Arthur T. Harris, Air Marshall Sir Douglas Evill, Air Marshall John J. Slessor, Major General Ira Eaker, the Honorable Robert A. Lovett, the Honorable John G. Winant, Air Marshall R. S. Sorley, Lieutenant Colonel Thomas Hitchcock, and Lieutenant Colonel Milton M. Turner. Air Marshall Leigh-Mallory must have pocketed his card, for Peggy never got it.

At that party he sat himself next to the famed "Bomber" Harris, a former ivory hunter and safari guide who was chief of the British bomber command and a fanatical advocate of strategic bombardments. He told Hitchcock that evening (May 12 or 13, 1943) that he was quite certain the war in Europe would be over within the year, largely because of the damage his bombers were inflicting. He was, of course, even more off target than his planes often were.

David Bruce said that among Hitchcock's unexpected skills as a housekeeper was the ability to find a good cook. This must be put down as the exaggeration of a loyal friend. The fact is that Hitchcock's early encounters with "the servant problem" were hilarious. When he first was sharing a house with Bruce he had a cook who, as he wrote Peggy, "has been a hell of a nuisance. She turned out to be a dope fiend." One evening, in the middle of a brass-decorated dinner party, she took off all her clothes, plopped down on the kitchen floor, and refused to move. Somehow, despite this unforeseen calamity, the dinner party sailed smoothly on, making him forever a hero in David Bruce's eyes. Preliminary negotiation with the naked cook he left to the maid. When that failed, he took to the telephone—as he put it, "to direct the logistics from a safe distance." In the end it required a doctor, an ambulance, and a policeman to get the cook into the hands of the proper authorities.

A second domestic farce erupted shortly after Bruce and he moved from their house to an apartment in October 1943. He wrote Peggy,

> *The nice maid we had to leave behind with Lady Kissman [the owner of the house]. I hired a new one, but she does not get on with the cook. She, the maid, is a vegetarian and a spiritualist. A good part of her time is spent in a trance. As a contact with the spirit world she uses a German soldier who was killed in the last war and an American Red Indian with feathers. When not in a trance, she fights with the cook. Whenever I talk with the cook, the maid imagines we are saying things about her. Every Friday morning the cook brings me the accounts and I give her enough cash to run the place for another week. Last Friday, the maid burst into the room and accused the cook and me of conspiring behind her back. She is as screwy as can be.*

A dope fiend and a paranoiac vegetarian spiritualist—not a good record even in wartime. It is no wonder that he wrote his wife that it would do people a lot of good when, after the war, everyone would have to put up with a lower standard of living.

Stateside domestic problems also occasionally preoccupied him after he returned to England in 1943. He was especially interested in what Alex was doing. The boy was in his last year at St. Paul's and Hitchcock counseled him to finish up there and take his college boards, especially if (as was apparently the case) he wanted to join the air force. When Alex was rejected for being color-blind, his stepfather told him not to be discouraged: as the war went on, the requirements for both flying and officer training schools were sure to be relaxed. But his mind was also on the future. He explored with Peggy the possibility of buying Broad Hollow Farm from his father's estate. "The upkeep is bound to be more," he wrote her, "as the place is larger [than Sand's Point] but the extra land will allow us to engage in any agriculture or husbandry that might meet our fancy and not wreck our pocket books. In any event the 80-some acres would provide ample land as building sites if ever our children wanted to settle near-by."

Yet the more he traveled about the country in his Beechcraft, the more restless he was to get into combat. Flying, moving about, talking always to young pilots like Avy, made the chains that tied him to his desk seem oppressive. In May he decided to write a report on gunnery instruction in the RAF and argued that the best way to do this was to take the course himself. On May 13 he went to Lincolnshire to enroll in the gunnery school at Sutton Bridge.

He was there for a month, working thirteen hours a day, four or five of them in the air flying Spitfires. Many of his fellow students were his age, and all of them had some combat experience. They were being trained, in fact, to carry the latest methods back to their squadrons. And he? Well, he wrote Peggy, a little sadly, he would be "able to instruct Alex and the twins in the latest wrinkles of aerial shooting." For the first time he was beginning to feel his age.

As he knew from the first war, aerial gunnery was something that was learned after flying had become a habit, just as horsemanship had to be instinctive when one played polo. He had not flown a Spitfire for a long time when he went up to Sutton Bridge, and then not for many hours. The first few days therefore were somewhat daunting.

Fighter-to-fighter tactics, Hitchcock discovered, were not all that different from what they had been "over the lines" in 1918, except for the vastly increased speed, a big except. Because the primary mission of his fellow students would be bomber-escort work, the first-instance problem was to avoid being surprised. At high altitudes this was extremely difficult. At 2,700 feet, a fighter pilot needed a head like an owl's and eyes like a hawk's. Moreover, at those heights the farthest one could see was two to five miles, and the wild blue yonder, of course, contained few visual clues against which to orient oneself to warnings of an attack. It was hard, in fact, to tell the difference between the "friendlies" and the "hostiles."

Once one was bounced (attacked), the standard maneuver, particularly in the handy Spitfires, was to turn sharply into the oncoming path of the enemy, thus redefining his problem and forcing him to come up with another solution. The solution, in the ideal case, was variously known in the air force slang as swinging into his stern or moving into his 6 o'clock, or (less elegantly) steering up his ass. From this position not only was the opponent defenseless—that is, unable to fire back—but one's own targeting problems were much reduced.

Later in the war, developments in gunnery made a certain degree of automatic sighting possible. But in 1943 a man's skill depended largely on his natural gifts, practice, and luck. After a month's work at it, Hitchcock was no longer mortified every evening when the class reviewed the day's "shooting" on the movie screen. Nonetheless he never fooled himself, as so many middle-aged men are apt to do, that he could keep up with the best of them. He believed he could, with time and experience, but he contented himself with the fact that at trap and skeet shooting (of which the pilots did a lot, as part of the course) he had a substantial edge over all of them. He still shot "like chain lightning," as Douglas Burden put it, but as he remarked to Peggy in a letter, "Unfortunately the war will not be won shooting skeet."

In the first three weeks of September 1943, he enrolled in another school, this one for would-be group and wing commanders. It was at Aston Downs in Gloucestershire and was as "close to the real thing" as he had come. The students, again flying Spitfires, operated as a full wing with three squadrons. One exercise involved making sweeps over Wales, where they would be bounced by a squadron of instructors. The object was to bag as many of them as possible, "dry-firing" at them with the cameras. Teamwork (made possible by the air-to-air radio) was of the essence in this sort of fighting, as it was in the other main exercise, bomber escort. He got the hang of it fairly quickly, and by the end of the course his only problem was "seeing enemy planes and giving proper warning" to the rest of the squadron. He caught the flavor of the exercises in a letter to Peggy dated September 13, 1943:

The day before yesterday I led the wing [three squadrons of three planes each] for the first time. Fortunately everything went well. We were on time at the rendevous [with the bombers they were to protect] and we all kept together well when "attacked." It is very easy, when taking evasive action, to get scattered about all over the sky, and then if the fighting keeps on, it is hard to get together again. . . . This afternoon I acted as the enemy and bounced some of the boys who were doing low-level attacks in pairs. I flew alone. There was a low cloud base in which you could take cover if things got too hot. I picked up a couple of pairs and got a pretty good squint in at one before he saw me. However, in the course of one of my flights, a third pair that I never saw came along and destroyed me. It is awfully hard to see everything, especially when you're alone. On the way home I tried some rolls and got them a little better, but not quite right yet. Also I tried some rolls off the top of a loop and to my surprise, after the first attempt I made two pretty fair ones.

He had written "a little better, but not quite right yet." His persistence in getting it right made him an idol in the eyes of the young RAF pilots with whom he trained. They knew who he was, of course, and they doubtless responded as well to his charm and force of personality. They also knew that he did not have to do what he was doing. In any other man this might have suggested play-acting, a grown-up trying to recapture his youth. But there was such an intensity in his approach, and such strong understanding and curiosity, that no one questioned his presence among them. They admired him as much as he admired them.

At Sutton Bridge a pilot by the name of Alan Smith invited him to his wedding. Hitchcock was touched by the gesture and flew with his roommate, Paul Birsky, to the little town of Kinross, sixty miles north of Edinburgh, to be at the ceremony. Later he wrote to his wife,

I have never understood why people cry at a wedding. Now I begin to understand. Tears came to my eyes when the music started to play in the church and a great surge of memories of our own happy life together swept over me and I felt so lonely for you and our family. . . .

*Enclosed are some postals of Kinross and a copy of the hymns we sang
at the wedding. The choir, everyone except me, could sing like a lark.*

He saw young Avy often during those months. He was a captain with
his own squadron, leading sweeps over the Continent in Thunderbolts,
the new American plane that was heavier and faster than the Spitfire
and thought to be better for low- and medium-altitude work, but which
the pilots did not like much. Sometimes when their leaves coincided on
a weekend, they went out together to Ronnie and Nancy Tree's house,
Ditchly, where they played tennis. Avy was getting better and better,
Tommy wrote to Helen, but he could still take him. He was also pleased
to report that Nancy Tree had lined up five of the prettiest girls in London for Avy. (Avy later married one of them, Brigit Eliot.)

September 26 was a day of triumph for the assistant military attaché
for air. Early that morning he sat down to write home,

*This is Sunday, a most beautiful day. The sun is pouring into the
southern windows of the new flat. As soon as I finish this letter I am
going to the U.S. field to do some flying. I hope to get a ride in the
new plane, the Merlin-Mustang, that I have been working on for so
long. The first ones have just arrived in this country. At the present
moment, the plan is to equip the Eagle boys with the first new planes.
Avy is delighted. It makes all the effort I have put in this doubly
worthwhile to have the planes go to Avy's outfit. . . ."*

The letter ended with an exultant postscript:

*I have just come in from flying. The plane is all and more than I hoped
for. I only had a short flight in it, no very high speeds, but it's easy as
an old shoe for acrobatics.*

The experience had but one effect on him. Flying the Mustang in
combat, preferably at the head of his own squadron, had until then been
a dream. He was determined to make it come true.

In retrospect it is almost incredible that Tommy Hitchcock was given the command he wanted, suddenly transferred from a London desk job to lead a fighter group then training in Texas. He was nearly forty-four years old. If there were any forty-four-year-old squadron commanders fighting in any theater of the war, they were professionals who had been flying military planes for years and who were considered for one reason or another unsuited to staff work. Hitchcock, on the other hand, had little or no experience in flying modern fighter planes; and, as the existence of the Merlin-Mustang proved, he was eminently suited to staff work. David Bruce more than once had tried to recruit him into the OSS; Jimmy Doolittle had wanted him on his staff. He had rejected all these offers, primarily because he wanted to complete the Merlin-Mustang project, but also because he knew that any other job than the embassy one would take him further from his primary goal of gaining a fighter command.

Yet despite all this, his ambition was not crazy. He was, for one thing, perfectly aware of his limitations. Just before finishing his gunnery course at Aston Downs, he had written Peggy. "I went to the school at about a zero player. After a month's hard work I may, with a little stretch of the imagination, be rated at one goal. When I quit in 1918 I was at least five goals. But the handicap committee was more lenient then and the game was not so fast." Even as a youth his adventurousness had been hedged with realism; it was no less so when he was middle-aged. Moreover, the job of group commander did not, strictly speaking, require him to fly every mission with his men or, if he flew, always to be the leader. The chief responsibilities were for organization and morale.

He had an extraordinary galvanizing effect on younger men. At the same time he did not propose to grow roots. As he told an interviewer just before taking over his group, "I shall do some fighting. . . . As commander, I'll do less than my subordinates [but] enough to convince my fliers that I am asking them to do nothing I cannot do myself. . . . Just how it will work out with me I cannot tell, until I have been in a scrap."

On Christmas Eve, in 1943, he arrived, alone, in Abilene, Texas, to assume command of the 408th Fighter Group. He had under him thirty-six pilots plus two backup personnel to service the group's thirty-six

Mustangs. It was just what he wanted, certainly, but how he got it is not clear. His persuasiveness, of course, could move bureaucratic mountains. Also, he was by that time closely acquainted with nine-tenths of the general staff of the U.S. Army Air Force. Still there was something magical about this transfer from a desk at the London embassy to a dirty Texas airfield that left him aghast. He wrote Peggy, with whom he had been briefly reunited on his way west:

> *The amount of work that must be done is staggering. In 90 days' time the group is supposed to be ready to fight for its life. A good many of the boys are fresh from flying school. . . . At the moment all their planes are grounded because of some defect in the engines. . . . When I look forward to the work and grief ahead of me I have some misgivings, and the thought occurs to me that I was a sucker to give up the London job. [But] ever since I returned to the army I have had an acute urge to get back into the fighter business. . . . I do not feel that I know all the answers, not by a long shot. [But] I have got what I wanted and it is up to me to make the very best of it.*

He set about making the "very best of it" immediately. Christmas Day he felt lonely, lonelier than he had felt since the Christmas twenty-six years before in Luneville, a novice pilot of seventeen newly arrived at Escadrille N-87. He had to attend a small dance to meet the officers of his group and their wives. "Not my style," Hitchcock wrote, "but I suppose I have to go. They would likely think me strange if I stayed away the first night."

Whether the new commanding officer realized it then, he knew soon enough that the arrival of a new commanding officer had caused something less than rejoicing among the thirty-six pilots in his group. The 408th was recently formed, but it had been in existence for several weeks and in that time had developed a certain esprit de corps. The focus of morale had been the former commanding officer. An officer not much older than his men, he had been with them from the outset of this crucial part of their training and had been a popular figure. This young officer and a number of his men naturally resented his being displaced by a desk flier old enough to be their father who had been sent all the way from a cushy London office to lord it over them. To make matters worse, the previous commanding officer remained with the group as Hitchcock's executive officer, but a disgruntled man.

The men of 408th had this preconception before they met Hitchcock. When they met him, much of the resentment evaporated in the excitement that he always generated in any undertaking. Still, some weeks would go by before Hitchcock stopped feeling like a wicked stepfather and fit comfortably into his new role. Peggy came out to Texas soon after Christmas, leaving the children behind at school. Tommy and Peggy stayed at first in a hotel, and then they moved to a small house on the outskirts of Abilene that seemed constantly blasted by hot dusty winds. Peggy remembered this interlude as one of her happiest experiences in the war. By now, she was over forty herself, but she was still as slim as a girl and as full of eager curiosity and high spirits. The town was full of young wives, many of them scarcely out of high school, and most had been hurriedly married to their sweethearts before they went overseas. She remembers how elated the young wives were to be away from their parents for the first time and how they dreaded going back home when their husbands went abroad. Abilene was their senior prom, their honeymoon, and their first home all in one.

Alex came for a brief visit. His color blindness had prevented him from getting his wings, but he had a flying job nonetheless, as a bomber radio operator. He was stationed in Gulfport, an awkward place from which to get to Abilene. But he made it and had a few days with his parents, though Hitchcock was then working day and night whipping the 408th together.

Ironically, many of his hours were spent behind a desk; he was, after all, a commanding officer. Still, there was plenty of flying to do, day after day leading the group in practice runs in which he stressed repeatedly the vital importance of staying together. In the afternoons and evenings, he conducted lectures and showed films of aerial combat. In all this his experience at the RAF schools was of enormous help. Not only had he taken those courses; he had taught them. Moreover, though he had seen no actual fighting in Europe, he had talked to literally hundreds of pilots, and knew the problems that they faced, better in some respects than they did.

Toward the end of the training, Hitchcock was completely at ease in his command and proud of the work his men were doing. He was eager to get into action. His wife had seen for herself the progress that the group made in formation flying. Often she would stand in the conning tower watching the thirty-six planes in their maneuvers, the Western sky a pale clear blue through which the 408th roared and swooped. They resembled nothing in nature; a Nieuport or a Spad might seem like a bird in flight, but only man could have created the spectacle of Mustangs in formation. Still, she thought, it was thrilling and beautiful, too.

Then suddenly Tommy's dream of a fighter command was all over. The bureaucratic machinery of the air force had other plans for the men of the 408th and for Lieutenant Colonel Hitchcock. In early February the unit was disbanded, the individual pilots sent abroad as replacements for men lost in action. Their commander, Hitchcock, was assigned to research and development work on the Mustang, the plane that he had done so much to create.

Hitchcock had never been more disappointed in his life. He was not used to defeat. Or, rather, the defeats he had experienced had always been part of a linked chain of challenges. He had been able to learn from them, "to get it right next time." But this was not that kind of defeat. He had not been sent back to square one; he had been knocked off the board. And the hand that did it acted without apology or explanation, and was beyond appeal. Disappointed, frustrated, helpless though he was, he soon recovered. In some ways this recovery was his greatest victory.

His orders were to return to England to take up the job of deputy chief of staff of the 9th Air Support Command, in charge of tactical research and development. He went via New York, and for a few short days he and Peggy, the two girls, and the twins were all together at 10 Gracie Square. Young Peggy remembers the day that he left. "I came home from school at lunch time to say goodbye to my father. We had said goodbye many times before, but that day, while waiting for the elevator to come up and take me back downstairs, I suddenly had the awful premonition that I might never see him again. I remember running back for one last glimpse of my father still sitting at the dining room table with my mother, and thinking to myself, I must fix his image in my mind so that I will never forget him. I was not quite ten at the time and absolutely idolized him."

Early one morning toward the end of March 1944, Hitchcock stood on the tarmac at Debden and watched his nephew Avy Clark take off for a rendezvous with an American bomber force over Germany. Clark was a captain, with many kills to his credit, and he alternated as leader of the group with his commanding officer, Captain Blakeslee. He was leading that day. The Mustangs rose from the field in threes, and their formations in the sky, like fingers of a skeletal hand, dwindled away against the light of the rising sun. If he felt any envy for his young nephew then, he suppressed it. Besides, he had been proud, a few minutes earlier, when he had sat in the back of the briefing room while Avy talked of the day's mission. It was a sketchy little talk, full of pilot's jargon: the squadron (twelve to sixteen planes in three or four flights) would coast in (to occupied territory) at such and such a point, and coast out at another point. The rendezvous with the bombers would occur at any of three or four points of intersection on the mission's course to and from the target or, as they called it, *the release point*.

These were experienced men, of course, so he did not have to mention that their primary function was to run interference against German fighter planes sent aloft to spoil the day's bombing. He did not have to remind them that the greatest danger lay in being surprised by bandits (identified enemy, as opposed to unidentified craft, which were known as bogies). And he did not have to tell them that on the way out they were welcome to take any targets of opportunity that came their way—airfields, railroad stations, troops. (Avy himself once scored a brace of kills on a target of opportunity that consisted of novice German pilots on a training flight, and when his mother had remarked that this was not sportsmanlike of him, he replied, "Well, Mother, you shoot doves, don't you?")

Listening to him during the briefing, Hitchock had felt great admiration, touched also with a sense of paternal pride. This was his blood, his family. He wrote Peggy the next day, "He is much better looking than he was when you saw him. He is thin, his face is older and in a way finer, less boyish; his look is kindly but there is a hard determination that comes from lots of fighting. He has destroyed 5 or 6 planes in this period, and he will destroy more and more until the unlucky moment arrives. He is doing the thing he likes most in the world, and he is doing it well."

Perhaps Avy was indeed doing what he liked most in the world. Was Hitchcock? Earlier, on his return to England, he had made one last try to command a group of his own. He took the plea to his new boss, General Elwood Quesada, chief of the 9th Air Support Command, who would soon be in charge of fighter operations in the Normandy invasion. Hitchcock pulled out all the stops during the interview—and got nowhere. Quesada was pleasant, even sympathetic, but replied with all the arguments that Hitchcock had been hearing for years: "Forty-four is just too old . . . young man's game . . . reflexes . . . how many G's can you pull without blacking out . . . services far more valuable here . . . nothing personal . . . too old." He heard it all and looked, Quesada thought, somewhat dejected.

But in fact his personal crisis had passed. Back in Texas, even before that, when he had first gone to war, he had accepted what every man must who would grow old with grace, that his youth belonged to the young, but it was still in some way his youth in them. Compared to many men he found it easy to be a father. At the gunnery school he had a shock of recognition, which he shared with his wife: "It is fun working hard, flying a lot and being physically tired at night. Also I enjoy being with young pilots again. It is funny that as a man gets older he seems to cling to life tenaciously. These boys do not seem the least bit concerned by the risks of their lives. Yet if they were 20 years older, most of them would become worried." He was twenty years older, and if he clung to life more tenaciously, it was not just because he had more to lose. Mostly it was because he had more to give.

Quesada remembered that quality of Hitchcock's most vividly. All during the winter and spring of 1944, the 9th Tactical Air Command was building up for D-Day. The groups, each with thirty-six men and planes, plus support staff and materiel, were arriving at the rate of two a week. To give them experience they were set to work escorting the Eighth Air

Force bombers. They would be in combat, in some cases, ten days after landing in England. "Tommy Hitchcock," Quesada told an interviewer, "had a tremendous dynamic and magnetic influence on these young men, and it was not because of his athletic prowess or reputation. Most of the boys in our fighter groups didn't know a thing about polo or give a damn about it. Their admiration for him was deeper and more sincere, and more worthy. He had an immediate electrifying effect on our young men. They quickly recognized his basic character, his depth of knowledge and the sympathy that comes with experience. He knew how to talk with them. He was a tremendous asset to my command."

And then, too, there was the Mustang itself, a child of a different sort. The Merlin-powered P-51 B, even in the short time that he had been away in the States, had proved to be the finest fighter plane in the skies. It was simply "the best." Already, with its enormously greater fuel capacity than the Spitfire's, it could fight on the far side of Berlin. And when it fought, it inflicted kills that were trustworthy. There were many statistics to confirm this, but the one Hitchcock liked best was something that he learned in March 1944. Avy, he wrote Helen, was "tremendously enthusiastic about the Mustangs," and he was pleased to tell her that the numbers gave him firm grounds for enthusiasm. In the previous eleven months, flying Thunderbolts, the squadron had shot down 120 enemy aircraft. In one month of flying Mustangs, they had shot down 160 enemy aircraft. Those were the sort of statistics that, had he been that sort of man, Tommy Hitchcock might have cited to claim that he had helped win the war.

The tactical research and development station headed by Hitchcock operated from an airfield near Salisbury, southwest of London. This was Constable country, a landscape of rolling hills, precious villages, and the vast Salisbury Plain, flowering then with the coming of spring. Flying over it, one could sometimes see herds of ponies running wild.

He lived for the most part in the officers' quarters at Quesada's headquarters in Middle Wallop, near Andover, sharing a small room there with another light colonel, Edward Kelso. As luck would have it, Kelso was a good tennis player, and when the weather improved, Hitchcock wrote Peggy, he hoped to see what he could do against him on the courts.

As he settled into the routine of the job, he wanted news and more news of home—whether the family had gone to Aiken over Easter, what Alex was doing, why the little boys had so many colds, what Juan Trippe thought of the American Export–American Airlines merger. In his last letter he delightedly noted that Avy's group "has been going great guns since switching over to Mustangs. They are now the highest scoring U.S. group in England . . . making deep penetrations into Germany and chasing German planes all around the tree tops." He also recommended that Alex's allowance be raised to $100 a month: "Even with his $50 from the Army, that does not give him too much."

The letter papered over a growing anxiety. His other nephew, Avy's younger brother, Tommy, had been reported missing after a low-altitude sweep over the coast of France. It was only his third operational mission. There had been some flak but no enemy-fighter interference. He was seen banking away back to the Channel while about forty miles into the mainland. He had not returned to his base, but as Hitchcock wrote his sister after the report came through, this did not mean that he had been killed. He could have been picked up by the Germans or the French resistance–either way one might not know for another six months. It was a vain hope. Thomas Hitchcock Clark had been killed.

There had been no hope at all for Peter Lehman, a pilot in Avy's group who had inexplicably plunged to the ground during a raid. Peculiar accidents of that sort had been happening more and more frequently among the Mustangs in recent weeks. As Quesada said later, "We found that we were getting an extraordinary number of airplanes—apparently without pilot error—just diving into the ground. We couldn't understand it, and Tommy couldn't. It was perhaps our most serious worry that spring. Obviously, you can't have a useful force that is going to destroy itself."

As deputy chief of staff, Hitchcock was expected to find out what was going wrong—and as fast as possible. The bombing had to continue. The bombers had to have fighter escort. The war could not be called off while the technicians went back to the drawing board. Yet each day the problem remained unsolved meant more and more losses.

Actually Hitchcock and the other technical people had a good hunch about what was going wrong. As the bombing raids were extended farther into the political heartland of the Reich, even the Mustang's fuel capacity became insufficient to carry them to the rendezvous over the release point, to fight there, then to return to England. To extend their range, the engineers devised a way to place a seventy-gallon fuel tank in the fuselage of the plane, behind the pilot's seat. This, of course, was supplementary to the ninety-gallon tanks in each wing and to the disposable tanks suspended under the wings. As the winter of 1944 turned to spring, more and more Mustangs were equipped with the new seventy-gallon tank. It was then, as Quesada put it, that all hell broke loose.

Obviously there was a connection between the new fuel tanks and the accidents, but what was it? Eyewitnesses knew only that one of their group, often in the middle of combat, would push the nose hard down, the throttle wide open, and begin a dive from which they failed to come out. The hunch was that the supplementary fuel tank was destabilizing the plane, forcing it to earth by creating a turbulence of air around the wings that froze the flaps in a downward position, the stick as immovable as if it had been plunged in a block of steel. This was the hypothesis that Hitchcock's group decided to test at once. If it were proven, the pilots would be put under the strictest orders to switch on the fuselage tank right after takeoff, thus burning as much of its fuel as possible before entering combat.

There was no question, apparently, about who would do the actual testing. Hitchcock would do it. It was not part of his job—not even part of his role as leader of the group. He had test pilots under him as qualified as he was. No one ordered him to do it. No one even expected it of him. But the expectations that Hitchcock had of himself at forty-four were as high as they had always been. He might have reasoned that this plane was in some sense "his," and because it was going wrong, he had an obligation to correct it. He might have believed that he had to set an example for his men or that he could test the plane better than anyone else. If someone had to take the risk, it might as well be he. He might have reasoned his way to the decision along any of these lines. Yet reason, one suspects, had little to do with it. To Tommy Hitchcock, it was a challenge to act.

Dr. Drury's favorite text read, "David hasted, and ran toward the army to meet the Philistine." All his life Hitchcock had run forward to meet challenge. He never had to be told to do it, never looked behind to see if others were following him or watching him. To say that he was ardent, brave, and persistent is true, but it also obscures the simplicity, the innocence, of his spirit. The flux of ordinary social experience seemed only, after a while, to remind him that he belonged elsewhere—in an endeavor that yielded clear results. For him a challenge was always a vocation, calling him back to himself, a kind of conscience. But it was also a deliverance, and so he ran forward to meet it.

He was at the field before 11:00 o'clock, most of his desk work done for the day. The Mustang was waiting for him, fully fueled and armed. Airborne, alone in the bright sunshine, he flew toward the bombing range. A luminous haze, the soil's breath in spring, lightly veiled the ground. If he looked straight down, even at fifteen thousand feet, he could see the earth, and as the target area came in view he readied himself for the dive.

The plane hit the ground almost perpendicularly, sending a thick ring of black smoke upward into the still air, where it soon dissipated. The date was April 18, 1944.*

---

*In addition to a letter of appreciation from the President of the United States, Franklin Delano Roosevelt, Tommy Hitchcock was posthumously awarded the Legion of Merit, the Bronze Star, and the Distinguished Flying Cross.

Epilogue: Tommy Hitchcock's Role in the Battle of the Atlantic*

My father, William H. Jackson, was packed off at age nine to board at Fay School in Massachusetts, where the corridors still echoed with Hitchcock's legendary exploits. The two first met in summer 1914 in Narragansett, Rhode Island, where Tommy, at fourteen, was already playing in the men's high goal games and my father, a year younger, was relegated to the boys' league. Undoubtedly, love of horses, polo, and a shared Southern heritage drew them together.

Over the years, Jackson seized every chance as a three-handicap player to be on the same polo field with Hitchcock, flew private planes with him at the Old Aviation Country Club, lived nearby in Long Island, and became Tommy's close friend and lawyer. Shared experience in World War II brought them even closer. I became aware of the extent of their friendship through the recent biography of my father cited below. Most dramatic to me and the focus of this epilogue was their wartime partnership in the Battle of the Atlantic, which, as Winston Churchill commented, was crucial to Allied victory in Europe.

Nelson Aldrich has amply documented in this book Tommy Hitchcock's pivotal role in developing the Mustang P-51B fighter, a game-changing breakthrough in World War II. What Aldrich could not have included because records were highly classified and until recently unavailable were Hitchcock's indefatigable efforts to reverse a disastrous U.S. Navy anti-submarine doctrine and implement a winning strategy of

---

*Vic Currier, *Good-bye, Lord, I'm Going to New York: The Secret Life of Belle Meade's William Harding Jackson*, Random House/Xlibris, 2015. Quotations below are excerpted, with the author's consent, from this book, and this epilogue would not have been possible without his ground-breaking research.

destroying German U-boats in the Bay of Biscay. Details of his involvement in this critical area have recently emerged from the Eisenhower and Truman Libraries and are included in the biography footnoted above.

As Aldrich writes, Hitchcock insisted that my father fly down to Washington with him just days after Pearl Harbor to enlist together as active duty fighter pilots in the coming war. Both were in their forties, and they were turned down flat by the chief of the Army Air Force, General "Hap" Arnold, despite flying experience, Hitchcock's heroic World War I record with the Lafayette Escadrille, and extensive lobbying with the top military brass. After several non-flying billets, Hitchcock was picked up by the American ambassador in London, his old history teacher and mentor at St. Paul's School, Gil Winant, to be assistant air attaché with responsibility for anti-submarine warfare. Meanwhile, my father was shifted to a less glamorous navy desk job close to his law office on Wall Street.

Hitchcock began his work on anti-submarine warfare with the RAF in London during April 1942, while Jackson started at the Anti-Submarine Command at 90 Church Street in New York during June. They would soon have reason to collaborate on one of the major strategic decisions of World War II. In the meantime, Jackson was responsible for recording all German submarine sightings in the eastern coastal region. In a pre-computer age, this involved mounting a ladder in the war room to place pins on a huge wall map for each sighting. He worked the night shift, allowing him to put in daytime hours at his law office. Jackson soon concluded that U.S. anti-submarine doctrine was a dismal failure and that some seven hundred German U-boats were operating with impunity from the French Bay of Biscay up to ten miles or less from New York and Boston. Although not a serious threat, in the Pacific as well the Japanese launched an aircraft from a submarine off the coast of Oregon. In the Gulf of Mexico too, twenty Nazi U-boats were operating and sank fifty ships off Texas and Louisiana.

Allied shipping losses were catastrophic, totaling some thirty-five hundred vessels, and the number was continuing to rise. For example, in the second half of 1940, U-boats sank 2.5 million tons of allied shipping,

2.9 million in the first half of 1941, 1.4 million in the second half, and rising to 4.1 million in the first half of 1942. Between January and June of 1942, German U-boats launched a concerted campaign off Cape Hatteras, which marine archaeology is only now bringing to light. Though they were usually caught, German submarines also regularly landed spies and saboteurs along the U.S. coast at sites from Hancock Point, Maine, to Ponte Vedra Beach, Florida. The bottom line was that, U.S. Navy propaganda notwithstanding, German U-boats dominated the Atlantic shipping lanes for the better part of five years under the command of Nazi Admiral Karl Doenitz, inflicting grievous losses at will.

Jackson sought and improbably received authorization to assemble a small staff to prepare an "Intelligence Estimate of the Situation" in which he documented overwhelming Allied losses, pilloried official U.S. Navy doctrine of separate U.S. responsibility for our coasts and British for theirs, and went on to recommend U.S. aircraft support for an all-out offensive against German U-boats in the shallow waters of the Bay of Biscay as they exited submarine pens in Brest, Lorient, St. Nazaire, La Rochelle, and Bordeaux. Throughout this critical period, whenever he was in the U.S. on Lend Lease or other missions, Hitchcock made a point to share anti-submarine intelligence with Jackson and to assure him that, "Between the two of us we can get all the information you need from the coastal command and, if necessary, from the British admiralty, where most of this stuff emanates." Jackson and Hitchcock shared intelligence with British Air Vice Marshall Sir John Slessor from whose *The Central Blue* (Frederick Praeger, 1957) Currier quotes:

"My case was that the Atlantic Ocean was one battlefield and that the Allies, the Americans and ourselves, had between us more than enough properly equipped long-range anti-submarine aircraft in the Atlantic, if only they were concentrated in sufficient numbers in the right place, which was where the opportunities offered to kill U-boats, on the convoys and in the Bay (of Biscay)."

The estimate was circulated in late 1942 just after a glowing commendation from Admiral Adolphus Andrews of the Eastern Coastal Command Center for claimed "successes" against German U-boats and was met with a firestorm from the navy brass. CNO Admiral King went ballistic and ordered that all copies of the intelligence estimate be immediately destroyed and that any further distribution of navy intelligence be embargoed to both the army and the air force group. As Ludwell Lee Montague, an officer in the wartime OSS and subsequently a senior CIA historian, put it in official histories of the CIA (1971 and 1992):

"Captain Jackson had the temerity to produce an analysis of the effectiveness of anti-submarine warfare as it was then being conducted off the U.S. East Coast. He showed that it was a dismal failure and urged that the Army units involved be sent to reinforce the RAF Coastal Command for a concerted attack on the German submarines at their source in the Bay of Biscay. Captain Jackson's report infuriated the U.S. Navy from Admiral King on down, but it delighted the Army-Air Force. Jackson was reassigned to be Assistant Military Air Attaché in London in liaison with the Coastal Command. His recommendation was eventually carried out, although it took the personal intervention of the Secretary of War to overcome the bitter opposition of the Navy."

The estimate thus stirred army-navy inter-service rivalries, but Jackson nevertheless received strong support from Navy Secretary James Forrestal, a prewar law client, as well as from Secretary of War Henry Stimson, a Long Island neighbor with whom he had worked as president of the New York Bar Association. Hitchcock, for his part, made sure that copies of the embargoed estimate quickly reached British Air Vice Marshall Slessor as well as Commodore and Chief of Combined Operations Lord Louis Mountbatten. The report also reached and was closely studied by U.S. Army Chief of Staff George Marshall and General "Hap" Arnold, commander of the army–air forces.

As soon as Secretary Stimson overrode Admiral King's resistance and took the Bay of Biscay decision transferring the focus of anti-submarine operations to the coast of France, Hitchcock arranged with Ambassador Winant for Jackson's rapid transfer to the embassy where they worked together to implement the decision, had adjacent offices, and, for a time, shared a house. Jackson arrived in London in late January 1943 as part of the air transport command's European wing, responsible for ferrying thousands of aircraft to Britain. He was soon promoted to major and then lieutenant colonel and worked closely with Assistant Secretary of War for Air Power Robert Lovett.

Fresh intelligence was critical to both Hitchcock and Jackson in implementing the Bay of Biscay decision, and Hitchcock proved as good as his word in this realm, acquiring advance copies directly from the British admiralty's first sea lord of the monthly *Royal Navy Red Book*, pinpointing the location of every known German submarine in the Atlantic or in port. Jackson wrote to Hitchcock's wife, Peggy, "I simply couldn't do my job without Tommy here." Equally important to their work together was a continuing close relationship with Slessor, a frequent visitor to Washington whose foremost concern was the U-boat menace. As the U.S. Navy delayed delivery of the promised Liberator bombers, Slessor strongly supported Hitchcock and Jackson's efforts to augment pressure on Washington to make the necessary resources available for antisubmarine warfare. Slessor arranged for both Hitchcock and Jackson to take part in separate extended anti-submarine missions along the French and Spanish coasts with British crews in B-24 Liberator bombers in order to have firsthand knowledge of the techniques involved.

In addition to Slessor, the Bay of Biscay decision was welcomed by the entire British high command including Churchill, who worked closely with Roosevelt to broaden it into the "Casablanca Directive on the Bomber Offensive," adopted at the Casablanca Conference on January 21, 1943, and specifically targeting destruction of German submarine yards as the highest Allied priority. And yet, despite this clear directive, Admiral King continued to drag his feet on the commitment to provide six squadrons of Liberators (seventy-two aircraft) for the Bay of Biscay. Slessor was appalled and complained directly to President Roosevelt during a June 24, 1943, private meeting at the White House set up for him by Harry Hopkins. Marshall and Stimson had already met directly with Churchill on the matter earlier in the month, and Jackson also returned to Washington in July 1943 to convey an urgent British request for the Liberators to Stimson, Marshall, and General Arnold. Finally in late July the impasse was broken, although General Marshall had to intervene on several further occasions to ensure U.S. Navy compliance.

Despite navy recalcitrance, the new anti-submarine strategy soon proved amply justified as growing pressure from Allied bombers, as well as Royal Navy sub-chasers, put German U-boats on the defensive for the first time and, in less than a year, five hundred were sunk in the Bay of Biscay and North Atlantic with loss of thirty thousand German personnel. Germany's five-year domination of the Atlantic was ended, paving the way for D-Day in June 1944.

Revisiting the chronology of 1943–44, it is almost impossible to imagine the pressures and tight deadlines that Allied officers, particularly Hitchcock, were operating under. Implementation of the Bay of Biscay decision and delayed arrival of the Liberator bombers to do the job was barely in time to sink the German U-boat fleet, winning the Battle of the Atlantic and ensuring control of the English Channel for the Normandy invasion. Almost simultaneously, Hitchcock was supervising tight production deadlines for the Mustang P-51B fighter and making the ultimate sacrifice to personally flight test the aircraft to correct a fuel tank stability issue, thus ensuring Allied air superiority over Normandy just two months later.

—Richard L. Jackson
Wellington, Florida

APPENDIX: MEMORIES OF A HERO

AMONG THE PHOTOGRAPHS IN MY LIBRARY ARE TWO OF THOMAS Hitchcock Jr., the only authentic hero I ever knew well. The first time I heard of him was at Fay School in Southborough, Massachusetts. He was two classes ahead of me and had graduated when I entered.

In the fall of 1912, I was looking at pictures of old Fay School football teams that lined the hall leading to the school library. An older boy, Ellis Jones, joined me, and pointing over my shoulder at one player, he said in an awestruck voice, "That's Tommy Hitchcock."

"Was he a very good player?" I asked.

"No," said Ellis, "He was not particularly good, but that's Tommy Hitchcock, honest to God it is."

There was something in the look of Tommy in this photograph of him as a twelve-year-old boy that enlisted me among his legions of hero worshippers, even before I saw him or had evidence of his potential for anything.

The summer of 1914, I met Tommy Hitchcock at Narragansett. Although there were boys' polo teams and boys' games, Tommy at fourteen played with the men in the high goal polo with Foxhall Keene handicapped at nine goals and others at six or seven, and possibly eight. I do not recall whether Tommy was handicapped at all, but he was as much of a prodigy at polo as his contemporary Bobby Jones was at golf. He had perfect form and had already developed the strength and timing to slice the ball on the near or fore side forward, and the same on the backhand. At that time Tommy seemed more interested in developing his technique and the strokes that no one had ever made consistently than in winning a particular game. Yet I doubt that any player at Narragansett that summer failed to recognize this boy as potentially the greatest polo player of all time. Seven years later he played on the American team against the British. The Americans won and brought the International Cup to America for the first time. The following year, 1922, Tommy was handicapped at ten goals, the highest a polo player can receive. It represents theoretical perfection in polo, and it forms the basis of all handicapping.

One of my pictures is a faded photograph of Hitchcock in action on a polo field. His pony is obviously a thoroughbred. Hitchcock has sliced the ball from in front of the goal his team is defending, toward the side boards and is just turning, much like a professional hockey player, before setting sail down the field. The pony is running at top speed and as he turns, the camera has caught him with all four feet off the ground. Tommy is in perfect cadence with his mount and, prepared for his next shot, he has the relaxed grace of a great golfer, matador, or ballet dancer.

Tommy's sister gave me that old photograph after his death and said that their father, once a nine-goal player himself, considered it the most typical and the best photograph ever taken of Tommy on the polo field.

From 1922 until his retirement from polo in 1939, except for one year following a serious injury when he was rated at nine goals, Hitchcock was handicapped at ten. For seventeen years he was at the top of his sport. There were, of course, other ten-goal players from time to time during these seventeen years, in Argentina, perhaps in England or India, and at least four that I can recall in the United States. But there are few, if any, athletes in any sport who have remained in the number one position for so long. There is certainly no such tennis player or golfer. Perhaps Hitchcock should be compared with baseball players such as Babe Ruth or Christy Mathewson.

Sometime in the late 1920s, I had the misfortune of playing against Hitchcock in a twenty-goal tournament match. Handicapped at ten himself, Tommy had to have three teammates with an aggregate of only ten goals. On the other hand, my team's total of twenty goals was more evenly balanced among the four players.

An incident occurred that was characteristic of Hitchcock. In the course of the game, I got the ball and hit it in the direction of the goal he was defending. He came in from my left to ride me off the ball at such speed and at such an angle that he knocked my pony to his knees and me out of the saddle. As I was falling off, he reached across with his left hand, in which he was holding the four reins of a double bridle, and pulled me back in the saddle. Tommy still had time to hit a near side backhand at the last split second a long way in the opposite direction. This not only showed unusual concern for an opponent on a polo field, but a mastery of the game itself that few other players possessed.

Playing on Tommy's team would make almost anybody look like a high-goal player. He was always a generous team player, and he could slice or fade or pull the ball with the accuracy of a good golfer, and often right in front of a teammate who was free. He played on a team in France one summer with Winston Churchill and acquired the future prime minister as an ardent fan and lifelong friend.

The details of Hitchcock's athletic supremacy have been given because they are so revealing of the man himself and particularly of the fighter pilot of both world wars: his generosity, his courage, complete confidence, security without the slightest need for self-assertion or conceit, natural leadership in any group without regard to rank, and, of course, perfect timing and the eye of a crack shot.

The second of my photographs of Tommy Hitchcock is the only posed picture I ever saw of him. His wife and I had conspired for many weeks in 1942 to persuade him to have it taken, and another two or three weeks were required to get him to wear his World War I decorations for the picture.

In 1917 Tommy was in the sixth form at St. Paul's school in New Hampshire. In April, at the age of seventeen, he left to join the Lafayette Escadrille and one of his teachers, Mr. Gil Winant, went with him. If Mr. Winant was not already a fan of Tommy, he certainly became an ardent admirer during World War I. As ambassador to the Court of St. James during World War II, he let Tommy, an assistant military air attaché, do anything he wanted to do, and he accepted almost every suggestion Tommy made, including the one that I also be made an assistant military air attaché as cover for my actual job.

In December 1917, Hitchcock had completed his training as a fighter pilot in the Lafayette Escadrille, and was sent to the front. Stationed at Luneville, one of the quietest sectors on the front, Tommy singlehanded stirred up the whole sector. Flying antiquated Nieuports, he was always in the air searching for the enemy far into Germany. He shot down two German planes and was wounded and shot down in Germany. In one of the most sensational escapes of the war, he jumped from a train full of Germans and made his way by night to Switzerland. He received the Croix de Guerre with four palms.

In the period between the World Wars, although playing superlative polo, Hitchcock managed to graduate from Harvard College in an abbreviated course for war veterans. He had little interest in academic education. The veterans of World War I were far too old in experience for their contemporaries in college. Unlike the veterans of World War II, and in the absence of a GI Bill of Rights, they did not show increased interest and diligence in pursuing an academic education. In Tommy's case, and in the light of his World War II contributions, I believe he should have become a mechanical engineer in which field he had great imagination and creativity.

After graduation from Harvard, Hitchcock worked for Lehman Brothers, an investment banking firm in downtown New York, and became a partner. Lehman Brothers owned the controlling stock of a shipping company, American Export Lines, and acting alone, as usual, Tommy conceived the idea that the shipping company should have a transport airline subsidiary to fly the Atlantic. Tommy, a member of the board of directors of the parent shipping company, became chairman of the board, and in effect the chief executive officer of the subsidiary, American Export Airlines. With only one airplane and only limited experience, Tommy then went head to head with Juan Trippe, the president of Pan American, who was a brilliant entrepreneur. He was not used to losing, but neither was Tommy. Trippe brought every pressure of which he was capable to persuade American Export Airlines to withdraw its challenge, but he had met his match. No force could persuade Tommy to withdraw his opposition to Pan Am's application for exclusive passenger flights across the Atlantic. He showed no more fear of Trippe than he had of anything or anybody else, and in the end a substantial proportion of the landing permits were withheld and Tommy had built an overseas airline out of whole cloth.

Although I never discussed politics with Tommy, I had understood from others in the late thirties that he favored the foreign policy of America first. I was surprised when he called me on the Monday morning following the attack on Pearl Harbor and asked:

"What are you going to get into?"

"I have not had time to think much about it," I said.

"Flying fighters will be the big game, like playing on the number one field," he said.

"For men of forty and forty-one?" I asked.

"Sure," he said. "Let's go to Washington tomorrow and look around."

Although I had not even decided to volunteer for any service in uniform, I agreed to go with him to Washington.

Flying down there the next morning we discussed the possibility of either of us getting our wings, much less achieving the exacting status of a fighter pilot. I had flown land planes ten to fifteen years later than Tommy, who had not flown a land plane, so far as I know, since he was shot down in 1918. He had, however, flown consistently in a pontoon sea plane, which he used to commute from his house on Long Island Sound at Sands Point.

Flying with Hitchcock in this commuter was an exciting experience in itself. One Saturday we went to Princeton for a football game and landed on Lake Carnegie. The ceiling was very low and neither of us could fly on instruments. We had to fly at three or four hundred feet where the air was very turbulent, and for most of the trip, we could not have reached any water if the single motor had quit. The weather deteriorated during the game. The ceiling was coming down, and I persuaded Tommy, with difficulty, to leave before the game was over. On our way down to Lake Carnegie from the stadium, we discussed where to drop me off in New York. I suggested that we go on to Sands Point, where there would be an easy landing off his beach and I could take the train back to New York. He said that was ridiculous and that he planned to drop me off at the ferry boat landing near my apartment at 84th Street.

"There are dangerous tides there," I said.

"The tides are about the same as at the foot of Wall Street," he replied. He landed in the East River off Wall Street almost every weekday, regardless of weather.

"The hell they are," I said. "I have seen them turn the ferry boat around."

He was the pilot and I was the guest, and he decided to land in the East River off the ferry boat landing.

The ceiling had now come down to about three hundred feet and the turbulence was so great that I thought the plane might break up. I saw Tommy reaching around in his briefcase. I thought he was looking for a map, which was necessary because we were, of course, flying contact and we were just above the freeway leading to the Lincoln Tunnel under the Hudson. Not at all. He handed me a sheaf of papers relating to the American Export Airlines and suggested that I look them over from a legal point of view.

"Well, I'll be damned," I said to myself.

The tides were ripping all right when we landed off East 86th Street. The plane surprisingly did not flip, thanks to Tommy's skill as a pilot. It would have been curtains for us both, as no swimmer could have survived in these currents and the cold water for long. The plane spun around three or four times when the pontoons hit the currents, but with nearly full throttle it crossed them to reach the ferry landing and help from on shore.

Tommy's take-off was almost equally difficult. The Triborough and the Hell Gate bridges were shrouded in fog, and the last I saw of Tommy that late afternoon, he was flying under both bridges on his way to Long Island Sound. He was surprised when I called him at his house to see if he had reached home safely.

When we arrived in Washington, if any of the Air Force brass had known of Tommy's experience with his seaplane, the conclusion could only have been that he had great skill in flying a slow seaplane and courage to the point of recklessness. This experience did not prove that Tommy could fly a land plane that was even as fast in the air and in landing as an Army Trainer. It certainly did not prove that at forty-one and in the absence of continuing experience with increasingly fast fighters, he had the stamina or the speed of reflex to fly fighters.

Tommy knew many of the air force generals and probably most of them knew him by reputation as a World War I pilot or as a top polo player or, perhaps, as the chairman of the board of a phantom overseas airline. We went right to the top, as was Tommy's custom, where we found General Arnold himself. Later, we saw many other air corps generals in their offices, at an airfield near Washington, and informally at our hotel, where we gave them all they would drink. Drunk or sober, no one gave either of us the slightest encouragement or held out any hope of our flying in World War II in any capacity.

Many offered one or both of us ground jobs and commissions in administration, and others recommended that we inquire in Air Corps Intelligence.

This was no surprise or disappointment to me. I had no particular desire to fly at all and no desire whatever to fly fighters. It was, however, a bitter disappointment to Thomas Hitchcock Jr. and an inauspicious beginning for a creative, imaginative, and ever-persevering engineer who in his own way and as a lieutenant colonel was to command a combat fighter group and ultimately receive the Distinguished Flying Cross. He would also have been on anyone's list of a hundred individuals in the European theater of operations who were indispensable to victory and irreplaceable in their jobs.

Turned down flat for flying in any capacity, even to flying Piper Cubs as observers or spotters, we took the advice we received and applied to Air Corps Intelligence then under G-2 or Army Intelligence. Tommy, as usual, knew someone there: Colonel Merion Cooper, a flyer in World War I and a prominent movie director after the war, who had gone back into air intelligence a year or two before the United States entered World War II. He wanted Tommy, and would accept me, to accompany him on a secret mission, which he implied was to China. Our commissions did not come through for a month or six weeks. Tommy was made a major and I a captain.

When we arrived in Air Force Intelligence, Colonel Cooper had disappeared and no one expected us. Tommy moved fast, and a friend of his, General Olds, commanding the Ferrying Command, afterward the Air Transport Command, requested and obtained his transfer to be in charge of freight. I moved more slowly and was picked up by Colonel Trubee Davison in Administration of Air Intelligence personnel. This was the last place I wanted to be. Tommy then effected almost at once my transfer to Ferrying Command to do law work. This was the first of several rescue jobs he did for me.

The job was ridiculously frustrating. I drew contracts in longhand using a packing box for a desk. My stenographer, with a low rating in the air force civilian personnel, could not take dictation and made hundreds of mistakes and typographical errors copying my drafts. The Ferrying Command, of course, had no law books.

Sometime during these months of my frustration, Tommy took a long and dangerous step in the direction of his ultimate objective. I assume he persuaded General Olds to get him a test by the Air Corps for his wings. The Lafayette Escadrille wings of World War I were his only credential. He resisted my suggestion that he take some private lessons and learn to fly the fastest planes available at a private school, even if he had to ask for a leave of absence from the Ferrying Command. So one afternoon I went with him to watch him take his test. It was the most painful afternoon I spent in World War II.

The Air Corps was not anxious to lose an applicant or one of its trainers. The trainer had dual controls and a back seat copilot accompanied him. Tommy was unaware of the strength of the torque or pull from the line of flight of a faster plane than he had ever flown and the necessity for quicker and more delicate rudder corrections as the speed increased. The plane went down the runway with the progress of a big snake. The copilot must have pulled the plane off as it approached the end of the field, although Tommy was then headed across wind.

Once in the air, Tommy, unaware of the steepness of the bank required for turning, skidded the plane all over the sky. Then he overshot the field three times in a row. After these three extremely dangerous passes, the copilot, by Tommy's own later admission, took over and landed the plane.

I walked out on the field when the plane stopped. The copilot got out first and muttered angrily to me, "I'll never fly with that one again," and walked off without waiting for Tommy or speaking to him.

On the way home, Tommy was obviously shaken and let me drive our car.

"Tommy," I said, "I think you flunked."

"I'm coming back here the first thing in the morning before it can be made official," he replied.

The next morning, Tommy and I were up early, but he could hardly walk.

"What's the matter?" I asked.

"My thighs are stiff," he said, "You know my knees shook pretty badly during that test."

Tommy never gave way to fear or showed it in any way. For the first time, I realized that he was even aware of danger.

"Do you think you could fly that trainer?" he asked.

"Yes, I do," I said, "It is very like my own plane."

"Well then, so can I," he said.

Fortunately, I had to go to the office and Tommy dropped me there.

He picked me up again at about dusk. He said at once, "I got my wings."

"How in God's name did you manage that?" I asked incredulously.

He had persuaded the commander of the field that if he were given some instruction, he could pass the test on the trainer before dark. For some mysterious reason never explained by Tommy or understood by me, the colonel in command fell for the suggestion and gave Tommy instruction himself all day long with a short break for lunch. The colonel began with the slowest land plane they had on the field and worked up to the official trainer. With Tommy's amazing aptitude for flying and with eight or nine hours of instruction, it was not surprising that he was able to fly the trainer alone and pass the test.

Two or three weeks later, the colonel, in his early thirties, came for drinks at our house. He told me that Tommy then could fly a trainer as well as anyone at the base. Tommy was on his way.

I heard of the formation of a school for air combat intelligence officers. Again with Tommy's indispensable help, I managed to obtain my assignment to the second session of this school at Harrisburg, Pennsylvania.

Before I left for Harrisburg, Tommy and I composed a letter to Ambassador Winant. This "Dear Gil" letter suggested that Mr. Winant ask for Hitchcock's assignment as an assistant military air attaché at the embassy in London. Tommy said that the Royal Air Force had the best training methods, doubtless true, of any air force in the world and that our air corps should be entirely clear that the only way to learn about training methods was to take the courses himself. Knowing Tommy's indomitable perseverance and his relationship to Mr. Winant, it was certain that was exactly what he would do. Mr. Winant and his American wings would be a sufficient introduction to the RAF training schools.

His transfer to the embassy in London came through. Tommy was now really on his way and part of his future in the air corps could be foreseen, but the extent of his success could not have been anticipated by anyone because no one suspected his hidden, creative abilities as a mechanical engineer.

The last phase of my military career in which Hitchcock participated with tremendous effect came after I graduated from the Harrisburg Intelligence School and ended up at the Anti-Submarine Command, with headquarters at 90 Church Street, not very far from my own office on Wall Street. This Air Corps Command was under the navy's Eastern Sea Frontier, commanded by Admiral Andrews.

The U.S. Navy anti-submarine strategy was clearly failing with German U-boats ranging at will from Maine to Florida, with enormous losses to American and British shipping. Finally, I inveigled my way into writing an intelligence estimate of the situation.

The timing of its completion and circulation in the spring of 1943 was unfortunate. Admiral Andrews, in charge of the Anti-Submarine Command, had just congratulated the Eastern Sea Frontier on its success against German submarines. The estimate came to the conclusion that the previous month had reached the peak of shipping losses to submarines attained in either World War. The authors, never having written an estimate before, went far beyond the scope of the intelligence paper and recommended U.S. aircraft support an all-out offensive against the submarines in the Bay of Biscay, where most of them were based in impenetrable concrete pens along the shore. This just happened to be the precise opposite of Admiral King's strategy, in which the United States would defend its half of the Atlantic and the British theirs.

Admiral Andrews was incensed by the paper. The estimate was justified on the grounds that it was based solely on navy data. When the commanding general of the Anti-Submarine Command found out about the navy's opposition, he gave the estimate the widest possible circulation, including a copy to British Coastal Command. The U.S. Navy's retaliation was to withhold all important current data on submarines from army and air corps intelligence at all levels. Frustration set in again, in earnest.

Then Hitchcock arrived from England on some mission, and called me at the Anti-Submarine Command headquarters. He was aware of the seriousness of the submarine situation and of Ambassador Winant's concern about it. As usual, he had a solution for me. Mr. Winant would have me assigned to the embassy in London as an assistant military air attaché.

"Between the two of us we can get all the information you need from Coastal Command and, if necessary, from the British Admiralty, where most of this stuff emanates," Tommy said.

"Does Mr. Winant want me?" I asked.

"Not yet," said Tommy.

My transfer orders came through almost immediately after Tommy got back to London, and when I reported to the embassy there it was still early spring of 1943. My office was next to Tommy's again, and we shared a house in London part of the time.

The first document I mentioned to Tommy as most urgently needed was a Royal Navy publication called the *Red Book*, issued every month, giving the estimated position of every known German submarine in the Atlantic or in port. This intelligence was compiled on the basis of the most highly classified information, observation on the ground by resistance workers placed in the vicinity of the Bay of Biscay ports, sightings at sea, radio intercepts, cryptography, minute calculations of speed and probable direction, etc. Unless current, the *Red Book* was practically useless. We had received it a month or two late in the Anti-Submarine Command, and after the circulation of our infamous estimate of the situation, not at all. Tommy promised to help me on the following Monday because he was flying to Scotland to shoot over the weekend.

On Monday, Tommy came into the office with the *Red Book* issued two days before. I could only give him my how-in-God's-name look of old.

"The First Sea Lord invited me to shoot with him in Scotland, and I flew him up there in the embassy plane," Tommy explained. Upon their return, they had stopped at the admiralty, where the First Sea Lord had given Tommy his own copy of the *Red Book* without even asking for a receipt.

Later that Monday afternoon, Tommy introduced me to his old friend, Air Marshall Slessor, commanding Coastal Command. Slessor had read the intelligence estimate sent to Coastal Command by the commander of our Anti-Submarine Command. He heartily approved the recommended offensive in the Bay of Biscay because he had already launched it before he read the estimate.

Several weeks later, Air Marshall Slessor asked me if I would like to fly an anti-submarine mission in a British B-24 or Liberator in the Bay of Biscay. This mission was in the new, continuous rectangular pattern over an area of the Bay where a German submarine of that time must surface twice in going across. I was still working hard to get six squadrons of Americans and American planes on the Bay. This was a fine opportunity for firsthand observation, and I readily accepted.

When I told Tommy about it, he arranged to go in another Liberator at about the same time in the early morning of a Saturday and offered to fly me down to southern England the preceding Friday afternoon. At this point, Tommy had made a study of, and incidentally himself graduated from, an RAF fighter pilot school and been checked out on Spitfires. He flew the embassy planes on every possible occasion to improve his instrument flying.

He improved his instrument flying on our way to the south of England. He would concentrate solely on the instruments, and it was my job in the copilot's seat to observe the horizon and other landmarks of contact flying and to notify him if he was flying off keel. Unfortunately he would sometimes get into clouds suddenly, and we would be entirely dependent on his instruments until we could see the ground again.

After he tired of instrument flying, he suggested that he navigate and I fly the plane. As usual as navigator, he fell asleep. He was soon rudely awakened when we dropped about twenty feet. I thought we had been attacked by the entire German Air Force. Actually, a squadron of Spitfires returning from France had come down very fast out of a cloud behind and above us and gone over and under and on either side of us.

"Spits," said Tommy, and went back to sleep. He slept peacefully the rest of the way almost to Land's End.

The next morning Tommy left on his mission before dawn and before I had breakfast. It seemed like an unnecessary mission for him as this patrolling of the enormous rectangle in the Bay of Biscay off the German submarine pens at the French ports was beginning to hurt the submarines. They were often escorted part way by German fighters and a submarine would fight back on the surface against a single, lightly armed Liberator bomber. Although Tommy's plane made no sighting, I believe his flight was very important to him in convincing him of the ultimately winning capacity of the Bay tactic, which had been devised mathematically largely by British civilian scientists. Once convinced, Tommy enlisted all-out in the cause of more planes patrolling under British Coastal Command in the Bay.

I was different because I was already convinced, but now I had Tommy's priceless support. My mission in fact had lifetime implications for me. It was more eventful than Tommy's when I spotted what I thought were two German Ju 88s in the distance. These planes outgunned us and our best hope would have been to outdistance them flying westward toward the Atlantic. My hand was on the intercom to warn the captain when I hesitated. The crew was experienced in these missions off France in the Bay of Biscay, and a number of them could see as well as I could, and especially the captain. I was the only officer aboard and an American at that. What if the planes were friendly? I would sweat it out for a little longer, and watch them. I waited in great discomfort, but not for long. The tail gunner rang the captain and I picked up the intercom. "Ju 88s at nine o'clock," said the tail gunner. "Bloody Beau fighters," replied the captain calmly, "you silly clown." I breathed a sigh of relief that I had not called the captain, but I was even more relieved that the approaching planes were friendly.

Soon after the Beau fighters scare on my part and that of the tail gunner, we were diverted westward to a spot where another Liberator was circling a German submarine proceeding westward on the surface. A single Liberator at that time was forbidden to make a bombing run against the surface gun power of a submarine. The submarine would presumably submerge at the approach of a supporting bomber. The spot was a good many miles distant, but we went at the top speed. We saw the submarine submerge as we approached, the only non-captive German submarine I ever saw in World War II. The other Liberator made its bombing run but I never knew whether it was successful or not.

The Sunday following our missions, Tommy and I started back to London via Debden, an old RAF base where Tommy's nephew, Avy Clark, was stationed with an American group of P-47 fighters. The flight was uneventful in surprisingly clear weather for England. In the course of this flight, Tommy decided to practice fighter attack on a small de Haviland Moth approaching us in the opposite direction. We dove at the Moth, and presumably an RAF fighter, returning home for Sunday, simulated the correct retaliatory measure and would have been in position to shoot us down. Tommy was delighted. He wagged his wings, as did the Moth pilot, and each proceeded on his way.

As we approached the area of Debden, a P-47 attacked us from above and slightly behind. Avy Clark, who had been "shaking it out" on Sunday and also watching for Uncle Tommy, flew across our prop at great speed and close enough for us to recognize him. He led us in to the landing field at Debden, and we had tea or drinks at the base. Then we flew on to where the two embassy planes were kept, which was still nearer London, and we had dinner in London that night.

The next morning, Tommy must have discussed the Bay of Biscay offensive with Ambassador Winant for shortly afterward the ambassador called me to his office, and we discussed this strategy at length. I pointed out that a great many more pilots and planes were necessary for the continuity that would sooner or later ensure success or effective victory over the German submarines. I do not know with whom Ambassador Winant discussed this strategy, surely with others of more authority, and perhaps certainly with Air Marshall Slessor.

As a captain, I often reminded myself of General Bedell Smith's story of the woodpecker who was pecking on an old oak tree. When a great wind blew the tree down, the woodpecker thought he had pecked it over.

Ambassador Winant sent me back for a brief visit to the United States and talks with our Anti-Submarine Command, but particularly with Secretary of War Stimson. I have no way of knowing how or for what reasons the final decision was made. I suspect it was Secretary Stimson himself, greatly influenced by his chief assistant Mr. Harvey Bundy, persuading or forcing it over Admiral King's dissent. But six squadrons of army and air force planes were decided to be withdrawn from the eastern sea frontier or elsewhere at about this time and placed under British Coastal Command in the Bay of Biscay. Although the total of six squadrons, or seventy-two planes, was never, I believe, actually reached, the number came at one time to five squadrons.

Then in early June 1943, an agreement was reached that the army would turn over all anti-submarine operations to the navy and the navy in theory would quit other long-range bombing. The navy was to man the agreed six squadrons in the Bay on September 1. By July, Admiral King was threatening to withdraw or not to supply or man any planes in the Bay of Biscay.

In July, Mr. Stimson and Mr. Bundy were in England, and I was summoned to their house in the country. The three of us drafted a letter to the secretary of the navy, and I believe to President Roosevelt for Mr. Stimson's signature. I am sure that Mr. Stimson had a talk with Air Marshall Slessor, and finally with the prime minister, who also intervened with President Roosevelt. Mr. Stimson took the firm position that the commitment in the Bay was that of the United States, and that the army planes would remain until the navy took over. This view prevailed, and when the navy did take over in the fall of 1943, I was transferred to ground forces.

When I left the embassy and joined the intelligence division of General Dever's staff, and not long after General Bradley's staff of 12th Army Group, I saw less of Tommy, although we often met for dinner or during other off hours. I never again had the help he had given me on anti-submarine war, or the support Mr. Winant gave me indirectly.

On one occasion, I remember when we were having difficulty getting very long-range bombers, Tommy heard of a disastrous flight of a group of two-motored B-26 bombers, which were then in great disrepute with American flyers. Tommy suggested that we go to the base of this group, so that he could fly one. He did this, and concluded that the plane was excellent, which they proved beyond a doubt in the balance of the war. When it came to offering them to British Coastal Command for use in the Bay of Biscay, it was then refused by the American Air Forces.

In addition to helping anyone to help to win, Tommy steadily pursued his own job, or the job he had prescribed for himself. After learning to fly Spitfire fighters at an RAF school, he was admitted, I believe in the late summer of 1943, to an RAF school for advanced gunnery and tactics. The attendance consisted solely of RAF pilots with combat experience—and Tommy. The other attendants were all approximately twenty years younger than Tommy, but he scored first in the gunnery course over these young men who were experienced fighter pilots and had survived in actual combat against young and very capable German members of the Luftwaffe.

After the gunnery course one of the young RAF pilots asked Tommy to serve as an usher in his wedding, to be held in Scotland. They were to fly up in the embassy plane, and I drove them to the airport.

On the way, Tommy commented on the low ceiling and generally bad weather.

"This is ideal for my work," said the young pilot, who flew intruder missions over France at high speed and at low altitude under the radar. Tommy glanced at him. I was surprised, for I don't believe anybody ever heard of Tommy turning back because of weather.

Although Tommy made outstanding contributions to the development of improved weapons and aircraft devices used in the European Theatre of Operations, and especially a machine gun sight, his greatest achievement was the acceptance by the United States of the Rolls-Royce Merlin–powered Mustang plane. The Mustang, built in the United States and powered by an American-built Alison motor, was used only by the British in the ETO (European Theater of Operations). This was the P-51A, or simply P-5 as it was then known. The excellent design of the P-51's, or more popularly Mustang's, air frame gave it less drag and more speed, despite the lack of power of the Alison motor. The great advantage of installing the two-stage Rolls-Royce Merlin in the American-built Mustang was immediately obvious to Tommy. This project and the plane that finally emerged was the P-51B. There was a general lack of interest in the project among high American officers and other officials in our air force, both in England and in the United States.

From May 1942, Tommy's greatest desire and all his available time were devoted to seeing our air force equipped with this fighter. It was first necessary, or certainly easier, to persuade the Rolls-Royce Company in England to put together the first model P-51B to be tested. So work was started at Boscombe Downs. The following is quoted from *The Central Blue*, by Marshall of the Royal Air Force, Sir John Slessor, page 332:

"This idea was taken up with great enthusiasm by Lieut. Colonel Tommy Hitchcock, the famous polo player, who was serving with the USAF in England, and was desperately anxious to see this American-built fighter make good. When it was on the point of undergoing flight trials, Tommy and I found ourselves together in the Pentagon, and bombarded General Arnold with curves and performance figures. Arnold was impressed, but not unnaturally said he would make up his mind when he saw how the results of the actual flight trials compared with the predicted program. Fortunately, a couple of days later we got a signal giving those results, which showed that the aircraft had in fact met and in some ways surpassed the calculated performance."

Tommy was soon back in England to test the P-51B himself. His nephew, Avy Clark, often spent his days on leave from routine fighter combat with his uncle and would fly with Tommy in the four-place Beechcraft used by the embassy. Avy's comments on the weather on such a flight with Tommy in the embassy plane, coming from a fighter pilot who was an ace many times over, are revealing:

"That was one of those days in England when you couldn't see anything, except straight down, haze. We had two bomber pilots in the back seat, just hooking a ride to this place we were trying to get to, and we got lost. We landed and asked where we were and found out. These guys took the train from there on."

Avy was visiting Tommy when he got back from America. Tommy, of course, took him in the Embassy Beechcraft when they went to see the P-51B. Referring to the day when the bomber pilots got off and took the train, Avy said, "It was the same kind of day. We flew up to Derby where the Rolls-Royce factory was. You'd better not fly that thing (the model P-51B); only the test pilot has ever flown it, and you're going to get lost."

Tommy said, in effect, to heck with it, and the man in charge of the plane, knowing who Thomas Hitchcock was and what he had done for the project, let him have it. After he had taken off with probably the best fighter bomber and the only model in existence, Avy said to the Rolls official, who had given permission, "Well, that's the last time you'll see that plane."

This put the Rolls official in a panic, and he telephoned all the airfields in the neighboring area. Tommy had gotten lost all right, but had managed to land the plane in a field about twenty miles away. Avy picked him up in a car. The plane was unhurt, but they left it in the field for the test pilot to fly back to Rolls-Royce in better weather. Finally, in justifying the whole procedure and ensuring that the plane was finally brought back to the Rolls Company, Avy gave the most enduring testimony to Tommy's part in the production of the P-51B.

"Oh yeah, he had a right to fly it. It was really his main idea."

In talking to me later, Tommy expressed the greatest confidence in the new plane based on its performance. He had flown it a great deal more than twenty miles and above the cloud cover and got lost trying to find his way back to the Rolls field descending through the clouds. He was now prepared to back the plane's statistics of rate of climb, speed, etc., on personal experience. He was also prepared to argue with anyone for the immediate production in the United States of the P-51B at highest priority and in large quantity. The only high officers or officials who would have any direct concern with the production of the plane with whom I don't believe Tommy did discuss it were the prime minister and the president of the United States, although I am not sure. I know that Tommy, shortly after his own test flight, made another trip to the United States and saw General Arnold again and, among others, I believe he saw both Harry Hopkins and Mrs. Franklin D. Roosevelt.

The United States Air Force went into production of the P-51B at high priority in 1943, and I know that Avy Clark's group was converted to flying these planes late in 1943.

The new planes arrived none too soon in the ETO. In the course of 1943, it became evident and particularly after Schweinfurt, that no strategic bombers, including the U.S. B-24s and the heavily armed B-17s, the Flying Fortress, could fly without fighter escort in a daylight raid deep in Germany. The Mustang with the Merlin motor was a high-level fighter with sharp rate of climb and great speed of four hundred miles an hour or more at high altitude. It also had extra built-in gasoline tanks and the longest range of any fighter. It could join the escort of the very long-range bombers beyond the range of other Allied fighters like the Spitfires, Thunderbirds, or Lightnings. I remember that Avy himself flew fighter escort in his new P-51B for the first time over Berlin. This plane is the tangible evidence of Tommy's contribution to victory. Without it the Allies would not have been winning the air war over Germany before D Day.

In December 1943, Lieutenant Colonel Hitchcock was given command of a fighter group flying Mustangs equipped with Merlin engines. He returned to the United States to take over his group. So far as I know, he had received but one day of training at that time by the Americans in the single day when he learned to fly the trainer and obtained his American wings, while he was assigned to the Ferrying Command as freight officer. He himself gave his group its advance training in fighter tactics, which was described as the most realistic in its simulation of actual modern fighting. When this group graduated and was transferred into combat, Tommy's was converted into a training command. This may have reflected the appreciation of the higher air force brass of his skill in final training of a group of fighters or the desire to save him for more valuable services out of combat because a group leader would customarily lead his group into combat and most surely Tommy would have done so. He returned to England in February 1944, as Deputy Chief of Staff of the 9th Air Support Command in charge of research and development.

On April 18, 1944, in a dive bombing test of a P-51B, the plane broke up in the air. He had no chance to jump and was killed instantly. It is thought that the plane's center of gravity was not right. It is known now that the plane cannot be subjected to maximum stress before some of its long-range tanks have been used up, or the plane has not been fully loaded at the start. However, I have not heard an official explanation except there was no pilot fault or escape. I believe that Tommy would have preferred to have been blamed himself than have any blame attached to that particular plane.

For his work leading to the development and acceptance of the P-51B and for his "brilliant airmanship and courage—in the execution of extremely hazardous test flights," Lieutenant Colonel Hitchcock was posthumously awarded the Legion of Merit and the Distinguished Flying Cross.

In the case of truly great men, they are especially hard to analyze because of the very fact that they are not average. Many people, while recognizing Tommy's greatness, would not have agreed on his outstanding qualities. Some said that one was his utter fearlessness. This would seem to be an oversimplification. He had outstanding determination, and in carrying it out his great courage overcame any fear. A life uninfluenced by fear was what made Hitchcock essentially different from most other people. It produced a total absence of malice arising out of jealousy. He seemed to be without envy. In fact, he had little to envy.

Many people would stress Tommy's competitiveness as his outstanding qualification. Tommy was, indeed, an all-out competitor in sports, flying, business, and other aspects of life. Here again this competitiveness came from deeper and greater qualities—his determination to win and the lack of restraint of fear permitted by his overriding courage. This produced a generous competitor, one who wished to win over his opponent's best game or effort. His victory or defeat were quietly accepted. I doubt that Tommy was capable of boasting. At least, I never heard him boast. Tommy Hitchcock was unique even then as one of the outstanding competitors of his time.

If Tommy had any scorn for others, it would be for those who, in his words, "put the ribbon above the game," the reward, the rank, the position, above the accomplishment.

The scorn was never applied, so far as I remember, to men who had not sought combat because of fear, but to men who feared to take, even in office jobs, the risk of jeopardizing rank or advancement in rank in the effort at accomplishment. Mr. Winant was never in combat, of course, in World War II, but he never hesitated to take these latter risks, or Tommy could not have worked for him. It need only be recalled that Tommy learned to fly Spitfire fighters at an RAF school and took an advanced gunnery school course for RAF fighter pilots, and was withdrawn temporarily from combat, when he was an assistant military attaché in our embassy. Still only a major, Tommy was arguing consistently about the P-51B with General Arnold, the head of the U.S. Air Force. The position advocated by Tommy was a square reversal of the air force policy, and specifically that of Wright Field. Tommy undoubtedly discussed the production of the model P-51B with Marshall of the Air Forces Portal, or someone else must have secured his approval on behalf of the Rolls-Royce Company. It is known also that Tommy saw Harry Hopkins at the White House, and perhaps the president. Surely at this level, Ambassador Winant might have been properly questioned as to the propriety of his own procedure out of channels until the vital necessity of the planes had been proven beyond a doubt in battle.

In carrying on his job, Tommy inspired hundreds of officers, young and old, with a little of his will to win. He brought his great qualities of leadership, resourcefulness, and judgment to the task of winning. I know Tommy always thought of improved planes and tactics in terms of improving the chances of his nephews, Avy and Tommy Clark, and the chances of all the other young pilots to whom he was so devoted.

Although Tommy completely ignored the fear, he was very mature and wise. He knew the dangers of flying fighters and the dangers of combat. He missed his family and wanted terribly to get home to them. In quiet moments, he worried about the right course for him to follow. He always came to the same answer. You either tried to win, or you didn't. His trying was of the all-out variety. Tommy was heroic in this war as he was in the last, because he couldn't be anything else. In this war it was different, however, because it was the deliberate heroism of a man.

—William H. Jackson
Undated manuscript, probably written in late 1960s

INDEX